The Women's Institute
big book of
baking

Liz Herbert

SIMON &
SCHUSTER
ILLUSTRATED

London · New York · Sydney · Toronto · New Delhi

A CBS COMPANY

Acknowledgements

With many thanks to those who provided essential back-up during the final days of writing *Cakes*, when our computer inexorably broke down.
And to my family who, during the writing of *Bread*, put up with drastically disrupted routines. Their consolation – an abundance of samples on offer!

This edition first published in Great Britain in 2012 by Simon & Schuster UK Ltd

Originally published as *Women's Institute Bread* and *Women's Institute Cakes* in 2009 by Simon & Schuster UK Ltd

A CBS COMPANY

10 9 8 7 6 5 4 3 2 1

SIMON & SCHUSTER ILLUSTRATED BOOKS
Simon & Schuster UK Ltd
222 Gray's Inn Road, London WC1X 8HB

www.simonandschuster.co.uk

Simon & Schuster Australia, Sydney
Simon & Schuster India, New Delhi

A CIP catalogue record for this book is available from the British Library

ISBN 978-1-47111-184-6

Project editor: Nicki Lampon
Design: Tiger Media Ltd, Fiona Andreanelli
Food photography: Chris Alack
Home economist: Lorna Brash
Stylist: Jo Harris (*Bread*), Sue Radcliffe (*Cakes*)

Printed and bound in China

Bread

Introduction

Bread forms a major part of our diet. It can be incorporated into every meal of the day – be it toast for breakfast, doughnuts with a cup of coffee, sandwiches at lunch time, a bun for tea or savoury bread to accompany a main meal.

Nowadays we are spoilt by the enormous variety of breads available. However, although mass-produced sliced bread is convenient, it is undoubtedly inferior to home-made. Making your own bread is both therapeutic and infectious! There is an undeniable satisfaction in the actual physical action of kneading the dough. This, coupled with the irresistible aroma of freshly baked bread, is reason enough to bake your own.

I hope that the following pages will inspire you to regularly incorporate bread making into your day, and to set aside a little time to create your own 'manna from heaven'.

Notes on the Recipes

All the recipes in this book have been made entirely by hand when testing. If using an electric mixer, food processor or bread machine, please refer to the manufacturer's instructions. If converting recipes for use in a bread machine, check the quantities carefully to make sure that your machine has enough capacity for the ingredients.

Always use exact measurements. Never mix imperial and metric quantities. If using metric measurements, add the final amount of liquid gradually to achieve a manageable dough.

The term 'scant' has been used in some recipes for the liquid. This means a little less than the quantity stated. You may not need the whole measure.

Fine sea salt is used throughout.

All breads are baked on the middle shelf of the oven unless stated otherwise.

Ingredients for Bread Making

It is very easy to detail all the dos and don'ts of how to create the perfect loaf. In the end it comes down to experience. However, it's also important to have some basic knowledge of the role of the main ingredients in bread making, and to appreciate how they interact and influence one another.

FLOUR

Wheat flour is best suited to bread making. Other flours contain a lower amount of gluten, and are often combined with wheat flour when making bread.

Wheat

Always choose flour specifically labelled for bread making as it has a high protein content. When water is added these proteins form gluten, and it is this that is responsible for forming the structure of the bread.

White bread flour is made from wheat that has had the bran and wheat germ removed during milling. Premium or very strong white bread flours are also available and produce a lighter, more aired bread. Wholemeal bread flour is much coarser, with a 'nutty' flavour. Stoneground wholemeal bread flour is just produced the old fashioned way, milled between two large, grooved stones. Brown bread flour is a combination of white and wholemeal flours and can be bought or mixed yourself at home. Breads made with wholemeal and brown flours

need more water and produce a denser loaf. The dough requires less kneading but takes longer to prove.

Malted grain flours are based on a mixture of white and wholemeal flours with malted grains to give a nutty, slightly sweet loaf. Semolina is made from hard durum wheat (used for pasta) and can be added to a dough or used to dust baking sheets.

Spelt

Spelt is an ancient form of wheat and can be bought in wholemeal or white form. Dough made with spelt should only be kneaded for 4–5 minutes and tends to prove quickly.

Cornmeal

Known as cornmeal in the USA and polenta in Italy, the latter tends to be more coarsely ground. Cornmeal is not to be confused with cornflour. Milled from sweetcorn kernels, it is gluten free, making it popular for those unable to tolerate wheat or gluten.

Oats

For bread making oats are usually incorporated whole as rolled oats or used as oatmeal. Oats do contain some gluten.

Barley

Barley flour is sold mixed with wheat flour or can be bought on its own over the Internet. Try substituting one-quarter wheat flour for barley flour.

Rice

Rice flour does not contain any gluten. It is available in white or brown (wholegrain) form but makes bread rather dry, so use in conjunction with another variety of flour when making wheat free bread.

Rye

Rye is very popular in Eastern Europe and America and has a poor gluten content, resulting in a fairly dense, chewy loaf. It is valued in bread making for adding flavour and colour.

Gluten free

There are a variety of gluten free flours available, such as gram (chickpea), soya and potato, as well as blends of different flours that have been pre-mixed to give good all-round results. As with other flours, do make sure that the packet states that it is suitable for bread making.

YEAST

Yeast is the raising agent used to make bread. It is a living organism and thrives in a warm, moist, sugary atmosphere. Salt, fat and sugar all slow down its progress, and consequently a longer time needs to be allowed for proving. In order to try and minimise this, bread can sometimes be made using a starter batter. This gives the yeast a head start so that when the other ingredients are added it has already begun to work. It is important to measure yeast accurately. Too little results in a heavy, poorly risen loaf; too much and the dough collapses on baking.

There are three forms of yeast available:

Dried yeast needs to be reconstituted in liquid with a little sugar before it can be used. After 15–20 minutes in a warm place, the liquid should be bubbly and frothing.

Fast action dried yeast (also known as easy blend) is added directly to the flour. Its main advantage is that the dough only requires one rise, which cuts down on proving time. The granules are much smaller than dried yeast so, if substituting one for another, it is not possible to do a straight switch.

Fresh yeast is no longer widely available. Some bakers may be able to sell you a small amount. If so, wrap in paper and keep in an airtight container in the fridge for up to two weeks. It is usually stirred into the liquid and then added to the flour.

SUGAR

Sugar helps to start the yeast working. White sugar is usually added to white dough. Wholemeal and brown breads taste good if flavoured with a more natural sugar, such as honey or muscovado. Malt extract or molasses are also sometimes used. Larger quantities of sugar are added to sweet breads, making the dough stickier and creating the need for a longer proving. Sweetened breads tend to have a closer texture, more like cake.

SALT

Salt helps to regulate how fast the dough rises. The more salt, the longer the dough will take to prove. Too little salt and you will be left with a sticky, unmanageable dough.

FAT

Butter, oils (sunflower, vegetable, olive and speciality), lard or white vegetable fat can all be used in bread making. Fat helps to keep the bread fresh and has a softening effect. Large quantities inhibit the action of yeast, so proving times may have to be increased accordingly.

EGGS

Enriched breads have added egg, which gives a yellow colour and softens the bread. Eggs give an overall richness to the dough and help it stay fresher for longer.

LIQUID

Liquid must be added in order to hydrate the yeast and to bind all the ingredients together. Water is usually added to basic dough. Milk is often used for enriched doughs. Milk also helps to keep the bread fresher for longer and results in a softer crumb and crust. It is very important that any liquid is warm. If it is cold the yeast will not start working, and if it is too hot it will kill the yeast. The ideal temperature is 38°C (100°F).

BREAD MIXES

There are many bread mixes available. They contain flour, yeast, salt and flavourings, together with flour improvers and emulsifiers to ensure a good end result. Some will make basic breads, others include added flavourings. Most simply require the addition of water.

STARTER DOUGHS

True starter doughs, also known as sour doughs because of their flavour, are made from just flour and water left over a period of days. They draw on bacteria from the air to cultivate into a yeasty batter. Each day a little more flour and water are added to keep it active. Rye flour makes a particularly good starter as its natural sugars are more easily broken down than those in wheat.

The resulting dough is sometimes known as the 'mother' starter. About a quarter of this is added to a basic recipe. The dough is then made as usual but, at the end, a quarter is kept back, ready to form the basis of the next new batch. Hence some of the original sour dough lives on as part of the make up of many loaves to come.

Biga, used in Italian breads (see Italian Semolina Bread page 27), uses a modern-day method in which baker's yeast is used in both the starter batter and the dough to speed up the process while still achieving the sour dough taste – combining the best of both worlds.

Stages of Bread Making

MIXING

A large bowl is usually best, but some people prefer to mix the dough on the work surface itself. In both cases, the liquid ingredients are poured into the dry ones, which are gradually incorporated. A wooden fork is ideal for mixing but use your hands to bring the last bits of flour together, leaving the sides of the bowl clean.

KNEADING

Bread dough is kneaded to develop the gluten in the flour, making it strong and elastic. White breads take longer to knead (about 10 minutes) than wholemeal and brown (about 5 minutes). The dough should end up silky and smooth.

To knead, place the dough on a work surface. Place both hands under the side furthest away and bring the dough towards you, folding it over to meet the near edge. Push down hard to seal, give it a quarter turn and repeat the action. You will gradually become faster and build up a rocking rhythm. Use the heel of your hand to push down. However, if you are working with relatively wet, sticky dough, it is easier to 'massage' it with your fingers, using both hands. It is not necessary to flour the work surface; in time the dough will become less sticky. However, if the dough is still sticky after 10 minutes, wash and dry your hands, lightly flour them and knead the dough just until it forms a ball.

PROVING

Dough needs to be proved (left to rise) in order to give the yeast an opportunity to work. A warm environment of about 32°C (90°F) is ideal – try an airing cupboard, a spot close to the boiler or a top oven with the one below switched on.

The dough should be left until it is about double its original size. This usually takes 1–1½ hours for white dough, longer for wholemeal and enriched breads. It is not possible to be specific as temperatures will fluctuate. If it is too cold the dough will take a long time to prove. If it is too hot the yeast will be killed and you will end up with a heavy, flat loaf. Dough left to rise slowly will have a better flavour, whereas those proved too quickly tend not to keep for so long and have a crumbly texture.

It is important to cover the dough so it does not dry out. A large, oiled polythene bag is good, or place the dough in a lightly oiled, clean bowl and cover with a clean, damp tea towel or cling film.

A recipe will have one or two provings. Fast action dried yeasts cut out the need to prove the dough twice. However, doing so will result in a denser loaf that has less flavour. The second proving will take about 45 minutes for loaves and 30 minutes for rolls. It should be slightly sticky to the touch when ready.

Knowledge of how temperature affects yeast gives you more control over your bread making, enabling you to slow down or speed up proving times to fit in with your schedule. If you halve the amount of yeast you use, you can even leave dough in the fridge for up to 12 hours. Bring it back to room temperature before shaping.

KNOCKING BACK

This is the term used for giving the dough a second, shorter kneading after it has proved. The purpose is to knock out air, which would lead to an uneven loaf with large air holes. The dough should be kneaded for a few minutes until it feels firm. After knocking back, the dough is shaped and put in a tin or on a baking sheet.

FINISHING TOUCHES

It is important to handle the dough very gently at the final stage to avoid knocking out any air and creating a dense, heavy bread.

Shaping
Some breads have a traditional finish, the shape being as much a part of the final bread as the ingredients. A good way to experiment is to divide a batch of basic dough into pieces and to shape them in different ways.

Cutting
Cuts can be made 1 cm (½ inch) deep with a very sharp knife before or after the dough has been proved and shaped.

Glazing
Certain glazes are associated with savoury bread and others with sweet breads. Likewise for wholemeal and white-based doughs. They may be applied before or after baking.

Topping
Toppings improve the appearance of the bread and add flavour and texture. They vary from a dusting of flour to a sprinkling of cereal flakes or grains, seeds, chopped nuts, herbs, coarse sea salt and grated cheese. Sweet breads are often topped with some form of sugar.

Crusts
Sugar and salt glazes both make the crust thicker.

A hard crust can be created by either spraying inside the oven with a fine mister a couple of minutes before you put in the dough or by placing a tin of boiling water on the bottom shelf when you turn the oven on. Be very careful when you open the oven as the steam will rush out. Alternatively, brush the crust with salted water or open the oven door for the last 5 minutes of baking.

A soft crust can be created by dusting the loaf with flour before baking, wrapping the bread in a clean, dry tea towel as soon as you take it out of the oven or adding fat and sugar to the dough. If you like a crisp crust, remove the bread from the oven 5 minutes before the end of its cooking time, take it out of the tin and return it to the oven on a baking tray.

BAKING

Always preheat the oven – too low a temperature and the dough will continue to prove, spilling over the tin. To test whether the bread is done, tap the bottom – it should sound hollow. Enriched breads are susceptible to burning and may need to be covered with foil or greaseproof paper after about 10 minutes.

STORING

Home made bread is best eaten warm or on the same day as baking. As soon as the bread is cooled, wrap in a paper bag or linen bread bag and store in a bread bin in a cool, dry place. Alternatively, seal in a polythene bag to keep fresh. Don't keep bread in the fridge.

It is always a good idea to double the quantity and put one loaf in the freezer. Wrap in a polythene bag and freeze as soon as it has cooled. Bread will keep for about 3 months, although crusty bread does not freeze well as the crust tends to flake off. To refresh day-old or defrosted bread, heat in a preheated oven at Gas Mark 4/180°C/350°F for 8–10 minutes.

BREAD MACHINES

There is no standard formula for converting recipes for use in a bread machine. Start with the recipes in the manufacturer's booklet. Once you become confident, these recipes can be adapted for use. The main thing is to check that the capacity of your bread maker matches the quantity of ingredients in the recipe. Remember that only fast action dried yeast is suitable for use in bread machines. Dough can also be mixed, kneaded and left to rise in a bread machine, then turned out on to a work surface to be shaped by hand, giving a home-made finish.

RESCUE REMEDIES

Poor rise and a heavy, close texture
The yeast was stale.
Too little yeast was used or it was not given enough time to work.
The liquid was too hot.
Too much salt was added.
The dough was not kneaded for long enough.

'Stretch marks' around the sides
The dough was under proved.

Dough spills over the tin
Too much dough was used for the size of the tin (generally bread made using 450 g/1 lb flour will need to be baked in a 900 g/2 lb tin).
Too much yeast was used.

Flat top
Not enough salt was used.
Too soft a flour was used.
The dough was over proved.
The dough was not properly shaped.

Sunken loaf
The loaf was undercooked.
Too much liquid was used.
Not enough salt was used.
The dough was over proved.

Large holes and uneven textured bread
The dough was not knocked back properly.

Sour, yeasty smell
The dough was over proved.
The yeast was old and 'going off'.
Too much yeast was used.

Crumbly crumb
The dough was put in too warm a place to rise.
Too soft a flour was used.
Too much yeast was used.
The dough was over proved.

Basic Breads

If you have never made bread before, or are in need of a refresher course, then this chapter is a good starting point. People are often wary of making bread, but the more bread you make, the better you become at judging whether the dough is right or not. Once the basics have been mastered, variations are often little more than fancy shaping. As with most things, with a little know-how you will find that complicated-looking breads are actually fairly simple. With practice comes experience, and with experience comes confidence.

French Country Bread, page 22

Basic White Bread (Farmhouse Loaf)

Makes: *1 loaf* **Preparation time:** *20 minutes + proving + 30–35 minutes baking*
Freezing: *recommended*

Try developing your own breads, using this recipe as a base and adding ingredients to create a sweet or savoury loaf.

450 g (1 lb) strong white bread flour, plus extra
    for dusting
25 g (1 oz) butter
1 teaspoon sugar
1 teaspoon salt
1 teaspoon fast action dried yeast
300 ml (½ pint) hand-hot water

1 Put the flour in a large mixing bowl and rub in the butter. Stir in the sugar, salt and yeast. Make a well in the centre, pour the water in all at once and mix well to combine the ingredients. After a little while it is easiest to dispense with the stirring utensil and use your hands to bring the dough together.

2 Turn out on to an unfloured surface and knead (page 8) the dough. It will take about 10 minutes for it to lose its 'craggy' appearance and take on a silky smoothness.

3 Place the dough in a large polythene bag that has been lightly oiled. Seal, allowing plenty of room for the dough to expand, and prove (page 8) in a warm place for about an hour or until it has doubled in size.

4 Grease a 900 g (2 lb) loaf tin and dust with flour.

5 Knock back (page 9) the dough for 2–3 minutes, making sure that all the air is dispelled. Shape into an oblong by putting both hands under the piece of dough furthest away and bringing it towards you, folding it over the rest of the dough. Push down to seal the edge nearest you. Give the dough a quarter turn and repeat until you have a smooth-shaped oblong. Lay it in the prepared tin, seam side down. Cover and leave to prove until doubled in size (about 45 minutes).

6 Preheat the oven to Gas Mark 8/230°C/450°F.

7 Using a very sharp knife, make a 1 cm (½ inch) deep cut down the centre of the loaf. Dust liberally with flour.

8 Bake for 30–35 minutes. If your baking tin is high and short, place the loaf one shelf below the centre of the oven. Longer, shallower loaf tins should be baked on the middle shelf.

9 Remove the bread from the tin and transfer to a wire rack to cool. The loaf should sound hollow on the bottom when tapped.

Tips: Do not flour the work surface. The dough becomes less sticky as you work it and the flour absorbs moisture. Adding too much flour at this stage results in a dry dough.

If you like a crisp crust, remove the loaf from the tin when baked, place it on a baking tray and return it to the oven for a further 5 minutes.

Easy Brown Bread

Makes: *1 loaf* **Preparation time:** *15 minutes + proving + 30–35 minutes baking*
Freezing: *recommended*

Brown bread is probably the best bread to make as an introduction to bread making as the dough handles beautifully. It does not require as long a kneading time as white bread and this recipe only rises once, so the dough is just mixed, kneaded, shaped, proved and baked.

300 g (10 oz) strong white bread flour
300 g (10 oz) strong wholemeal bread flour
25 g (1 oz) white vegetable fat
   or sunflower oil
1¼ teaspoons sugar
1¼ teaspoons salt
1¼ teaspoons fast action dried yeast
375 ml (13 fl oz) hand-hot water

1 Grease a 900 g (2 lb) loaf tin.

2 Combine the flours in a large mixing bowl. Rub in the fat and stir in the sugar, salt and yeast. Make a well in the centre (if using oil, add at this stage) and pour in the water. Gradually incorporate the dry ingredients, mixing to a soft dough. Use your hands to bring the last crumbs together.

3 Turn out on to an unfloured surface and knead (page 8) for about 5 minutes until smooth.

4 Shape the dough into an oblong by putting both hands under the piece of dough furthest away and bringing it towards you, folding it over the rest of the dough. Push down to seal the edge nearest you. Give the dough a quarter turn and repeat until you have a smooth-shaped oblong. Lay it in the prepared tin, seam side down. Using a sharp knife, make a cut down the centre of the loaf. Place the tin in an oiled polythene bag and prove (page 8) in a warm place until doubled in size.

5 Preheat the oven to Gas Mark 8/230°C/450°F.

6 Bake for 30–35 minutes. If your baking tin is high and short, place the loaf one shelf below the centre of the oven. Longer, shallower loaf tins should be baked on the middle shelf.

7 Turn out on to a wire rack. The bottom should sound hollow when tapped. For a crisp crust, leave out of the tin and return to the oven for a further 5 minutes.

Note: Slightly more flour is used than in the basic white bread recipe, as brown and wholemeal varieties do not rise to the same extent as white loaves.

Wheatgerm Bread

Makes: *1 loaf* **Preparation time:** *15 minutes + proving + 30–35 minutes baking*
Freezing: *recommended*

Wheatgerm gives this bread a wonderful golden crumb, as well as boosting its nutritional value.

225 g (8 oz) strong wholemeal bread flour
225 g (8 oz) strong white bread flour
50 g (2 oz) wheatgerm
1 tablespoon muscovado sugar
1 teaspoon salt
1 teaspoon fast action dried yeast
2 tablespoons sunflower oil
325–350 ml (11–12 fl oz) hand-hot water

1 Lightly grease a 900 g (2 lb) loaf tin.

2 Combine the flours, wheatgerm, sugar, salt and yeast in a large mixing bowl. Make a well in the centre and add the oil and water. Mix to a soft dough.

3 Turn the dough out on to an unfloured surface and knead (page 8) for about 5 minutes until smooth.

4 Shape the dough into an oblong by putting both hands under the piece of dough furthest away and bringing it towards you, folding it over the rest of the dough. Push down to seal the edge nearest you. Give the dough a quarter turn and repeat until you have a smooth-shaped oblong. Lay it in the prepared tin, seam side down. Using a sharp knife, make a cut down the centre of the loaf. Cover and prove (page 8) in a warm place until doubled in size.

5 Preheat the oven to Gas Mark 7/220°C/425°F.

6 Bake the bread one shelf below the middle of the oven for 30–35 minutes. Remove from the tin and cool on a wire rack.

White Seeded Loaf

Makes: *1 loaf* **Preparation time:** *25 minutes + proving + 25–30 minutes baking*
Freezing: *recommended*

In this loaf, six types of seed are mixed into the dough to create a
bread full of flavour and crunch.

450 g (1 lb) strong white bread flour
1 teaspoon sugar
1 teaspoon salt
1 teaspoon fast action dried yeast
1 tablespoon each of sesame, linseed, millet,
   pumpkin, poppy and sunflower seeds
1 tablespoon sunflower oil
scant 300 ml (½ pint) hand-hot water (page 4)
For the topping:
milk
2 teaspoons mixed seeds

1 Combine the flour, sugar, salt, yeast and
   seeds in a bowl. Make a well in the centre and
   add the oil and water. Mix to a soft dough.

2 Turn the dough out on to an unfloured surface
   and knead (page 8) for about 10 minutes until
   smooth. Place in an oiled polythene bag and
   prove (page 8) in a warm place until doubled
   in size.

3 Grease a baking sheet.

4 Knock back (page 9) the dough for a few
   minutes to knock out all the air. Shape into a
   round. Place on the baking sheet and, using
   a sharp knife, slash three lines across the top
   to a depth of about 1 cm (½ inch). Cover and
   prove until doubled in size.

5 Preheat the oven to Gas Mark 7/220°C/425°F.

6 Brush the surface of the dough with milk and
   sprinkle with seeds. Bake for 25–30 minutes
   until golden. Cool on a wire rack.

Tip: If you prefer, use just one variety of seed,
or a mixture of two or three favourites.

Wholemeal Stoneground Loaf

Makes: *1 loaf* **Preparation time:** *15 minutes + proving + 30–35 minutes baking*
Freezing: *recommended*

Adding a little more yeast than normal helps to lighten wholemeal and stoneground loaves. Alternatively, substitute some of the wholemeal flour with white bread flour.

550 g (1¼ lbs) strong wholemeal or
stoneground bread flour
1 teaspoon brown sugar
1 teaspoon salt
1¼ teaspoons fast action dried yeast
2 tablespoons sunflower or vegetable oil
375–400 ml (13–14 fl oz) hand-hot water

1 Combine the flour, sugar, salt and yeast in a large mixing bowl. Make a well in the centre and add the oil and enough water to bind the ingredients together. Using a wooden spoon, mix to a soft dough, gradually drawing in the dry ingredients. When it is almost mixed, put aside the spoon and use your hands to form a ball of dough.

2 Turn out on to an unfloured work surface and knead (page 8) for about 5 minutes until smooth. Place in a lightly oiled polythene bag and leave in a warm place to prove (page 8) until the dough has doubled in size. This can take 1–1½ hours.

3 Grease a 900 g (2 lb) loaf tin.

4 Turn the dough out again and knead for a few minutes to knock out the air. Shape into an oblong with the short end nearest to you. Putting your fingertips under the piece of dough furthest away, bring the dough towards you, folding it in half. Press down, then give the dough a quarter turn. Repeat this, shaping several times until you have a smooth-shaped oblong. Place in the prepared tin, seam side down.

5 Cover and leave in a warm place to prove until the bread rises to just above the top of the tin.

6 Preheat the oven to Gas Mark 7/220°C/425°F.

7 Bake for 30–35 minutes one shelf below the middle of the oven if you have a short, squat tin, or on the centre shelf if you have a longer, shallow tin.

8 Remove from the tin and cool on a wire rack. The loaf should sound hollow on the bottom when tapped. If you prefer a crisp crust, then place the bread on a baking tray and return to the oven for a further 5 minutes.

Tip: If you would like to make a good sized cob loaf, simply shape the knocked back dough into a round, mark with a cross and, after a second proving, bake in the centre of the oven for 25–30 minutes.

Malted Mixed Grain Bread

Makes: *1 loaf* **Preparation time:** *15 minutes + proving + 25 minutes baking*
Freezing: *recommended*

This is a fairly dense, slightly sweet, chewy bread packed with flavour.

450 g (1 lb) malted grain bread flour
1 teaspoon salt
1 teaspoon fast action dried yeast
2 tablespoons malt extract
2 tablespoons sunflower oil
275 ml (9 fl oz) hand-hot water

1 Lightly grease a baking sheet.

2 Combine the flour, salt and yeast in a bowl. Make a well in the centre and add the malt extract, oil and water. Mix to a soft dough.

3 Turn out on to an unfloured surface and knead (page 8) for about 10 minutes until smooth. The malt makes this dough very sticky – do not panic! Keep working it the best you can and you will be left with a beautifully soft dough.

4 Give the work surface a good scrape down. Scrub any dough off your hands and then dust them with a little flour. Form the dough into a sausage shape about 20 cm (8 inches) in length. Place the dough on the baking sheet, cover and prove (page 8) in a warm place until doubled in size.

5 Preheat the oven to Gas Mark 8/230°C/450°F.

6 Bake for 25 minutes until the loaf sounds hollow when tapped on the base. Cool on a wire rack.

Milk Bread (Bridge Rolls)

Makes: *18 rolls* **Preparation time:** *25 minutes + proving + 15 minutes baking*
Freezing: *recommended*

Soft and golden, these little rolls are perfect for filling with sausages, caramelised onions and relish. Space them on the baking sheet so that they are almost touching and you will end up with soft-sided, tall rolls.

450 g (1 lb) strong white bread flour
50 g (2 oz) butter
1 tablespoon caster sugar
1 teaspoon salt
1 teaspoon fast action dried yeast
300 ml (½ pint) warm semi-skimmed milk

1 Put the flour in a large mixing bowl and rub in the butter. Stir in the sugar, salt and yeast and mix to a soft dough with the milk.

2 Turn out on to an unfloured surface and knead (page 8) for about 10 minutes until smooth. Cover and prove (page 8) in a warm place until doubled in size.

3 Grease a baking sheet.

4 Divide the dough into 18 pieces, each weighing approximately 40 g (1½ oz). Keep them covered while you shape one at a time.

5 Using your fingertips, roll each piece of dough out into an 8 cm (3¼ inch) long sausage shape. Arrange the rolls in two rows on the baking sheet, side by side and almost touching. Cover and prove.

6 Preheat the oven to Gas Mark 6/200°C/400°F.

7 Bake the rolls for 15 minutes. Remove from the oven to a wire rack and cover with a clean tea towel so that they have a traditional soft crust.

Tip: The same quantity of dough can also be used in mini individual tins to produce soft rolls that are perfect for a dinner party.

French Country Bread

Makes: *1 loaf* **Preparation time:** *20 minutes + 1–2 days fermenting + proving + 30–35 minutes baking* **Freezing:** *recommended*

This classic, rustic style French loaf, made with white and wholemeal flours, has a sour taste achieved by fermenting the yeast a day or two before making the bread.

175 g (6 oz) strong white bread flour, plus
**   extra for dusting**
175 g (6 oz) strong wholemeal bread flour
25 g (1 oz) butter
1 teaspoon salt
½ teaspoon fast action dried yeast
175 ml (6 fl oz) hand-hot water
For the starter dough:
115 g (4 oz) strong white bread flour
½ teaspoon fast action dried yeast
150 ml (¼ pint) warm water

1 Begin the starter dough 24–48 hours before making the bread. Combine the flour for the starter dough with the yeast and stir in the water to make a thick batter. Cover with a damp tea towel and leave in a cool place to ferment for 1–2 days. Stir occasionally, and check frequently to make sure that the tea towel remains damp.

2 When you are ready to make the actual bread, combine the flours in a bowl. Rub in the butter. Stir in the salt, yeast, starter dough and water and mix to form a soft dough.

3 Turn out on to an unfloured surface and knead (page 8) for 8–10 minutes until smooth. Cover and prove (page 8) in a warm place until doubled in size.

4 Grease a baking sheet and dust with flour.

5 Knock back (page 9) the dough and form into a round. Place on the baking sheet and, using a sharp knife, slash the surface with 4–5 deep lines one way and then the other. This will give you a diamond effect. Cover and prove.

6 Preheat the oven to Gas Mark 6/200°C/400°F.

7 Dust the loaf liberally with flour and bake for 30–35 minutes until golden and crisp. Cool on a wire rack.

Illustrated on page 13

Rye Bread

Makes: *1 loaf* **Preparation time:** *20 minutes + proving + 25–30 minutes baking*
Freezing: *recommended*

Rye flour has a low gluten content and produces a loaf with quite a close, dense texture. It has a distinctive 'chewiness' to it.

225 g (8 oz) wholemeal rye flour, plus extra for
dusting
225 g (8 oz) strong white bread flour
1½ teaspoons salt
1½ teaspoons fast action dried yeast
1½ teaspoons caraway seeds
2 tablespoons molasses sugar
325–350 ml (11–12 fl oz) hand-hot water

1 Combine the flours in a large mixing bowl. Stir
in the salt, yeast and caraway seeds. Rub the
molasses sugar through the mixture to remove
any lumps. Add the water and mix to a soft
dough.

2 Turn out on to an unfloured surface and knead
(page 8) for approximately 8 minutes until
smooth. Cover and prove (page 8) in a warm
place until doubled in size.

3 Grease a baking sheet.

4 Knock back (page 9) the dough for a couple
of minutes to distribute any air bubbles, then
shape into a log or round. Place on the baking
sheet and slash a single deep line down the
length of the dough, slightly off centre. Dust
with a little flour if wished. Cover and prove.

5 Preheat the oven to Gas Mark 7/220°C/425°F.

6 Bake the bread for 25–30 minutes. Cool on a
wire rack.

Tip: Rye bread usually contains caraway
seeds. This recipe contains just enough to
give the bread a little flavour; you may wish to
increase the quantity if you prefer a stronger
taste.

Barley Bread

Makes: *1 loaf* **Preparation time:** *45 minutes + 20 minutes cooking + proving + 30–35 minutes baking* **Freezing:** *recommended*

Barley is an old style grain that now only tends to be used in casseroles and malt extract. This bread uses barley in its flour and grain form, resulting in a moist, textured loaf, full of flavour. I have used a flour mix, Barleycorn. If you wish to make your own mix, you can buy pure barley flour on the Internet.

50 g (2 oz) pearl barley
350 g (12 oz) Barleycorn bread flour
¾ teaspoon salt
¾ teaspoon fast action dried yeast
2 teaspoons runny honey
1 tablespoon sunflower oil
175 ml (6 fl oz) hand-hot water

1 Rinse the pearl barley. Place it in a small saucepan and cover with plenty of cold water. Bring to the boil and simmer for 20 minutes. Drain and run under cold water to cool. Turn out on to a plate lined with several sheets of kitchen paper to drain thoroughly.

2 Combine the Barleycorn flour, salt and yeast in a bowl. Make a well in the centre and add the honey, oil, water and cooked barley. Mix to a soft dough.

3 Turn out on to an unfloured surface and knead (page 8) for 8–10 minutes until smooth. Cover and leave to rise slowly at room temperature until doubled in size. The slower rise helps develop the flavour.

4 Grease a 900 g (2 lb) loaf tin.

5 Knock back (page 9) the dough and shape into an oblong by putting both hands under the piece of dough furthest away and bringing it towards you, folding it over the rest of the dough. Push down to seal the edge nearest you. Give the dough a quarter turn and repeat until you have a smooth-shaped oblong. Place in the tin, cover and leave to rise slowly for about 1 hour.

6 Preheat the oven to Gas Mark 7/220°C/425°F.

7 Bake for 30–35 minutes on one rung below the centre of the oven. Cool on a wire rack.

Tip: This can also be shaped in a more rustic way by lining a basket or tin with a clean linen tea towel, dusting it with flour, placing the shaped dough inside, sprinkling a little more flour on top and folding the tea towel over to encase it. Once the dough has doubled in size carefully tip out on to a greased baking sheet and cook as above but on the middle shelf of the oven.

Wholemeal Spelt Bread

Makes: *1 loaf* **Preparation time:** *20 minutes + proving + 35–40 minutes baking*
Freezing: *recommended*

Spelt flour used to be very popular, but went into decline when manufacturing costs increased due to the difficulty in separating the tough husk from the grain. Now enjoying a revival, both white and wholemeal varieties are available. Although a cousin to wheat flour, its protein structure is different, and consequently some people who have an intolerance to wheat may be able to eat spelt.

450 g (1 lb) stoneground strong spelt bread flour, plus extra for dusting
25 g (1 oz) butter
1 teaspoon muscovado sugar
1 teaspoon salt
1½ teaspoons fast action dried yeast
300–325 ml (10–11 fl oz) hand-hot water

1 Lightly grease a 900 g (2 lb) loaf tin.

2 Put the flour in a large mixing bowl and rub in the butter. Stir in the sugar, salt and yeast and mix to a soft dough with the water.

3 Turn out on to an unfloured surface and knead (page 8) for 4 minutes only. Shape into an oblong by putting both hands under the piece of dough furthest away and bringing it towards you, folding it over the rest of the dough. Push down to seal the edge nearest you. Give the dough a quarter turn and repeat until you have a smooth-shaped oblong. Place in the prepared loaf tin. Cover and prove (page 8) in a warm place until doubled in size.

4 Preheat the oven to Gas Mark 7/220°C/425°F.

5 Dust the bread with flour and bake for 35–40 minutes. Turn out on to a wire rack to cool.

Tip: Spelt has a more delicate gluten structure than wheat flour, so the dough does not require such a long kneading time. It also tends to rise more quickly than ordinary bread, so keep an eye on it and bake as soon as the loaf has doubled in size.

Italian Semolina Bread

Makes: *1 loaf* **Preparation time:** *25 minutes + 24–36 hours standing + proving + 35–40 minutes baking* **Freezing:** *recommended*

This is an Italian form of sour dough bread made with a 'biga' starter. There is nothing rushed about this bread – it also has a long first proving to allow the alcohols given off by the yeast to flavour the dough.

225 g (8 oz) fine semolina, plus extra for
    sprinkling
225 g (8 oz) strong white bread flour, plus
    extra for dusting
115 g (4 oz) strong wholemeal bread flour
1½ teaspoons salt
1 teaspoon fast action dried yeast
2 tablespoons olive oil
350 ml (12 fl oz) hand-hot water
For the biga:
115 g (4 oz) strong white bread flour
½ teaspoon fast action dried yeast
150 ml (¼ pint) hand-hot water

1 Prepare the biga the day before you wish to make the bread. Place the flour and yeast in a small bowl and blend in the water to make a paste. Cover with a damp tea towel and leave in a cool place for 24–36 hours.

2 The next day, place the semolina and flours in a large bowl and stir in the salt and yeast. Make a well in the centre, add 115 g (4 oz) of the biga, the olive oil and the water. Mix to a soft dough.

3 Turn out on to an unfloured surface and knead (page 8) for 8–10 minutes until smooth. Cover and prove (page 8) at room temperature until doubled in size – this takes about 2 hours.

4 Knock back (page 9) the dough and shape into a round.

5 Dust a linen tea towel with flour and use it to line a large mixing bowl. Place the dough inside, with the smooth side facing down. Dust with a little flour and fold over the tea towel to encase the dough. Prove slowly at room temperature until doubled in size.

6 Preheat the oven to Gas Mark 7/220°C/425°F. Grease a baking sheet and sprinkle with a little semolina.

7 Very carefully tip the dough out on to the baking sheet. Using a sharp knife, slash lines across the top to make a diamond effect. Dust with a little white flour.

8 Bake for 35–40 minutes, opening the oven door for the final 5 minutes if you like a crisp crust. Cool on a wire rack.

Rice Bread

Makes: *1 loaf* **Preparation time:** *25 minutes + proving + 15 minutes cooking + 30 minutes baking*
Freezing: *recommended*

The beauty of breads with added cooked grain (such as Barley Bread, page 24) is that, unlike most home-made breads that are stale in a day or two, the grain helps keep the loaf moist. This milk bread is a particular favourite with children, and is lovely spread with butter and jam.

40 g (1½ oz) Arborio or risotto rice
¾ teaspoon salt, plus extra for rice
350 g (12 oz) strong white bread flour
1 teaspoon fast action dried yeast
⅛ teaspoon freshly grated nutmeg
1 tablespoon runny honey
25 g (1 oz) butter, softened
1 teaspoon vanilla essence
225 ml (8 fl oz) warm semi-skimmed milk, plus
extra to glaze

1 Place the rice in a small pan. Cover with water, add a little salt, bring to the boil and simmer for 15 minutes. Drain and run under a cold tap to cool. Transfer to a double thickness of kitchen paper to remove any excess water.

2 Combine the flour, salt, yeast and nutmeg in a bowl. Stir in the cooked rice. Make a well in the centre and add the honey, butter, vanilla essence and milk. Mix to a soft dough.

3 Turn out on to an unfloured surface and knead (page 8) for 8–10 minutes until smooth. Place in an oiled polythene bag and prove (page 8) in a warm place until doubled in size.

4 Grease a 900 g (2 lb) loaf tin.

5 Knock back (page 9) the dough and form into an oblong by putting both hands under the piece of dough furthest away and bringing it towards you, folding it over the rest of the dough. Push down to seal the edge nearest you. Give the dough a quarter turn and repeat until you have a smooth-shaped oblong. Place in the prepared tin, cover and prove until doubled in size.

6 Preheat the oven to Gas Mark 7/220°C/425°F.

7 Brush the loaf with a little milk and bake for about 30 minutes. Leave in the tin for 5 minutes before turning out on to a wire rack to cool.

Honey and Oat Bread

Makes: *1 loaf* **Preparation time:** *15 minutes + proving + 30 minutes baking*
Freezing: *recommended*

Honey gives this bread a lovely golden, thick crust, full of flavour, and a delicious lightly sweetened taste. Sweet and savoury toppings go well with this loaf. Once it is a day old it is best eaten toasted.

350 g (12 oz) strong white bread flour
80 g (3 oz) medium oatmeal, plus extra for sprinkling
50 g (2 oz) rolled oats, plus extra for sprinkling
1 teaspoon salt
1½ teaspoons fast action dried yeast
3 tablespoons runny honey
2 tablespoons sunflower oil
225–250 ml (8–9 fl oz) warm semi-skimmed milk, plus extra to glaze

1 Grease a 900 g (2 lb) oblong loaf tin and sprinkle lightly with a little oatmeal and rolled oats.

2 Combine the flour, oatmeal, oats, salt and yeast in a large bowl. Make a well in the centre and add the honey, oil and warm milk. Mix to a soft dough.

3 Turn out on to an unfloured surface and knead (page 8) for 8–10 minutes until smooth.

4 Shape into an oblong by putting both hands under the piece of dough furthest away and bringing it towards you, folding it over the rest of the dough. Push down to seal the edge nearest you. Give the dough a quarter turn and repeat until you have a smooth-shaped oblong. Place in the prepared tin, brush with a little milk and sprinkle with oatmeal and rolled oats. Cover and prove (page 8) in a warm place until doubled in size.

5 Preheat the oven to Gas Mark 7/220°C/425°F.

6 Bake the bread for about 30 minutes until golden. Remove from the tin and cool on a wire rack.

Polenta Bread

Makes: *1 loaf* **Preparation time:** *15 minutes + proving + 25 minutes*
Freezing: *recommended*

Polenta (or maize flour) has a slightly grainy texture and a
vivid yellow colour that makes an everyday loaf a little more
interesting.

350 g (12 oz) strong white bread flour
115 g (4 oz) polenta, plus extra for sprinkling
1 teaspoon sugar
1 teaspoon salt
1 teaspoon fast action dried yeast
25 g (1 oz) butter, melted
275–300 ml (9–10 fl oz) hand-hot water

1 Combine the flour, polenta, sugar, salt and
yeast in a mixing bowl. Add the butter and
water and mix to a soft dough.

2 Turn out on to an unfloured surface and knead
(page 8) for 8–10 minutes until smooth. Cover
and prove (page 8) in a warm place until
doubled in size.

3 Grease a baking sheet and sprinkle with
polenta.

4 Knock back (page 9) the dough and shape
into an 18 cm (7 inch) long oval. Place on the
baking sheet. Using a sharp knife, make deep
cuts on alternate sides of the loaf, roughly
equidistant, starting two thirds across the top,
and finishing on the baking tray.

5 Cover and prove until doubled in size.

6 Preheat the oven to Gas Mark 7/220°C/425°F.

7 Sprinkle liberally with polenta and bake for
about 25 minutes until golden. Cool on a wire
rack.

Soya Flour Bread

Makes: *1 loaf* **Preparation time:** *20 minutes + proving + 30 minutes baking*
Freezing: *recommended*

Soya flour is not an obvious choice for making bread, but it does create a lovely golden loaf with a soft, cake-like crumb that keeps well for a couple of days. Soya flour is readily available from health food shops.

300 g (10 oz) strong white bread flour
80 g (3 oz) soya flour
80 g (3 oz) wholemeal rye flour
1 teaspoon muscovado sugar
1 teaspoon salt
1¼ teaspoons fast action dried yeast
2 tablespoons sunflower oil
300–325 ml (10–11 fl oz) hand-hot water
For the topping:
1 egg
1 tablespoon water
a handful of golden linseeds

1 Combine the flours in a large mixing bowl with the sugar, salt and yeast. Make a well in the centre and stir in the oil and water to make a soft dough.

2 Turn out on to a floured surface and knead (page 8) for 8–10 minutes until smooth. Cover and prove (page 8) in a warm place until doubled in size.

3 Grease a 900 g (2 lb) loaf tin.

4 Knock back (page 9) the dough and shape into an oblong by putting both hands under the piece of dough furthest away and bringing it towards you, folding it over the rest of the dough. Push down to seal the edge nearest you. Give the dough a quarter turn and repeat until you have a smooth-shaped oblong. Place in the prepared tin, cover and prove until doubled in size.

5 Preheat the oven to Gas Mark 7/220°C/425°F.

6 Beat the egg with the water and brush the loaf with the egg glaze. Sprinkle linseeds liberally over the surface. Bake one shelf below the middle of the oven for 30 minutes. Cool on a wire rack.

Tip: Soya makes this bread quite sticky to work with, so you may need to sprinkle a little flour periodically on to the work surface whilst kneading.

Plain and Savoury

One of the great advantages of bread making is how a few standard ingredients can be built upon to make so many different variations. This chapter begins with basic breads that use very few ingredients other than the essentials. Shaping the dough in different ways means you can produce a wide range of alternative breads. Then, by adding other ingredients, the scope widens still further to produce a wealth of delicious alternatives.

Sweet Chestnut Bread, page 59

French Bread

Makes: *2 baguettes* **Preparation time:** *20 minutes + proving + 20 minutes baking*
Freezing: *recommended*

Some plain flour is mixed in with bread flour in this recipe to provide a texture more reminiscent of true French bread, which is traditionally made with French flour.

350 g (12 oz) strong white bread flour, plus extra for dusting
115 g (4 oz) plain white flour
1 teaspoon sugar
1 teaspoon salt
1½ teaspoons fast action dried yeast
300 ml (½ pint) hand-hot water

1 Combine the flours, sugar, salt and yeast in a large bowl. Add the water and mix to a soft dough.

2 Turn out on to an unfloured work surface and knead (page 8) for about 10 minutes until smooth. Cover and prove (page 8) in a warm place until doubled in size.

3 Grease and flour two baking sheets.

4 Divide the dough into two equal pieces. Without knocking back, roll out on a lightly floured surface to a rectangle measuring 38 x 30 cm (15 x 12 inches). Roll up tightly from the long edge, pinching the seams together. Place diagonally on the baking sheets, seam side down, and make deep, diagonal cuts at 6 cm (2½ inch) intervals. Prove, uncovered, until doubled in size.

5 Preheat the oven to Gas Mark 7/220°C/425°F. Place a large, shallow dish on the bottom shelf of the oven and carefully half fill this with boiling water.

6 Dust the baguettes with a little flour and bake for 20 minutes, until golden. Cool on a wire rack and eat the same day.

Tips: The water in the oven will create steam, which will give the bread a crisp crust. Be very careful to stand well back when you open the oven, otherwise the steam may catch you in the face.

This recipe produces a loaf with a matt finish. If you prefer your bread to be shiny, brush the dough with an egg white, beaten with 1 tablespoon water.

Pitta Bread

Makes: *6 breads* **Preparation time:** *25 minutes + proving + 6–8 minutes baking*
Freezing: *recommended*

Pitta bread is a very basic bread, made from just a few simple ingredients. I have recommended quite a short cooking time. This does not brown the breads as they are often toasted before eating.

350 g (12 oz) strong white bread flour, plus
  extra for dusting
½ teaspoon sugar
¾ teaspoon salt
¾ teaspoon fast action dried yeast
225 ml (8 fl oz) hand-hot water

Tip: These are delicious filled with hot or cold meats and salad, or sliced into strips to accompany dips.

1 Combine the flour, sugar, salt and yeast in a bowl. Stir in the water to make a soft dough.

2 Turn out on to an unfloured work surface and knead (page 8) for 10 minutes until smooth. Rest the dough for 10 minutes.

3 Dust two baking sheets with flour.

4 Divide the dough into six equal pieces. On a lightly floured surface, roll out each piece into a 20 cm (8 inch) by 12 cm (4½ inches) oval. Score a line across the centre of each to make the breads easier to tear. Place well apart on the baking sheets, cover and prove (page 8) for 20 minutes only, until they are just starting to puff up.

5 Preheat the oven to Gas Mark 7/220°C/425°F.

6 Bake for 6–8 minutes until just cooked through. Transfer to a wire rack to cool.

Naan Bread

Makes: *6 breads* **Preparation time:** *25 minutes + proving + 10 minutes baking*
Freezing: *recommended*

Naan bread may be cooked in the oven or under a very hot grill. Cooking in the oven creates a more uniform finish, without the trademark blistering.

450 g (1 lb) strong white bread flour
2 teaspoons sugar
1 teaspoon salt
1½ teaspoons fast action dried yeast
1½ teaspoons black onion seeds
1 teaspoon baking powder
50 g (2 oz) butter, melted
175–200 ml (6–7 fl oz) warm semi-skimmed
   milk
150 ml (¼ pint) natural yogurt

1 Mix together the flour, sugar, salt, yeast, black onion seeds and baking powder. Make a well in the centre and add 25 g (1 oz) of the melted butter, the milk and yogurt. Combine to make a soft dough.

2 Turn out on to an unfloured work surface and knead (page 8) for about 10 minutes until smooth. Cover and prove (page 8) in a warm place until doubled in size. Grease two baking sheets.

3 Divide the dough into six. Using floured hands, form each piece into a 20 cm (8 inch) long teardrop shape that is thicker at the edges than in the centre. Place well apart on the baking sheets. Cover and prove for 20 minutes, or until the dough is just beginning to puff up.

4 Preheat the oven to Gas Mark 7/220°C/425°F.

5 Bake the breads for 10 minutes. When they come out of the oven, brush with the remaining melted butter and either wrap in foil to keep warm or transfer to a cooling rack.

Variation: This makes a plain naan. If you prefer something a little spicier, mix some roasted and crushed coriander, fennel and cumin seeds in with the flour.

Bagels

Makes: *8 bagels* **Preparation time:** *35 minutes + proving + 15 minutes baking*
Freezing: *recommended*

To achieve an authentic chewy texture, bagels must be dropped into boiling water for a minute before baking in the oven – thereby cooking them twice.

450 g (1 lb) strong white bread flour
3 tablespoons caster sugar
1½ teaspoons salt
1¼ teaspoons fast action dried yeast
300 ml (½ pint) warm water
For the glaze:
1 egg yolk
1 tablespoon water

1 Grease two baking sheets or line with baking parchment.

2 Place the flour, sugar, salt and yeast in a large bowl. Make a well in the centre and add the water. Mix to a soft dough.

3 Turn out on to an unfloured work surface and knead (page 8) for 8–10 minutes until smooth. Place in an oiled polythene bag and prove (page 8) in a warm place until doubled in size.

4 Knead the dough for a couple of minutes to even out any air bubbles. Divide the dough into eight and roll each piece out to about 25 cm (10 inches). Wet one end and press firmly together with the other to form a ring. Place well apart on the baking sheets, cover and prove for 30 minutes, until they are just over half their original size.

5 Preheat the oven to Gas Mark 6/200°C/400°F and bring a large pan of water to the boil.

6 Using a lightly floured slice, very carefully transfer one of the bagels to the boiling water. Simmer for 30 seconds before turning over. Simmer for a further 30 seconds, then remove with a slotted spoon. Drain well and set back on the baking sheet. Repeat with the remaining bagels.

7 Beat together the egg yolk and water and glaze each bagel. Bake for 15 minutes until golden. Cool on a wire rack.

Tips: If your pan is big enough, you can simmer two to three bagels at a time.

Try scattering seeds over the top before baking – linseed, poppy, sesame or black onion seeds all work well.

Pikelets

Makes: *around 26 pikelets* **Preparation time:** *10 minutes + proving + 30 minutes total cooking*
Freezing: *recommended*

These are great fun. Serve lightly toasted and buttered. Any left over will keep well for a couple of days or freeze beautifully.

225 g (8 oz) strong white bread flour
1 teaspoon caster sugar
½ teaspoon salt
1 teaspoon fast action dried yeast
¼ teaspoon bicarbonate of soda
175 ml (6 fl oz) warm semi-skimmed milk
175 ml (6 fl oz) hand-hot water
sunflower or vegetable oil, for brushing

1 Stir the flour, sugar, salt, yeast and
bicarbonate of soda together in a mixing bowl.
Gradually blend in the milk and water to make
a smooth batter. Beat for a couple of minutes
with a balloon whisk, cover with a clean,
damp tea towel and leave in a warm place
until the mixture becomes light and frothy. This
may take up to 1½ hours.

2 Beat the batter again, this time for about
1 minute, until it is smooth.

3 Warm a large, non-stick frying pan over a
medium heat. Brush the surface very lightly
with oil. Carefully spoon a tablespoon of
the batter into the pan to make a round.
Depending on the size of your pan, you
may be able to cook three or four spoonfuls
at a time.

4 Cook the pikelets for about 2 minutes,
until the bubbles have burst and the batter is
almost set. Turn over and continue cooking for
about 30 seconds until they are just starting to
colour. The underside should be a light golden
colour.

5 Repeat until all the batter has been used,
greasing the pan lightly between batches.
Cool on a wire rack.

Tip: This recipe can also be used to make
crumpets. Cook 2 tablespoons of batter in
greased 8 cm (3¼ inch) egg rings or biscuit
cutters. The cooking time will be a little
longer. Alternatively, downsize and make
mini pikelets to use as a base for canapés.

Irish Soda Bread

Makes: *1 loaf* **Preparation time:** *15 minutes + 35–40 minutes baking*
Freezing: *not recommended*

This traditional Irish bread uses bicarbonate of soda rather than yeast. Plain flour is also used as, in the past, Ireland's wet climate meant that hard varieties of wheat could not be grown there.

225 g (8 oz) plain flour, plus extra for dusting
225 g (8 oz) plain wholemeal flour
1 tablespoon muscovado sugar
2 teaspoons bicarbonate of soda
1 teaspoon salt
50 g (2 oz) toasted pumpkin seeds
250 g (9 oz) carton buttermilk made up to
   300 ml (½ pint) with water
1 medium egg, beaten

1 Preheat the oven to Gas Mark 6/200°C/400°F. Lightly grease a baking sheet.

2 Mix together the flours, sugar, bicarbonate of soda, salt and pumpkin seeds in a large bowl. Make a well in the centre and add the watered buttermilk and egg. Stir to form a soft dough.

3 Turn out on to a lightly floured surface and work quickly and gently to just bring the mixture together into a ball. Place on the baking sheet and flatten slightly. Using a sharp knife, score a deep cross on to the bread.

4 Bake for 35–40 minutes until golden and the base sounds hollow when tapped.

American Pumpernickel

Makes: *1 loaf* **Preparation time:** *20 minutes + proving + 40–45 minutes baking*
Freezing: *recommended*

Traditional German pumpernickel bread is made from rye flour and rye berries using a sourdough starter. This recipe is the American version and produces a lighter loaf. The texture is more bread-like than the German version and is best left unsliced for a day to develop a more 'chewy' texture.

175 g (6 oz) strong white bread flour
80 g (3 oz) strong wholemeal bread flour
80 g (3 oz) wholemeal rye flour
1 teaspoon sugar
1 teaspoon salt
1½ teaspoons fast action dried yeast
2 tablespoons cocoa powder
1 teaspoon instant coffee powder
2 tablespoons molasses
1 tablespoon sunflower oil
225 ml (8 fl oz) hand-hot water
For the glaze:
1 egg white
1 teaspoon water

1 Combine the flours, sugar, salt, yeast, cocoa powder and coffee powder in a bowl. Make a well in the centre and add the molasses, oil and water. Mix to a soft dough.

2 Turn out on to an unfloured work surface and knead (page 8) for 5–6 minutes until smooth. Place in an oiled polythene bag and prove (page 8) in a warm place until doubled in size.

3 Grease a 900 g (2 lb) loaf tin.

4 Knock back (page 9) the dough and shape into an oblong by putting both hands under the piece of dough furthest away and bringing it towards you, folding it over the rest of the dough. Push down to seal the edge nearest you. Give the dough a quarter turn and repeat until you have a smooth-shaped oblong. Lay it in the prepared tin, seam side down, cover and prove until doubled in size.

5 Preheat the oven to Gas Mark 4/180°C/350°F.

6 Beat the egg white with the water and use to glaze the top of the loaf. Bake for 40–45 minutes. Cool on a wire rack.

English Muffins

Makes: *around 12 muffins* **Preparation time:** *30 minutes + proving + 12–15 minutes baking*
Freezing: *recommended*

These are a lovely standby to have in the freezer as they defrost quickly and toast beautifully.

450 g (1 lb) strong white bread flour
50 g (2 oz) butter
2 teaspoons caster sugar
1 teaspoon salt
1 teaspoon fast action dried yeast
300 ml (½ pint) warm semi-skimmed milk
around 3 tablespoons fine semolina

1 Place the flour in a large mixing bowl and rub in the butter. Stir in the sugar, salt and yeast. Make a well in the centre, pour in the milk and mix to a soft dough.

2 Turn out on to an unfloured work surface and knead (page 8) for 8–10 minutes. Place in an oiled polythene bag and prove (page 8) in a warm place until doubled in size.

3 Grease four baking sheets and sprinkle them with the semolina.

4 Knock back (page 9) the dough and roll out to measure 1 cm (½ inch) thick. Using an 8 cm (3¼ inch) plain round cutter, cut out 11–12 muffins, re-rolling the dough as necessary. Space well apart on two of the prepared baking sheets, cover and prove in a warm place until doubled in size.

5 Preheat the oven to Gas Mark 7/220°C/425°F.

6 Carefully place a prepared baking sheet upside down on top of each tray of muffins. Bake for 12–15 minutes until golden. Cool on a wire rack.

Tips: The heavier the baking sheet on top of the muffins, the flatter they will be. You may need to shorten the baking time accordingly if the muffins are considerably squashed!

Split these in half to make quick mini pizza bases – spread with a little tomato purée or ketchup, pile on some flaked tuna and sweetcorn, finish with a little grated cheese and grill until golden.

Ciabatta

Makes: *1 large loaf* **Preparation time:** *15 minutes + overnight + proving + 15–20 minutes baking*
Freezing: *recommended*

As this needs starting the day before, it is well worth making this large loaf, half of which may be frozen for another time. Choose very strong or premium bread flour for this recipe as it is a very wet dough.

350 g (12 oz) very strong white bread flour,
    plus extra for dusting
1 teaspoon salt
1 teaspoon yeast
3 tablespoons extra virgin olive oil
200 ml (7 fl oz) hand-hot water
For the starter batter:
115 g (4 oz) very strong white bread flour
1 teaspoon sugar
½ teaspoon fast action dried yeast
150 ml (¼ pint) hand-hot water

1 Make the starter batter the night before. Place the flour, sugar and yeast in a small bowl and blend in the water. Mix to a smooth batter and cover with a damp tea towel.

2 The following day, mix together the flour, salt and yeast in a very large bowl. Make a well in the centre and add the starter batter, olive oil and a little of the water. Beat to a smooth paste, gradually adding all the water. You should end up with a thick batter. Cover with the damp tea towel and prove (page 8) for a couple of hours, until it almost triples in size.

3 Grease and flour a large baking sheet with sides.

4 Very carefully (so as not to knock out any of the air), tip the dough on to the baking sheet. Flour your hands well and pat and coax the dough into a long slipper shape, tucking the sides and ends under to plump up the dough. You should end up with a shape around 35 x 14 cm (14 x 5½ inches). Dust with what seems like an excessive amount of flour and prove, uncovered, for 45 minutes.

5 Preheat the oven to Gas Mark 7/220°C/425°F.

6 Bake for 15–20 minutes. Cool on a wire rack.

Olive and Feta Breads

Makes: *2 breads* **Preparation time:** *35 minutes + proving + 13–15 minutes baking*
Freezing: *recommended*

These delicious slipper breads make an ideal accompaniment to a main course salad in the summer.

350 g (12 oz) strong white bread flour
1 teaspoon caster sugar
1 teaspoon salt
1 teaspoon fast action dried yeast
1 teaspoon dried oregano
scant 225 ml (8 fl oz) hand-hot water (page 4)
3 tablespoons olive oil, plus 1 tablespoon for
   drizzling
50 g (2 oz) Feta cheese, cubed
25 g (1 oz) pitted black olives, roughly
   chopped

1 Combine the flour, sugar, salt, yeast and oregano in a mixing bowl. Make a well in the centre and add the water and 3 tablespoons olive oil. Mix together to form a dough.

2 Turn out on to an unfloured work surface and knead (page 8) for about 10 minutes until smooth. Work in the Feta cheese and olives. Divide the dough in two and place in an oiled polythene bag. Allow to rest for 10 minutes.

3 Grease a baking sheet.

4 Take one piece of dough and, using your hands, allow it to hang so that it takes on a teardrop shape measuring about 23 cm (9 inches) long and 13 cm (5 inches) in the widest part. The edges will be slightly thicker than the middle. Place on the baking sheet and repeat with the second piece of dough. Cover and prove (page 8) in a warm place until doubled in size.

5 Preheat the oven to Gas Mark 7/220°C/425°F.

6 Drizzle a little oil over the breads and bake for 13–15 minutes until golden. Cool on a wire rack.

Tip: Soft, black olives that have been preserved in salt are ideal for this recipe, even if it does mean going to the trouble of rinsing them and removing the stones.

Roasted Pepper Calzone

Makes: *6 calzone* **Preparation time:** *20 minutes + proving + 40–45 minutes cooking + 20–25 minutes baking* **Freezing:** *recommended*

Calzone are an Italian version of Cornish pasties. I have filled these with a medley of peppers – ideal for vegetarians.

350 g (12 oz) strong white bread flour, plus
extra for dusting
¾ teaspoon fast action dried yeast
¾ teaspoon salt
2 tablespoons extra virgin olive oil
scant 250 ml (8 fl oz) hand-hot water (page 4)
For the filling:
1 red, 1 yellow and 1 orange pepper,
de-seeded and sliced
400 g (14 oz) fresh tomatoes, halved
1 medium red onion, sliced
3–4 garlic cloves, unpeeled
2 sprigs of rosemary
3 tablespoons extra virgin olive oil
salt and freshly ground black pepper

1 Preheat the oven to Gas Mark 7/220°C/425°F.

2 Combine the flour, yeast and salt in a bowl. Make a well in the centre and pour in the oil and water. Mix to a soft dough.

3 Turn out on to an unfloured work surface. Knead (page 8) for about 10 minutes until smooth. Cover and prove (page 8) in a warm place until doubled in size.

4 Meanwhile, put the peppers, tomatoes, onion, garlic and rosemary into a large roasting pan so that they are in a single layer. Drizzle the oil over the top and season. Cook at the top of the oven for 40–45 minutes, turning half way through. Remove from the oven, cool and remove the skins from the garlic. Mash the flesh and mix into the roasted vegetables.

5 Grease two baking sheets and lightly dust with flour.

6 Divide the dough into six pieces. On a lightly floured surface, roll out each to an 18 cm (7 inch) circle. Place one sixth of the filling in the centre of each. Brush the edges with a little water. Turn over half of the dough to make a semi-circle and encase the filling. Pinch the edges together to seal, making a pattern as you wish. Place on the baking sheets, cover and prove for 30 minutes.

7 Bake for 20–25 minutes until golden. Serve warm or cold.

Garlic Butter Swirls

Makes: *12 rolls* **Preparation time:** *35 minutes + proving + 15–20 minutes baking*
Freezing: *recommended*

Serve these warm as an accompaniment to meatballs or spaghetti Bolognese, encouraging everyone to tear off a portion.

350 g (12 oz) mixed grain bread flour
25 g (1 oz) butter
¾ teaspoon salt
1 teaspoon fast action dried yeast
scant 250 ml (8 fl oz) hand-hot water (page 4)
For the garlic butter:
50 g (2 oz) butter, melted and cooled
2 garlic cloves, crushed
a squeeze of lemon juice
2 tablespoons chopped fresh parsley
salt and freshly ground black pepper

1 Lightly grease a shallow, 25 x 17 cm (10 x 6½ inch) baking tin.

2 Place the flour in a bowl and rub in the butter. Stir in the salt and yeast. Make a well in the centre and add enough water to make a soft dough.

3 Turn out on to an unfloured work surface and knead (page 8) for 8–10 minutes until smooth. Place in an oiled polythene bag for 10 minutes to give the dough a chance to relax.

4 Lightly flour the work surface and roll the dough out to 35 x 25 cm (14 x 10 inches). Mix together the butter, garlic and lemon juice and drizzle evenly over the dough, taking it right to the edges. Scatter the parsley over the top and season lightly.

5 Roll up the dough tightly from the long edge and pinch the seam together to seal. Using a sharp knife, cut the roll into 12 equal pieces. Turn the pieces so that the spiral is facing upwards and space evenly in the prepared tin. Pour any leftover garlic butter over the surface, cover and prove (page 8) in a warm place until doubled in size.

6 Preheat the oven to Gas Mark 7/220°C/425°F.

7 Bake the bread for 15–20 minutes until golden. Allow to cool slightly on a wire rack before serving warm.

Variation: Sprinkle a few chilli flakes over the garlic butter before rolling up the dough.

Onion and Poppy Seed Bread

Makes: *1 loaf* **Preparation time:** *35 minutes + proving + 20–25 minutes baking*
Freezing: *recommended*

Rye flour gives this bread a lovely colour as well as adding to its flavour. This is a great loaf to take on a picnic and goes well with cheese.

3 tablespoons extra virgin olive oil

1 large onion, chopped

225 g (8 oz) strong white bread flour, plus extra for dusting

115 g (4 oz) wholemeal rye flour

1 teaspoon muscovado sugar

1 teaspoon salt

1 teaspoon fast action dried yeast

2 teaspoons poppy seeds

250 ml (8 fl oz) hand-hot water

1 Heat 1 tablespoon of the oil in a small pan and soften the onion for 5–10 minutes until golden. Cool.

2 Mix together the flours, sugar, salt, yeast and poppy seeds. Make a well in the centre and add the water and remaining oil. Mix to a soft dough.

3 Turn out on to an unfloured work surface and knead (page 8) for 10 minutes until smooth. Knead in the softened onion. Don't worry that the dough becomes wet and sticky at this stage – keep kneading until it becomes smooth again. Place in an oiled bag to relax for 10 minutes.

4 Preheat the oven to Gas Mark 7/220°C/425°F. Grease a baking sheet.

5 Lightly flour the work surface and roll out the dough to 28 x 18 cm (11 x 7 inches). Roll up from the long side and place on the baking sheet with the join on the bottom. Make random snips in the top using scissors, so that the bread has a spiky appearance. Cover and prove (page 8) in a warm place until doubled in size.

6 Bake for 20–25 minutes until golden and hollow when tapped on the base. Cool on a wire rack.

Mixed Seed Flower Pot Loaves

Makes: *2 loaves* **Preparation time:** *20 minutes + proving + 25–30 minutes baking*
Freezing: *recommended*

This method of baking recreates the clay ovens that used to be widely used and are still found in some parts of the world. The pots give the bread a lovely crust and provide a novel shaped loaf.

lard or white vegetable fat, for greasing
225 g (8 oz) strong wholemeal bread flour
225 g (8 oz) strong white bread flour
1 teaspoon salt
1¼ teaspoons fast action dried yeast
8 tablespoons mixed seeds (sunflower,
    pumpkin, hemp and linseeds), toasted
1 tablespoon sunflower oil
1 teaspoon runny honey
325 ml (11 fl oz) hand-hot water
For the topping:
1 teaspoon salt, dissolved in 1 tablespoon
    boiling water, cooled
sunflower seeds and linseeds, for sprinkling

1 'Season' two new 13 cm (5 inch) earthenware flower pots. Grease with lard or white vegetable fat and stand on a baking sheet. Bake in a hot oven for 5 minutes, then allow to cool. Repeat this process at least four times to ensure that you have a waterproof seal.

2 In a large bowl, combine the flours, salt, yeast and seeds. Make a well in the centre and add the oil, honey and water. Mix to a soft dough.

3 Turn out on to an unfloured work surface and knead (page 8) for 5 minutes until smooth. Divide the dough into two. Shape each piece into a round, and then elongate slightly so it fits when placed in a flowerpot. Cover and prove (page 8) in a warm place until doubled in size and the dough is level with the top of the flowerpot.

4 Preheat the oven to Gas Mark 7/220°C/425°F.

5 Stand the flowerpots on a baking tray and brush with the salt water. Sprinkle liberally with seeds. Bake one rung below the centre of the oven for 25–30 minutes, covering with parchment paper if they brown too fast. Turn out on to a wire rack to cool.

Tips: Do take care when handling the pots as they will retain heat. Afterwards, clean them by wiping with a damp cloth – don't put them in water as this may break the waterproof seal you created.

If you do not wish to use flowerpots this quantity of dough is sufficient for two 450 g (1 lb) loaves, or one 900 g (2 lb) loaf. Alternatively, divide into 12 rolls.

Sage, Pancetta and Potato Bread

Makes: *1 loaf* **Preparation time:** *30 minutes + proving + 20 minutes simmering + 20–25 minutes baking* **Freezing:** *recommended*

This is delicious served warm from the oven with soups or casseroles.

175 g (6 oz) floury potatoes, peeled
350 g (12 oz) very strong white bread flour
¾ teaspoon salt
1½ teaspoons fast action dried yeast
freshly ground black pepper
175 ml (6 fl oz) hand-hot water
105 g (3½ oz) packet smoked pancetta slices, snipped
15 g (½ oz) fresh sage, chopped, plus 5 sage leaves to garnish
1 tablespoon extra virgin olive oil

1 Put the potatoes in a pan, cover with cold water, bring to the boil and simmer for 15–20 minutes until tender. Drain well and mash until smooth. Press a piece of clingfilm on to the surface of the mash to prevent it from drying and leave to cool slightly.

2 Combine the flour, salt and yeast in a mixing bowl. Season with pepper. Rub in the potato (which can be added while still warm). Make a well in the centre and add the water. Mix to a soft dough.

3 Turn out on to an unfloured work surface and knead (page 8) for 5–6 minutes until smooth. Oil a large mixing bowl, place the dough in it and cover with a damp tea towel. Prove (page 8) in a warm place until doubled in size.

4 Heat a small saucepan over a medium heat. Add the pancetta and cook for 2 minutes until it starts to crisp up and any fat runs out. Stir in the chopped sage and cook for a further 30 seconds. The pancetta should be very crisp. Set aside to cool.

5 Grease a baking sheet or 23 cm (9 inch) round sandwich cake tin.

6 Knead the pancetta, sage and any fat from the pan into the dough. For a rustic appearance, form roughly into a square or oblong and place on the baking sheet. Alternatively, shape into a ball and place in the prepared tin. Cover and prove until doubled in size. Preheat the oven to Gas Mark 7/220°C/425°F.

7 Dip each sage leaf in oil and arrange in a pattern on top of the loaf. Drizzle the remaining oil over the surface of the dough. Bake for 20–25 minutes until golden and the base sounds hollow when tapped. Cool on a wire rack.

Tip: If the dough is too sticky to handle, beat it with a wooden spoon instead of kneading and scrape the mixture into the tin.

Tomato and Red Pepper Tear 'n' Share Bread

Serves: *8–10* **Preparation time:** *30 minutes + proving + 25 minutes baking*
Freezing: *recommended*

Based on focaccia bread, this is similar to a vegetarian pizza but is best eaten as an accompaniment, rather than as a main meal.

350 g (12 oz) strong white bread flour
1 teaspoon sugar
¾ teaspoon salt
1 teaspoon fast action dried yeast
2 tablespoons extra virgin olive oil
225 ml (8 fl oz) hand-hot water
For the topping:
1 tablespoon sun-dried tomato paste
50 g (2 oz) small cherry tomatoes, halved
half a 290 g jar chargrilled red peppers in oil, drained and sliced
80 g (3 oz) mild, soft goat's cheese
50 g (2 oz) grated mozzarella
8 sprigs of fresh basil leaves
freshly ground black pepper
1 tablespoon extra virgin olive oil

1 Grease a 22 x 33 cm (8½ x 13 inch) Swiss roll tin.

2 Combine the flour, sugar, salt and yeast in a mixing bowl. Stir in the oil and water and mix to a soft dough.

3 Turn out on to an unfloured work surface and knead (page 8) for about 10 minutes until smooth. Leave to relax for 10 minutes. Press the dough evenly into the base of the prepared tin. Cover and prove (page 8) in a warm place until doubled in size.

4 Using your fingers, make dents all over the surface of the dough, pushing right through to the bottom of the tin. Gently spread the tomato paste over the surface. Push in the cherry tomatoes and scatter strips of peppers evenly over the top. Dot the goat's cheese over the dough in about ½ teaspoon measures and sprinkle with mozzarella. Scatter basil over the top and season with pepper. Finally, finish with a drizzle of olive oil. Leave to rise for a further 20–30 minutes.

5 Preheat the oven to Gas Mark 6/200°C/400°F.

6 Bake for about 25 minutes. Cool slightly before presenting at the table and inviting everyone to help themselves.

Tip: Always useful to have as a standby, it is just as quick to make up double the quantity of dough and freeze half. This can also be made in a 28 cm (11 inch) flan tin.

Fennel, Oregano and Pine Nut Ring

Makes: *1 loaf* **Preparation time:** *40 minutes + proving + 20–25 minutes baking*
Freezing: *recommended*

The fennel gives this bread a subtle flavour and keeps it moist. Like most home-made breads it is best eaten warm from the oven.

25 g (1 oz) butter
1 small fennel bulb, finely chopped
400 g (14 oz) strong white bread flour
50 g (2 oz) wholemeal rye flour, plus extra for dusting
1 tablespoon muscovado sugar
1 teaspoon salt
1½ teaspoons fast action dried yeast
2 teaspoons dried oregano
40 g (1½ oz) pine nuts, toasted
300 ml (½ pint) hand-hot water

1 Melt the butter in a pan, add the fennel and cook gently for about 10 minutes until softened but not browned. Leave to cool.

2 Meanwhile, mix together the flours, sugar, salt, yeast, oregano and pine nuts. Make a well in the centre and add the water. Stir to form a soft dough.

3 Turn out on to an unfloured work surface and knead (page 8) for 10 minutes until smooth. Gradually work in the cooked fennel. The dough will become sticky, so flour your hands if necessary. Place the dough in an oiled bag for 10 minutes to allow it to relax.

4 Grease a baking sheet.

5 Using your hands, shape the dough into a log and roll it until it is 50 cm (20 inches) long. Transfer to the prepared baking sheet and form it into a ring, sealing the ends together well. Make sure that the seam is underneath. Using a sharp pair of scissors, snip a pattern all around the top of the ring. Cover and prove (page 8) in a warm place until doubled in size.

6 Preheat the oven to Gas Mark 7/220°C/425°F.

7 Dust the bread with a little rye flour and bake for 20–25 minutes until golden. Cool on a wire rack.

Tip: This is a lovely bread for cheese sandwiches, or try it toasted the next day and spread with Marmite.

Beer Bread

Makes: *1 loaf* **Preparation time:** *15 minutes + proving + 20–25 minutes baking*
Freezing: *recommended*

It is always difficult to guess a dedicated beer drinker's reaction to bread made with beer. Will it be welcomed, or regarded as sacrilege? In fact the end product is quite subtle, producing a bread with universal appeal. It is great with a ploughman's lunch or if used to make sandwiches.

225 g (8 oz) strong white bread flour
115 g (4 oz) wholemeal rye flour, plus extra for dusting
¾ teaspoon salt
1 teaspoon fast action dried yeast
225 ml (8 fl oz) ale or stout
1 tablespoon sunflower oil
2 teaspoons runny honey

Tip: When you measure the beer, allow the frothy head to subside to ensure that you have the exact quantity needed.

1 Lightly grease a baking sheet.

2 Combine the flours, salt and yeast in a mixing bowl. Stir in the beer, oil and honey to make a soft dough.

3 Turn out on to a work surface and knead (page 8) for 7–8 minutes until smooth. Shape into a round, place on the baking sheet and, using a sharp knife, make five slashes across the top of the loaf. Cover and prove (page 8) in a warm place until doubled in size.

4 Preheat the oven to Gas Mark 6/200°C/400°F.

5 Dust the bread with a little rye flour and bake for 20–25 minutes. Cool on a wire rack.

Mushroom and Melted Cheese Pie

Serves: 6 **Preparation time:** *35 minutes + proving + 30 minutes baking*
Freezing: *recommended*

This is an unexpected pie, almost a ready-made cooked sandwich.

350 g (12 oz) strong white bread flour
1 teaspoon sugar
¾ teaspoon salt
1 teaspoon fast action dried yeast
2 tablespoons extra virgin olive oil
225 ml (8 fl oz) hand-hot water
a little oil for brushing
For the filling:
25 g (1 oz) butter
225 g (8 oz) flat field mushrooms, wiped,
    halved and thinly sliced
1 fat garlic clove, crushed
salt and freshly ground black pepper
115 g (4 oz) Fontina cheese, cubed
50 g (2 oz) grated mozzarella
2 teaspoons chopped fresh thyme
For the topping:
a few sprigs of fresh thyme
1 tablespoon extra virgin olive oil
coarse sea salt

1 Grease a 23 cm (9 inch) flan ring or loose bottomed sandwich tin.

2 Combine the flour, sugar, salt and yeast in a mixing bowl. Stir in the oil and water and mix to a soft dough.

3 Turn out on to an unfloured work surface and knead (page 8) for about 10 minutes until smooth. Cover and prove (page 8) in a warm place until doubled in size.

4 Meanwhile, melt the butter in a pan and sauté the mushrooms and garlic, continuing to cook until the juices have been reabsorbed by the mushrooms or have evaporated off. Season and leave to cool.

5 Halve the dough and press one half into the base of the prepared tin. Brush a little oil around the edge of the dough. Spoon the mushroom mixture evenly over the top to within 1 cm (½ inch) of the edge. Scatter the cheeses over the top and sprinkle with thyme. Take the remaining dough and roll out on a lightly floured surface to a 23 cm (9 inch) round. Place on top of the filling and press the edges down well to seal. The dough should completely cover the bottom layer.

6 With your fingertips, make random, deep indents all over the surface, pushing through to the filling without making any actual holes. Push sprigs of thyme into the dough and drizzle with the oil. Scatter a little sea salt over the top. Cover and prove for about 20 minutes, until the dough is puffy.

7 Preheat the oven to Gas Mark 6/200°C/400°F.

8 Place the pie on a baking sheet and bake for 30 minutes until golden. Leave in the tin for 5 minutes before removing and serving warm.

Variation: Pont L'Evêque and Taleggio cheeses melt beautifully and would work well instead of Fontina.

Brie and Redcurrant Bites

Makes: *24 rolls* **Preparation time:** *45 minutes + proving + 20–25 minutes baking*
Freezing: *recommended*

These are brilliant for a tear-and-share starter. Put them in the centre of the table and invite your guests to help themselves. They look especially pretty in the summer when thyme is young and tender.

225 g (8 oz) strong white bread flour
25 g (1 oz) butter
½ teaspoon sugar
½ teaspoon salt
¾ teaspoon fast action dried yeast
150 ml (¼ pint) hand-hot water
For the filling:
2 tablespoons redcurrant jelly
115 g (4 oz) Brie (not too ripe), cut into 24 cubes
2 tablespoons fresh thyme leaves
For the topping:
1 egg
1 tablespoon water
a handful of sesame seeds
fresh thyme leaves

1 Put the flour in a bowl and rub in the butter. Stir in the sugar, salt and yeast and mix to a soft dough with the water.

2 Turn out on to an unfloured work surface and knead (page 8) for 10 minutes until smooth. Place in an oiled polythene bag and leave to rest for 10 minutes.

3 Grease a 23 cm (9 inch) sandwich tin.

4 Divide the dough into 24 pieces. Working with one piece at a time while the others remain covered, press out into a 6 cm (2½ inch) disc using your fingertips. Place ¼ teaspoon redcurrant jelly in the centre, followed by a piece of Brie and a sprinkling of thyme leaves. Bring up the edges of the dough to encase the filling and pinch together to seal. Roll gently in your hand to form a ball shape. Place in the prepared tin.

5 Repeat with the remaining dough, placing the balls sealed side down in rings in the tin. Cover and prove (page 8) in a warm place until doubled in size.

6 Preheat the oven to Gas Mark 6/200°C/400°F.

7 Beat the egg and water together. Either brush the rolls with the egg glaze and sprinkle with sesame seeds, or just top each roll with some thyme leaves. Doing half and half takes longer but looks very attractive. Bake for 20–25 minutes. Cool for 5 minutes then turn out on to a wire rack.

Tip: Serve these warm while the cheese is still melted.

Golden Grain Finger Rolls

Makes: *16 rolls* **Preparation time:** *25 minutes + proving + 10–12 minutes baking*
Freezing: *recommended*

These rolls are tasty and sweet and have added texture from the grains and seeds. The egg gives them more of a 'cakey' texture.

450 g (1 lb) malted grain bread flour
50 g (2 oz) butter
1 tablespoon muscovado sugar
1 teaspoon salt
1½ teaspoons fast action dried yeast
25 g (1 oz) golden linseeds, toasted
25 g (1 oz) sunflower seeds, toasted
2 medium eggs, beaten
175 ml (6 fl oz) warm semi-skimmed milk
For the topping:
1 egg
1 tablespoon water
a handful of mixed linseeds and sunflower
    seeds

Tip: These are delicious filled or as an accompaniment to soup.

1 Lightly grease a baking sheet.

2 Put the flour in a bowl and rub in the butter. Stir in the sugar, salt, yeast and seeds. Add the eggs and milk and mix to a soft dough.

3 Turn out on to an unfloured work surface and knead (page 8) for about 10 minutes until smooth. Do not worry if the dough is quite sticky – keep working it and it will become more manageable. Divide the dough into 16 pieces, shape into sausages and place side by side, almost touching, on the baking sheet. Cover and prove (page 8) in a warm place until doubled in size.

4 Preheat the oven to Gas Mark 6/200°C/400°F.

5 Beat the egg and water together. Brush the rolls with the egg glaze and sprinkle with the seeds. Bake for 10–12 minutes. Cool on a wire rack.

Sweet Chestnut Bread

Makes: *2 batons* **Preparation time:** *20 minutes + proving + 25 minutes baking*
Freezing: *recommended*

If you don't know, it is hard to tell what ingredients have gone into this bread. The sweet chestnuts, enhanced with a little vanilla, produce a wonderful loaf that works well as a sweet or savoury accompaniment.

350 g (12 oz) strong white bread flour
115 g (4 oz) wholemeal rye flour
25 g (1 oz) butter
1 tablespoon sugar
1 teaspoon salt
1¼ teaspoons fast action dried yeast
100 g (3½ oz) vacuum-packed chestnuts, finely chopped
300 ml (½ pint) semi-skimmed milk
½ teaspoon vanilla essence

Tip: Use leftover chestnuts to flavour any of the more basic breads in this book, such as Polenta Bread (page 30) or Soya Flour Bread (page 31).

1 Combine the flours in a bowl and rub in the butter. Stir in the sugar, salt, yeast and chestnuts. Add the milk and vanilla essence and mix to a soft dough.

2 Turn out on to an unfloured work surface and knead (page 8) for 8–10 minutes until smooth. Cover and prove (page 8) in a warm place until doubled in size.

3 Grease a large baking sheet.

4 Divide the dough in half and shape each piece into a baton about 30 cm (12 inches) long. Place well apart on the baking sheet and make diagonal cuts across the top of each. Cover and prove until doubled in size.

5 Preheat the oven to Gas Mark 6/200°C/400°F.

6 Bake for 25 minutes until golden. Cool on a wire rack.

Illustrated on page 33

Gruyère Baps

Makes: *8 giant baps* **Preparation time:** *30 minutes + proving + 15 minutes baking*
Freezing: *recommended*

These baps look enormous, but because the dough is so light they can afford to be huge. If you prefer, you can divide the dough into 12.

450 g (1 lb) strong white bread flour
50 g (2 oz) unsalted butter
1 teaspoon sugar
1 teaspoon salt
1½ teaspoons fast action dried yeast
2 medium eggs, beaten
175 ml (6 fl oz) warm semi-skimmed milk
200 g (7 oz) Gruyère cheese, finely grated
For the glaze:
1 egg
1 tablespoon water

1 Place the flour in a large mixing bowl and rub in the butter. Stir in the sugar, salt and yeast. Make a well in the centre and add the eggs and milk. Mix to a soft dough.

2 Turn out on to an unfloured work surface and knead (page 8) for 10 minutes until smooth. Place in an oiled polythene bag and leave in a warm place to prove (page 8) until doubled in size.

3 Lightly grease two baking sheets.

4 Knead most of the cheese into the dough, saving about 25 g (1 oz) for the top. Divide the dough into eight. Shape into rounds and hammer each one down hard with the heel of your hand to flatten. The baps should

measure about 10 cm (4 inches) across. Space well apart on the baking sheets, cover and prove until doubled in size.

5 Preheat the oven to Gas Mark 6/200°C/400°F.

6 Beat the egg and water together. Brush each bap twice with the egg glaze and sprinkle the remaining cheese over the tops. Bake for 15 minutes.

7 Remove from the oven and transfer to a cooling rack. Cover at once with a clean tea towel (this will give them a soft crust) and leave to cool.

Tip: These make a lovely lunchtime meal, filled with sliced ham, mustard and cress.

Chorizo and Tomato Bread

Makes: *1 loaf* **Preparation time:** *25 minutes + proving + 30–35 minutes baking*
Freezing: *recommended*

This bread is full of colour and flavour – vivid orange with a 'kick' from the chorizo. It is ideal as an accompaniment to a main course salad.

350 g (12 oz) strong white bread flour

2 teaspoons sugar

¾ teaspoon salt

¾ teaspoon fast action dried yeast

½ teaspoon dried thyme

1 tablespoon tomato purée

1 tablespoon olive oil

scant 225 ml (½ pint) hand-hot water (page 4)

50 g (2 oz) semi-dried tomatoes in olive oil, roughly chopped

40 g (1½ oz) thinly sliced chorizo, chopped

1 Combine the flour, sugar, salt, yeast and thyme in a bowl. Stir in the tomato purée, olive oil and enough water to make a soft dough.

2 Turn out on to an unfloured work surface and knead (page 8) for 8–10 minutes until smooth. Place in an oiled polythene bag and prove (page 8) in a warm place until doubled in size.

3 Grease a baking sheet.

4 Knead the tomatoes and chorizo into the dough. Form into a rugby ball shape, place on the baking sheet and, using a sharp knife, slash three times lengthwise along the top of the dough. Cover and prove until doubled in size.

5 Preheat the oven to Gas Mark 6/200°C/400°F.

6 Bake for 30–35 minutes. Remove to a wire rack and serve warm or cold.

Walnut and Raisin Bread

Makes: *1 loaf* **Preparation time:** *20 minutes + proving + 20–25 minutes baking*
Freezing: *recommended*

This bread is delicious topped with pears and cheese – try a soft, mild goat's cheese or a creamy blue such as Gorgonzola, dolcelatte or St. Agur.

175 g (6 oz) strong wholemeal bread flour
175 g (6 oz) strong white bread flour
115 g (4 oz) wholemeal rye flour, plus extra for dusting
1 teaspoon salt
1 teaspoon fast action dried yeast
115 g (4 oz) walnuts, toasted and chopped
80 g (3 oz) raisins
2 tablespoons walnut oil
1 tablespoon runny honey
325 ml (11 fl oz) hand-hot water

Tip: To toast the walnuts, fry them gently in a dry frying pan until they are golden brown.

Variation: Try substituting chopped dried apricots for the raisins.

1 Grease a baking sheet.

2 Combine the flours, salt, yeast, walnuts and raisins in a large mixing bowl. Stir in the oil, honey and water. Mix to a soft dough.

3 Turn out on to an unfloured work surface and knead (page 8) for 5–6 minutes until smooth. Shape into an 18 cm (7 inch) oblong, and place on the baking sheet. Using a sharp knife, make a cut along the length slightly to one side. Dust with a little rye flour. Cover and prove (page 8) in a warm place to double in size.

4 Preheat the oven to Gas Mark 6/200°C/400°F.

5 Bake for 20–25 minutes. Cool on a wire rack.

American Rye Bread

Makes: *1 loaf* **Preparation time:** *20 minutes + proving + 35–40 minutes baking*
Freezing: *recommended*

Traditional rye bread uses a sourdough starter to give it its distinctive taste. This American version takes a short cut, using natural yogurt instead to achieve a similar flavour.

300 g (10 oz) wholemeal rye flour
175 g (6 oz) strong white bread flour
1 tablespoon molasses sugar
1 teaspoon salt
1¼ teaspoons fast action dried yeast
200 ml (7 fl oz) hand-hot water
150 ml (5 fl oz) natural yogurt

1 Combine the flours, sugar, salt and yeast in a bowl. Make a well in the centre and add the water and yogurt. Mix to a soft dough.

2 Turn out on to an unfloured work surface and knead (page 8) for 5–6 minutes until smooth, scraping off the work surface as necessary. Place in an oiled bag and prove (page 8) in a warm place until doubled in size.

3 Grease a baking sheet.

4 Using floured hands, knock back (page 9) the dough and shape into a round. Place on the baking sheet and, using a sharp knife, make a deep cut down the centre. Cut three diagonal lines off this on each side to make a tree-like effect. Cover and prove once more until doubled in size.

5 Preheat the oven to Gas Mark 6/200°C/400°F.

6 Bake for 35–40 minutes, until golden and the base sounds hollow when tapped.

Tip: Rye flour handles differently to strong wheat flour. Just keep working the dough and don't be tempted to add extra flour, as you will end up with a dry loaf.

Sea Salt and Cracked Pepper Grissini

Makes: *24 grissini* **Preparation time:** *25 minutes + proving + 18–20 minutes baking*
Freezing: *recommended*

There are some wonderful sea salts available that are mixed with seaweed, spices, seeds and herbs, including their flowers. These all blend beautifully with this dough.

semolina, for sprinkling
350 g (12 oz) strong white bread flour
1 teaspoon sugar
1 teaspoon coarse sea salt
¾ teaspoon fast action dried yeast
1 teaspoon dried green peppercorns, lightly
  crushed
2 tablespoons extra virgin olive oil
scant 225 ml (8 fl oz) hand-hot water (page 4)
sunflower oil, for oiling

Tip: Delicious in the summer with a well-chilled aperitif, the dough could be made up without any flavourings, and then halved, and various ingredients added to each batch, such as sesame, fennel or poppy seeds. Alternatively, brush with garlic butter, or sprinkle with finely grated Parmesan.

1 Grease two baking sheets and sprinkle lightly with semolina.

2 Combine the flour, sugar, salt, yeast and peppercorns in a bowl. Make a well in the centre and add the olive oil and water. Mix to a soft dough.

3 Turn out on to an unfloured work surface and knead (page 8) for 10 minutes until smooth. Oil a patch of the work surface with sunflower oil, place the dough on it and cover with a tea towel. Leave to rest for 10 minutes.

4 Using a sharp knife, divide the dough into 24 pieces. Cover the pieces you are not working with. Using your fingers, and working from the middle outwards, roll out each piece into 28 cm (11 inch) lengths.

5 Place the breadsticks on the baking sheets, ensuring that they do not touch, and sprinkle lightly with semolina if you wish. Cover again and prove (page 8) in a warm place for 45 minutes.

6 Preheat the oven to Gas Mark 6/200°C/400°F.

7 Bake for 18–20 minutes until crisp and golden. Cool on a wire rack.

Onion Kuchen

Serves: *6–8* **Preparation time:** *35 minutes + proving + 30 minutes baking*
Freezing: *not recommended*

Kuchen means cake in German. Although most of the kuchen served in German coffee shops are sweet varieties, this is a savoury recipe.

225 g (8 oz) strong white bread flour
25 g (1 oz) butter
1 teaspoon caster sugar
½ teaspoon salt
¾ teaspoon fast action dried yeast
150–175 ml (5–6 fl oz) warm semi-skimmed
    milk
For the topping:
25 g (1 oz) butter
225 g (8 oz) onions, sliced
1 fat clove garlic, crushed
175 g (6 oz) mascarpone
salt and freshly ground black pepper
1 teaspoon poppy seeds

1 Grease a 20 cm (8 inch) sandwich tin.

2 Place the flour in a mixing bowl and rub in the butter. Stir in the sugar, salt and yeast and mix to a soft dough with the milk.

3 Turn out on to an unfloured work surface and knead (page 8) for about 10 minutes until smooth. Cover and leave to relax for 10 minutes.

4 Meanwhile, heat the butter in a fairly large saucepan. Add the onions and garlic and cook for about 10 minutes until softened but not coloured, stirring frequently. Turn out on to a plate and leave to cool.

5 Press the dough into the prepared tin, working it to the edges with your fingers and ensuring that it is an even thickness. Cover and prove (page 8) in a warm place until doubled in size.

6 Preheat the oven to Gas Mark 5/190°C/375°F.

7 Beat the mascarpone in a small bowl and stir in the onions and garlic until thoroughly combined. Season to taste. Spread the onion mixture evenly over the dough, leaving a 1 cm (½ inch) rim around the edge. Sprinkle with poppy seeds.

8 Bake for 30 minutes until the onion is tinged dark brown. Remove from the oven, run a knife around the edge of the tin and allow to stand for 10 minutes before transferring to a cooling rack. Serve warm.

Tip: Sprinkle with ⅛ teaspoon crushed dried chillies just prior to baking for an added kick.

Fiery Chicken and Pesto Pizzas

Makes: *2 pizzas* **Preparation time:** *35 minutes + proving + 30 minutes cooking + 10–12 minutes baking* **Freezing:** *not recommended*

These flavoursome pizzas are so much nicer than shop bought ones. The chilli flakes add a little kick.

225 g (8 oz) strong white bread flour
½ teaspoon salt
¾ teaspoon fast action dried yeast
1 tablespoon extra virgin olive oil, plus extra for brushing
150 ml (¼ pint) hand-hot water
semolina, for sprinkling
For the tomato sauce:
400 g can chopped tomatoes
1 garlic clove, crushed
1 tablespoon tomato purée
1 tablespoon extra virgin olive oil
½ teaspoon red wine vinegar
½ teaspoon dried oregano
sugar, salt and freshly ground black pepper, to taste
For the topping:
115 g (4 oz) cooked, diced chicken breast tossed in 2 teaspoons extra virgin olive oil and ⅛ teaspoon crushed chilli flakes
50 g (2 oz) buffalo mozzarella, torn into small pieces
4 teaspoons basil pesto
2 tablespoons grated Parmesan
a handful of fresh basil leaves

1 Combine the flour, salt and yeast in a bowl. Make a well in the centre and pour in the oil and water. Mix to a soft dough.

2 Turn out on to an unfloured work surface. Knead (page 8) for about 10 minutes until smooth, cover and prove (page 8) in a warm place until doubled in size.

3 Combine all the tomato sauce ingredients in a small saucepan. Bring to the boil and simmer, uncovered, for about 30 minutes, until thickened. Allow to cool.

4 Preheat the oven to Gas Mark 8/230°C/450°F. Grease two baking sheets and sprinkle them with semolina.

5 Divide the dough in two and roll out on a lightly floured surface to make two 25 cm (10 inch) discs. Place each on a baking sheet and brush lightly with olive oil.

6 Spread the tomato sauce to within 2.5 cm (1 inch) of the edge. Scatter over the chicken and mozzarella. Dot over the pesto and sprinkle with Parmesan.

7 Bake for 10–12 minutes until the base is crisp and the cheese has melted. Serve at once, sprinkled with fresh basil leaves.

Sesame Bread

Makes: *1 loaf* **Preparation time:** *20 minutes + proving + 15–20 minutes baking*
Freezing: *recommended*

The joy of this loaf is that it is actually formed from rolls that are joined together – built-in portion control! Using sesame oil in the dough brings out the flavour of the seeds and gives a deep underlying sesame taste.

350 g (12 oz) strong white bread flour
½ teaspoon sugar
¾ teaspoon salt
¾ teaspoon fast action dried yeast
1 tablespoon toasted sesame oil
225 ml (8 fl oz) hand-hot water
For the topping:
**1 teaspoon salt dissolved in 1 tablespoon
    boiling water, cooled**
1 tablespoon sesame seeds

1 Combine the flour, sugar, salt and yeast in a bowl. Add the sesame oil and water and mix to a soft dough.

2 Turn out on to an unfloured work surface and knead (page 8) for 8–10 minutes to a smooth dough. Cover and prove (page 8) in a warm place until doubled in size.

3 Grease a large baking sheet.

4 Without kneading the dough, cut into nine equal pieces. Place these on the baking sheet, offsetting the rolls, left and right, so that they touch and overlap the ones to each side by half. They will join up when proved to form an irregular shaped baton. Cover and prove in a warm place until doubled in size.

5 Preheat the oven to Gas Mark 7/220°C/425°F.

6 Brush the loaf with the salt water wash and sprinkle liberally with sesame seeds.

7 Bake for 15–20 minutes until golden. Cool on a wire rack.

Wild Herb Focaccia

Makes: *1 loaf* **Preparation time:** *25 minutes + proving + 20 minutes baking*
Freezing: *recommended*

You can use any herbs for this bread. Some are stronger than others, so vary the amount depending on which you choose.

350 g (12 oz) strong white bread flour
¾ teaspoon salt
¾ teaspoon fast action dried yeast
4 tablespoons extra virgin olive oil
scant 225 ml (8 fl oz) hand-hot water (page 4)
2 tablespoons chopped fresh herbs (such as thyme, rosemary or oregano)
¼ teaspoon coarse sea salt

1 Combine the flour, salt and yeast in a bowl. Make a well in the centre and add 2 tablespoons of the oil and the water. Mix to a soft dough.

2 Turn out on to an unfloured work surface and knead (page 8) for about 8–10 minutes until smooth. Allow to rest for 10 minutes.

3 Grease a 23 cm (9 inch) flan ring and place on a baking sheet.

4 Press the dough into the flan ring. Cover and prove (page 8) in a warm place until doubled in size.

5 Flour your fingertips and make indentations all over the surface of the dough. Push the herbs into the holes and drizzle with the remaining olive oil. Sprinkle with coarse sea salt, cover and leave to rise for another 20–30 minutes.

6 Preheat the oven to Gas Mark 7/220°C/ 425°F.

7 Bake for 20 minutes until golden. Transfer to a wire rack and serve warm or cold.

Stromboli

Serves: *8–10* **Preparation time:** *40 minutes + proving + 30–35 minutes baking*
Freezing: *not recommended*

This is an easy-cutting bread that creates ready-made sandwiches. Traditional Italian '00' flour makes a lovely smooth dough. Just remember to read the label and check that it is for bread making and contains at least 11 g protein per 100 g flour.

450 g (1 lb) strong white bread flour or '00' white flour
1 teaspoon salt
1 teaspoon fast action dried yeast
3 tablespoons extra virgin olive oil
300 ml (½ pint) hand-hot water
extra virgin olive oil, for brushing
For the filling:
75 g (2¾ oz) Parma, Prosciutto or Serrano ham
150 g (5 oz) mozzarella, torn
150 g (5 oz) Fontina cheese, cut into small cubes
25 g (1 oz) grated Parmesan
half a 280 g jar chargrilled artichoke hearts, cut into small pieces
half a 280 g jar chargrilled red peppers, thickly sliced
15 g (½ oz) fresh basil leaves
freshly ground black pepper

1 Combine the flour, salt and yeast in a large mixing bowl. Make a well in the centre and add the olive oil and water. Mix to a dough.

2 Turn out on to an unfloured work surface and knead (page 8) for about 10 minutes until smooth. Cover and prove (page 8) in a warm place until doubled in size.

3 Grease a baking sheet.

4 On a lightly floured work surface, roll out the dough to 40 x 28 cm (16 x 11 inches). Lay the ham over the surface to within 2 cm (¾ inch) of the edge. Scatter over the cheeses, artichoke hearts, peppers and basil leaves. Season with pepper.

5 Starting from the long edge, fold the third of the dough nearest to you over the filling, then fold the top third over. Place on the baking sheet, making sure that the join is underneath. Tuck the ends under, cover and prove for about 30 minutes.

6 Preheat the oven to Gas Mark 6/200°C/400°F.

7 Using a skewer, spike the dough randomly right through to the baking sheet. Brush the surface of the dough with olive oil and bake for 30–35 minutes until golden. Allow to cool slightly before serving warm or serve cold.

Variation: Alter the filling to suit your taste. Olives or semi-dried tomatoes would work equally well.

Pretzels

Makes: *12 pretzels* **Preparation time:** *30 minutes + proving + 15–20 minutes baking*
Freezing: *recommended*

Pretzels have a distinctive shape that might look complicated but is easy to create.

350 g (12 oz) strong white bread flour
½ teaspoon sugar
1 teaspoon salt
1 teaspoon fast action dried yeast
225 ml (8 fl oz) hand-hot water
For the topping:
1 egg yolk
1 tablespoon water
coarse sea salt

Variation: If you prefer a sweet version, omit the egg glaze and salt, lightly brush with water when they come out of the oven and toss them in a combination of ½ teaspoon cinnamon mixed with 4 teaspoons caster sugar.

Tip: You may need to lightly flour your hands when rolling out the strands if the dough is sticky.

1 Grease two baking sheets. Place the flour, sugar, salt and yeast in a large bowl. Make a well in the centre and add the water. Mix to a soft dough.

2 Turn out on to an unfloured work surface and knead (page 8) for 8–10 minutes until smooth. Place in a polythene bag and prove (page 8) in a warm place until doubled in size.

3 Knock back (page 9) the dough and divide into 12 pieces. Roll each out into a strand measuring 40 cm (16 inches). Take an end in either hand. Loop one end around, almost into a circle, so that the end just extends beyond the far side of the arc. Repeat with the other end to create a pretzel shape. Place on a baking sheet and repeat with the remaining stands. Cover and prove for about 30 minutes.

4 Preheat the oven to Gas Mark 6/200°C/400°F.

5 Beat the egg yolk and water together. Brush the pretzels with the egg glaze and sprinkle with a little sea salt. Bake for 15–20 minutes. Cool on a wire rack.

Pissaladière

Makes: *1 pizza* **Preparation time:** *50 minutes + proving + 20–25 minutes baking*
Freezing: *recommended*

This is a French version of pizza. It can be made with a bread or pastry base and with or without tomato. It has a strong flavour so only needs a green salad to accompany it.

225 g (8 oz) strong white bread flour
½ teaspoon salt
¾ teaspoon fast action dried yeast
2 tablespoons extra virgin olive oil
scant 150 ml (¼ pint) hand-hot water (page 4)
For the topping:
25 g (1 oz) butter
1 tablespoon extra virgin olive oil
450 g (1 lb) large Spanish onions, thinly sliced
2 garlic cloves, crushed
1 teaspoon sugar
1 tablespoon chopped fresh thyme
freshly ground black pepper
50 g (2 oz) can anchovy fillets, drained and
    halved lengthways
65–80 g (2½–3 oz) pitted black olives

1 Mix together the flour, salt and yeast. Make a well in the centre and add the oil and water. Mix to a soft dough.

2 Turn out on to an unfloured work surface and knead (page 8) for 8–10 minutes until smooth. Cover and allow to rest for 10 minutes.

3 Grease a 28 cm (11 inch) flan ring.

4 Press or roll out the dough and fit in the ring. Place on a baking sheet, cover and prove (page 8) in a warm place until doubled in size.

5 Preheat the oven to Gas Mark 7/220°C/425°F.

6 Heat the butter and oil in a large pan. Stir in the onions and cook over a low to medium heat for 15 minutes. Add the garlic and sugar, increase the heat and cook for a further 5 minutes, stirring occasionally, until golden. Remove from the heat and allow to cool. Stir in 2 teaspoons of the thyme and season with pepper.

7 Spread the topping over the dough. Arrange the anchovies over the top to form a lattice pattern. Stud each space with an olive.

8 Bake for 20–25 minutes. Serve warm.

Fougasse

Makes: *4 breads* **Preparation time:** *20 minutes + proving + 15–20 minutes baking*
Freezing: *recommended*

A flat bread from the Provence area of France, Fougasse has
a distinctive leaf-shaped appearance and is similar to Focaccia
(page 69). This is a plain version, but the dough may be
flavoured to make sweet or savoury breads.

450 g (1 lb) strong white bread flour
1 teaspoon salt
1½ teaspoons fast action dried yeast
6 tablespoons extra virgin olive oil
scant 300 ml (½ pint) hand-hot water (page 4)
flour or semolina, for dusting

1 Combine the flour, salt and yeast in a large
mixing bowl. Add 4 tablespoons of olive oil
and the water. Mix to a soft dough.

2 Turn out on to an unfloured work surface and
knead (page 8) for 8–10 minutes until smooth.
Place in an oiled polythene bag and prove
(page 8) in a warm place until doubled in size.

3 Grease two baking sheets and dust with flour
or semolina.

4 Knock back (page 9) the dough and divide
into four equal pieces. With your hands, or by
rolling out on a lightly floured surface, shape
these into 20 cm (8 inch) long and 13 cm
(5 inch) wide ovals.

5 Make two short cuts down the centre of each
bread, leaving a space between. Then make
3–4 diagonal cuts on either side, radiating
almost from the middle, to give a leaf effect.
Flour your finger and run it around each cut to
enhance the slit and ensure that it does not
close up when proved.

6 Place two fougasse on each baking sheet.
Cover and leave to prove for just 30 minutes.

7 Preheat the oven to Gas Mark 7/220°C/425°F.

8 Drizzle the breads with the remaining oil and
bake for 15–20 minutes until golden. Transfer
to a wire rack to cool.

Tip: A craft blade works well for making clean
cuts in the dough.

Apricot Loaf

Makes: *1 loaf* **Preparation time:** *25 minutes + overnight soaking + proving + 25 minutes baking*
Freezing: *recommended*

Soaking the apricots in Amaretto the night before gives them an added depth of flavour and soft chewiness. Use the partially rehydrated variety if you can.

150 g (5 oz) no-need-to-soak dried apricots, chopped
4 tablespoons Amaretto
225 g (8 oz) strong white bread flour
50 g (2 oz) strong wholemeal bread flour
50 g (2 oz) wholemeal rye flour
¾ teaspoon salt
1 teaspoon fast action dried yeast
scant 200 ml (7 fl oz) hand-hot water (page 4)

Tips: If you prefer your bread crusty, open the oven door for the final 5 minutes of cooking.

Try this as the base for bruschetta – sprinkled with a little olive oil, toasted in the oven and topped with mild goat's cheese and watercress.

1 Place the chopped apricots in a small bowl and pour over the Amaretto. Cover and leave overnight. Stir the next morning and then use when required.

2 Combine the flours in a mixing bowl and stir in the salt and yeast. Make a well in the centre and add the soaked apricots with any juices, plus the water. Mix to a soft dough.

3 Turn out on to an unfloured work surface and knead (page 8) for 8–10 minutes until smooth. You may need to flour your hands now and then as the apricot makes this dough quite sticky. Cover and prove (page 8) in a warm place until doubled in size.

4 Grease a baking sheet.

5 Knead the dough for a couple of minutes until smooth. Shape into an oblong and place on the baking sheet. Taking a sharp knife, make a deep slit lengthwise down the top and again just to one side. Cover and prove again until doubled in size.

6 Preheat the oven to Gas Mark 7/220°C/425°F.

7 Bake for 25 minutes. Cool on a wire rack.

Sugar and Spice

In many countries sweet breads are eaten in preference to biscuits and cakes. Germany has its Kaffé und Kuchen – coffee and cake – and France is renowned for its tantalising selection of patisseries. But there are many traditional English breads too, such as Sally Lunn or Bath Buns, and there is nothing more English than afternoon tea with a West Country split or toasted teacakes. As more ingredients are added, the distinction between bread and cake blurs, with some so rich or sweet they can double up as puddings.

Currant Buns, page 99

Danish Pastries

Makes: *16 pastries* **Preparation time:** *30 minutes + resting + proving + 15 minutes baking*
Freezing: *not recommended*

These taste and look spectacular! For a selection of pastries, divide the dough into four and use different fillings.

For the basic dough:
250 g (9 oz) butter, softened
450 g (1 lb) strong white bread flour
25 g (1 oz) caster sugar
1 teaspoon salt
1½ teaspoons fast action dried yeast
150 ml (¼ pint) semi-skimmed milk
2 medium eggs, beaten

1 Take the butter and place between two sheets of greaseproof paper, and then roll out into an oblong measuring 23 x 13 cm (9 x 5 inches). Chill to firm up while you make the dough

2 Combine the flour, sugar, salt and yeast in a mixing bowl. Make a well in the centre and add the milk and eggs. Mix to a soft dough. Turn out on to a work surface and knead (page 8) for 8–10 minutes until smooth. Cover and allow to rest for 10 minutes.

3 On a lightly floured work surface, roll out the dough into a 25 cm (10 inch) square. Place the butter in the middle and fold the long edges over to encase the butter, ensuring that they overlap. Press down to seal, making sure you also seal the ends.

4 Roll the dough into a strip measuring 40 x 18 cm (16 x 7 inches). Fold the top third down and the bottom third up to make an oblong. Press to seal. Place in a greased bag and refrigerate for 10 minutes. Repeat the rolling and folding process twice before using the dough to make one of pastries on pages 79–80.

Tips: Make the dough the night before and keep it in the fridge. It rolls out beautifully in the morning, and you can have freshly made pastries by coffee time!

When rolling out the dough, push the rolling pin down on the dough in short bursts to help distribute the butter before rolling out completely.

It is important that the baking sheet has a raised edge to catch any butter that comes out of the pastries during cooking.

Caramel Toffee Plaits

¼ quantity Danish Pastry basic dough
1 medium egg, beaten
2 tablespoons dulce de leche (caramel toffee)
25 g (1 oz) pecan nuts, chopped
For the glaze:
1 tablespoon sieved apricot jam
1 teaspoon boiling water

1 On a lightly floured surface, roll out the dough into a 25 x 20 cm (10 x 8 inch) oblong. Cut into four 13 x 10 cm (5 x 4 inch) rectangles and brush with beaten egg.

2 Spread 1½ teaspoons of caramel in a line down the length of one of the pieces of dough. Sprinkle an eighth of the nuts on top. Cut diagonal lines at 1 cm (½ inch) intervals, from the caramel to the edge of the dough. Fold alternate sides over the filling to make a plait, overlapping the dough in the centre. Repeat with the remaining dough.

3 Place on a greased baking sheet, brush with beaten egg and sprinkle with the remaining nuts. Allow to prove (page 8) slowly at room temperature for 20–30 minutes until slightly puffed up. Bake for about 15 minutes at Gas Mark 6/200°C/400°F

4 Remove to a cooling rack and brush with the apricot jam mixed with water while still warm.

Tutti Frutti Pinwheels

¼ quantity Danish Pastry basic dough
15 g (½ oz) butter, melted
1 tablespoon caster sugar
80 g (3 oz) dried tropical fruit, finely chopped
1 medium egg, beaten
For the glaze:
1 tablespoon sieved apricot jam
1 teaspoon boiling water

1 On a lightly floured surface, roll out the dough into a rectangle 30 x 13 cm (12 x 5 inches). Brush with melted butter, sprinkle with sugar and scatter the chopped dried fruit evenly over the top.

2 Roll up the dough, starting from the short edge, and seal well. Using a sharp knife, cut into four even-sized pieces. Place on a greased baking sheet and flatten down firmly with your hand so that each pastry is about 8–9 cm (3¼–3½ inches) in diameter. Brush with the beaten egg.

3 Allow to prove (page 8) slowly at room temperature for 20–30 minutes until slightly puffed up. Bake for about 15 minutes at Gas Mark 6/200°C/400°F.

4 Remove to a cooling rack and brush with apricot jam mixed with water.

Cherry Stars

¼ quantity Danish Pastry basic dough
1 medium egg, beaten
50 g (2 oz) stoned Morello cherries
   (from a jar or tin)
1 tablespoon no-added-sugar black
   cherry jam
For the icing:
50 g (2 oz) icing sugar, sifted
1½ teaspoons boiling water

1 On a lightly floured surface, roll out the dough
   into a 20 cm (8 inch) square. Divide into four
   equal pieces and brush with beaten egg.

2 Combine the cherries and jam and place
   a spoonful in the centre of each square of
   dough. Taking a sharp knife, make a cut from
   the cherries to each corner. Fold each corner
   to the middle, overlapping the cherries. Seal
   with beaten egg.

3 Allow to prove (page 8) slowly at room
   temperature for 20–30 minutes until slightly
   puffed up. Bake on greased baking sheets
   with raised edges for about 15 minutes at Gas
   Mark 6/200°C/400°F

4 Remove to a cooling rack. Mix together the
   icing sugar and water until smooth and drizzle
   over the warm pastries.

Apple Diamonds

1 medium cooking apple, peeled, cored and
   thinly sliced
1 tablespoon sultanas
1 tablespoon sugar
2 teaspoons water
large pinch of cinnamon
¼ quantity Danish Pastry basic dough
1 egg, beaten
For the glaze:
1 tablespoon sieved apricot jam
1 teaspoon boiling water

1 Place the apple, sultanas, sugar and water in
   a small pan and simmer until soft. Mash and
   stir in the cinnamon. Cool.

2 On a lightly floured surface roll out the
   dough into a 20 cm (8 inch) square. Cut into
   quarters. Cut along the pastry 1cm (½ inch)
   from the edge, leaving an uncut section at two
   opposite corners. Brush with beaten egg.

3 Place one quarter of the apple mixture in
   the centre of each square. Take one of the
   cut edges and fold it across to the opposite
   corner. Repeat with the other edge to form
   a diamond. Brush again with egg. Allow to
   prove (page 8) slowly at room temperature
   for 20–30 minutes until slightly puffed up.
   Bake on greased baking sheets with raised
   edges for about 15 minutes at Gas Mark
   6/200°C/400°F.

4 Remove to a cooling rack and brush with
   apricot jam mixed with water while still warm.

Chelsea Buns

Makes: *9 buns* **Preparation time:** *30 minutes + proving + 25 minutes baking*
Freezing: *recommended*

These buns make their own glaze – the butter and sugar combining to make a delicious, sticky butterscotch sauce at the bottom of the tin.

175 g (6 oz) strong white bread flour
25 g (1 oz) caster sugar
½ teaspoon salt
25 g (1 oz) unsalted butter, softened
1 medium egg, beaten
25 g (1 oz) unsalted butter, melted and cooled slightly
65 g (2½ oz) light muscovado sugar
115 g (4 oz) dried fruit and mixed peel
For the yeast batter:
1½ teaspoons dried yeast (not fast action)
½ teaspoon sugar
90 ml (3 fl oz) warm semi-skimmed milk
50 g (2 oz) strong white bread flour

1 First, make the yeast batter. Sprinkle the yeast and sugar over the milk and leave for 5 minutes. Stir in the flour to make a smooth batter and leave for another 15–20 minutes until frothy.

2 Combine the flour, sugar and salt in a mixing bowl. Make a well in the centre and add the softened butter, egg and yeast batter. Mix to make a soft dough.

3 Turn out on to an unfloured work surface and knead (page 8) until smooth. Cover and prove (page 8) in a warm place until doubled in size. Butter a shallow 18 cm (7 inch) square cake tin.

4 Lightly flour the work surface and roll out the dough, without knocking back, to 30 x 23 cm (12 x 9 inches). Pour the butter over the surface, spreading it evenly. (Do not worry that there are puddles, the sugar will soak these up.) Sprinkle the sugar on top, almost to the edges, followed by the dried fruit and mixed peel.

5 Roll up the dough tightly, starting from the long edge. Seal the edge well, making sure it is underneath the roll. Using a sharp knife, cut the dough into nine pinwheel buns. Place them cut side down in rows in the prepared tin. Cover and prove until the buns have joined up and the dough has doubled in size.

6 Preheat the oven to Gas Mark 6/200°C/400°F

7 Bake for 25 minutes (covering with a piece of foil or baking parchment after 10 minutes). Turn out onto a wire rack and serve warm.

Teacakes

Makes: *10 teacakes* **Preparation time:** *25 minutes + proving + 15 minutes baking*
Freezing: *recommended*

Split these generous-sized teacakes in half, toast and serve dripping with melted butter – delicious!

700 g (1½ lbs) strong white bread flour
50 g (2 oz) white vegetable fat
50 g (2 oz) caster sugar
1 teaspoon salt
1½ teaspoons fast action dried yeast
425 ml (¾ pint) warm semi-skimmed milk
80 g (3 oz) currants
25 g (1 oz) candied peel, finely chopped

1 Lightly grease two baking sheets.

2 Place the flour in a large mixing bowl and rub in the vegetable fat. Stir in the sugar, salt and yeast. Make a well in the centre, add the milk and mix to a soft dough.

3 Turn out on to an unfloured work surface and knead (page 8) for 10 minutes until smooth. Work in the currants and candied peel until evenly dispersed.

4 Divide the dough into 10 and shape into buns. Flatten these down firmly to 1 cm (½ inch) thick. Space the teacakes evenly on the baking sheets. Cover and prove (page 8) in a warm place until doubled in size.

5 Preheat the oven to Gas Mark 7/220°C/425°F

6 Bake the teacakes for about 15 minutes, or until they are golden and sound hollow when tapped on the base. Transfer to a wire rack to cool.

Sally Lunn

Makes: *1 loaf* **Preparation time:** *20 minutes + proving + 25 minutes baking*
Freezing: *recommended*

Sally Lunn is believed to have originated in Bath and is thought to be named after the French refugee who created the recipe. The loaf is traditionally split into three horizontally and filled with clotted cream and jam.

175 g (6 oz) strong white bread flour
25 g (1 oz) butter
25 g (1 oz) caster sugar
½ teaspoon salt
grated zest of 1 lemon
1 medium egg
For the starter batter:
2 teaspoons dried yeast (not fast action)
1 teaspoon caster sugar
175 ml (6 fl oz) warm semi-skimmed milk
50 g (2 oz) strong white bread flour
For the glaze:
1 tablespoon granulated sugar
1 tablespoon boiling water
1 tablespoon semi-skimmed milk

1 First, make the starter batter. Stir the yeast and sugar into the milk and beat in the flour. Do not worry that the mixture looks lumpy at this stage. Leave in a warm place for about 20 minutes until the mixture becomes frothy and smells yeasty.

2 Line a 15 cm (6 inch) round, loose-bottomed cake tin with a double thickness of baking parchment, ensuring it comes about 5 cm (2 inches) above the top of the tin.

3 Place the main quantity of flour in a bowl and rub in the butter. Stir in the sugar, salt and lemon zest. Beat the egg into the frothy yeast mixture. Tip this into the dry ingredients and, using a wooden spoon, beat for 1–2 minutes to give a smooth batter. Pour into the prepared tin and level the surface. Cover and prove (page 8) in a warm place until doubled in size. This can take 1½ hours.

4 Preheat the oven to Gas Mark 7/220°C/425°F.

5 Bake the bun one shelf below the centre of the oven for about 25 minutes, until set and golden.

6 While the loaf is baking, dissolve the sugar for the glaze in the boiling water and stir in the milk. Glaze the top of the bread as soon as it comes out of the oven. Leave to stand in the tin for 5 minutes before turning out on to a wire rack to cool.

Bath Buns

Makes: *7 buns* **Preparation time:** *30 minutes + proving + 15 minutes baking*
Freezing: *recommended*

These originate in Bath in Somerset and are based on a beaten batter rather than kneading. Mace, which used to be a popular spice, is traditionally used. Dried sour cherries make an interesting, tangy variation.

175 g (6 oz) strong white bread flour
25 g (1 oz) butter
40 g (1½ oz) caster sugar
½ teaspoon salt
¼ teaspoon ground mace
80 g (3 oz) sultanas or raisins
50 g (2 oz) sour cherries, roughly chopped
1 medium egg
For the starter batter:
2 teaspoons dried yeast (not fast action)
1 teaspoon caster sugar
150 ml (¼ pint) warm semi-skimmed milk
50 g (2 oz) strong white bread flour
For the glaze:
1 egg
1 tablespoon water
1 teaspoon caster sugar
coarsely crushed sugar cubes or sugar nibs

1 First, make the starter batter. Stir the yeast and sugar into the milk and beat in the flour. Do not worry that the mixture looks lumpy at this stage. Leave in a warm place for about 20 minutes until it produces a frothy head and smells yeasty.

2 Place the flour in a bowl and rub in the butter. Stir in the sugar, salt, mace and all the dried fruit. Beat the egg into the frothy yeast mixture. Tip into the dry ingredients and, using a wooden spoon, beat for 2–3 minutes to create a smooth batter. Cover and prove (page 8) in a warm place until doubled in size.

3 Grease two baking sheets. Preheat the oven to Gas Mark 6/200°C/400°F.

4 Beat the batter again, just for a minute, to knock out the air. Place seven large spoonfuls, spread well apart, on the baking sheets. Cover and prove.

5 Beat the egg, water and sugar together and glaze the buns. Sprinkle with a little crushed sugar. Bake for about 15 minutes, or until golden. Cool on a wire rack.

Saffron Flower Bread

Makes: *8 rolls* **Preparation time:** *20 minutes + proving + 15–20 minutes*
Freezing: *recommended*

Saffron has a unique flavour and an alluring colour. Something also happens to the texture of the dough when saffron is added, resulting in a soft roll that goes well with savoury Indian-style dishes or can be served as a sweet bun.

¼ teaspoon saffron strands
1 tablespoon boiling water
225 g (8 oz) strong white bread flour
25 g (1 oz) unsalted butter
25 g (1 oz) caster sugar
½ teaspoon salt
¾ teaspoon fast action dried yeast
50 g (2 oz) sultanas
150 ml (¼ pint) warm semi-skimmed milk
1 egg, beaten, to glaze

Tip: Baking the rolls together in a sandwich tin gives a flower-like appearance.

1 Crush the saffron strands in a pestle and mortar. Pour on the boiling water and leave the colour to seep out while you prepare the remaining ingredients.

2 Lightly grease a 20 cm (8 inch) round sandwich tin. Place the flour in a bowl and rub in the butter. Stir in the sugar, salt, yeast and sultanas. Make a well in the centre of the flour. Pour the milk on to the saffron liquid and stir to combine, then pour into the well. Mix to a soft dough.

3 Turn out on to an unfloured work surface and knead (page 8) for about 10 minutes until smooth. Divide the dough into eight even-sized pieces. Shape into rounds and space around the edge of the tin, with one round in the centre. Cover and prove (page 8) in a warm place until doubled in size.

4 Preheat the oven to Gas Mark 6/200°C/400°F

5 Brush the rolls with egg and bake for 15–20 minutes. Cool on a wire rack.

Croissants

Makes: *12 croissants* **Preparation time:** *35 minutes + relaxing + proving + 15–20 minutes baking*
Freezing: *recommended*

Croissants are not difficult to make but there are several stages of rolling and folding. Choose a time when you have something else to do and work the stages round it!

200 g (7 oz) unsalted butter, softened
450 g (1 lb) strong white bread flour
2 teaspoons sugar
¾ teaspoon salt
1½ teaspoons fast action dried yeast
1 medium egg, beaten
scant 225 ml (8 fl oz) hand-hot water (page 4)
For the glaze:
1 egg
1 tablespoon water

1 Place 175 g (6 oz) of the butter between two sheets of greaseproof paper. Roll out to a rectangle measuring 25 x 15 cm (10 x 6 inches). Refrigerate.

2 Place the flour in a mixing bowl and rub in the remaining butter. Stir in the sugar, salt and yeast. Add the egg and water and mix to a soft dough. Turn the dough out on to an unfloured work surface and knead (page 8) for about 10 minutes until smooth. Place in an oiled polythene bag and leave to relax for 10 minutes.

3 Flour the work surface and roll the dough out to measure 2.5 cm (1 inch) wider than the rolled butter. Take the butter from the fridge and place it in the centre of the dough. Fold the bottom third of the dough up, and the top third down. Press the edges down firmly with the rolling pin to seal. Repeat the rolling and folding, wrap the dough in greaseproof paper and chill for 10 minutes.

4 Repeat the rolling and folding process twice more, then chill for 20–30 minutes.

5 Repeat step 4. Grease two baking sheets with raised edges.

6 Flour the work surface again and roll out the dough into a rectangle measuring 46 x 30 cm (18 x 12 inches). Trim the edges and cut the dough into six squares. Cut each square in half diagonally to make 12 triangles.

7 Brush a little egg on one tip of the triangle. Roll the triangle up, starting from the opposite side. Place the croissant on the baking sheet, making sure that the egg-glazed tip is underneath the croissant to seal it. Curve the ends inwards to form a crescent shape. Repeat with the remaining triangles. Cover and prove (page 8) in a warm place for about 30 minutes until puffy. Preheat the oven to Gas Mark 7/220°C/425°F

8 Beat the egg and water together and brush the croissants with the glaze. Bake for 15–20 minutes, until golden. Cool slightly on a wire rack and serve warm.

Petit Pain au Chocolat

Makes: *18 petit pains* **Preparation time:** *35 minutes + relaxing + proving + 13–15 minutes baking*
Freezing: *recommended*

A variation on plain Croissants (opposite), these are delicious for a weekend treat.

200 g (7 oz) unsalted butter, softened
450 g (1 lb) strong white bread flour
1 tablespoon sugar
¾ teaspoon salt
1½ teaspoons fast action dried yeast
1 medium egg, beaten
scant 225 ml (8 fl oz) hand hot water (page 4)
175 g (6 oz) plain chocolate drops
1 egg, for brushing
For the glaze:
1 egg
1 tablespoon water

1 Follow the recipe for Croissants, steps 1–5 (opposite).

2 Flour the work surface again and roll out the dough into a rectangle measuring 46 x 30 cm (18 x 12 inches). Trim the edges and cut into three strips, each measuring 46 x 10 cm (18 x 4 inches).

3 Sprinkle one third of the chocolate drops down each strip of dough. Brush the dough with egg on either side of the chocolate, and fold the dough over to encase. Using the back of a heavy knife, push down on the dough 1 cm (½ inch) from the edge to seal thoroughly.

4 Cut each strip into six and place on the baking sheets. Cover and prove (page 8) in a warm place for about 30 minutes, until puffy. Preheat the oven to Gas Mark 7/220°C/425°F.

5 Beat the egg and water together and glaze the petit pains. Bake for about 13–15 minutes, until golden. Transfer to a wire rack and serve warm.

Doughnuts

Makes: *11 doughnuts* **Preparation time:** *30 minutes + proving + 15 minutes cooking*
Freezing: *not recommended*

These are absolutely scrummy!

450 g (1 lb) strong white bread flour
50 g (2 oz) unsalted butter
50 g (2 oz) caster sugar
1 teaspoon salt
1½ teaspoons fast action dried yeast
225 ml (8 fl oz) warm semi-skimmed milk
1 medium egg, beaten
½ teaspoon vanilla essence
5½ teaspoons stiff seedless red jam
vegetable or sunflower oil
caster sugar, for dusting

1 Grease two baking sheets well.

2 Place the flour in a large bowl and rub in the butter. Stir in the sugar, salt and yeast. Make a well in the centre and add the milk, egg and vanilla essence. Stir to make a soft dough.

3 Turn out on to an unfloured work surface and knead (page 8) until smooth. The dough will be quite wet and sticky but do not add any more flour. Keep working the dough with your fingertips until you end up with a smooth, silken ball. This will take 10–12 minutes.

4 Divide the dough into 11 pieces, form each piece into a ball and then flatten into a disc. Place half a teaspoon of jam in the centre of each, gather up the edges and pinch the dough to encase the jam. Carefully re-roll in the palm of your hand to make a ball. Place, well spaced, on the baking sheets, cover and prove (page 8) in a warm place until doubled in size.

5 Pour about 5 cm (2 inches) of cooking oil into a wide, heavy based pan. Heat until a cube of bread dropped into the oil browns in 30 seconds. Add 3–4 doughnuts and fry for 3 minutes, turning frequently until golden and puffy. Remove using a slotted spoon and drain on kitchen paper. While still warm, dust with caster sugar. Repeat with the remaining dough.

Variation: Try a chocolate and hazelnut spread filling or coating the doughnuts with a mixture of cinnamon and sugar.

Sugary Spice Dough Ball Ring

Serves: *8–10* **Preparation time:** *30 minutes + proving + 25 minutes baking*
Freezing: *not recommended*

This is a fun bread to share – simply pull off the individual pieces of dough! Adding cream cheese gives a lovely flavour and soft crumb.

350 g (12 oz) strong white bread flour
40 g (1½ oz) caster sugar
¾ teaspoon salt
1 teaspoon fast action dried yeast
80 g (3 oz) full fat cream cheese
150 ml (¼ pint) warm semi-skimmed milk
1 medium egg, beaten
For the topping:
50 g (2 oz) unsalted butter, melted and cooled
80 g (3 oz) caster sugar
1 teaspoon ground cinnamon

1 Combine the flour, sugar, salt and yeast in a bowl. Make a well in the centre and add the cream cheese, milk and egg. Mix to a soft dough.

2 Turn out on to an unfloured work surface and knead (page 8) for about 10 minutes, until smooth. The dough will be sticky, but persevere without adding any flour if you can. Flour your hands lightly and knead the dough into a smooth ball. Divide this into 24 little pieces. Shape into balls and place in an oiled polythene bag while you prepare the coating.

3 Pour the cooled butter into a small bowl. Combine the sugar and cinnamon in another bowl. Lightly grease a 1 litre (1¾ pint) ring tin. If you do not have a ring tin, use a 20 cm (8 inch) deep cake tin.

4 Take a couple of pieces of dough. Dunk them in the butter, then toss them in the cinnamon sugar to coat. Pop them randomly into the prepared tin (they will level themselves out on proving). Repeat with the remaining dough balls, then pour any remaining melted butter or sugary mixture over the top. Cover and prove (page 8) in a warm place until doubled in size. (The coating will crack slightly as it stretches.)

5 Preheat the oven to Gas Mark 6/200°C/400°F.

6 Place the ring mould on a baking sheet and bake for about 25 minutes, covering with a piece of greaseproof paper or foil after 10 minutes to prevent the top from browning too much. Turn out and cool on a wire rack.

Swiss Buns

Makes: *10 buns* **Preparation time:** *25 minutes + proving + 10–12 minutes baking*
Freezing: *recommended before icing*

These are a long established favourite in bakeries up and down the country.

450 g (1 lb) strong white bread flour
25 g (1 oz) butter
25 g (1 oz) caster sugar
1 teaspoon salt
1 teaspoon fast action dried yeast
300 ml (½ pint) warm semi-skimmed milk
For the icing:
350 g (12 oz) icing sugar, sifted
approximately 4 tablespoons hot water

Tip: Add a couple of drops of pink food colouring to the icing to make a pretty pastel pink alternative.

1 Lightly grease two baking sheets.

2 Place the flour in a large mixing bowl and rub in the butter. Stir in the sugar, salt and yeast and mix to a soft dough with the milk.

3 Turn out on to an unfloured work surface and knead (page 8) for about 10 minutes until smooth. Divide the dough into 10 pieces and shape into 15 cm (6 inch) sausage-shaped rolls. Place well apart on the baking sheets, cover and prove (page 8) in a warm place until doubled in size.

4 Preheat the oven to Gas Mark 7/220°C/425°F.

5 Bake the rolls for 10–12 minutes. Transfer to a wire rack, cover them with a clean tea towel (this softens the tops) and leave to cool.

6 To make the icing, put the icing sugar in a small bowl and gradually add enough hot water to make a fairly stiff paste. Spoon this along the top of each bun and leave to set.

West Country Splits

Makes: *6 splits* **Preparation time:** *30 minutes + proving + 12–14 minutes baking*
Freezing: *recommended before filling*

Also known as Cornish or Devonshire Splits, West Country splits are spread thickly with clotted cream and sandwiched with jam.

225 g (8 oz) strong white bread flour
25 g (1 oz) butter
1 rounded tablespoon caster sugar
½ teaspoon salt
¾ teaspoon fast action dried yeast
150 ml (¼ pint) warm semi-skimmed milk
For the filling:
clotted cream
strawberry conserve
sifted icing sugar, for dusting

1 Lightly grease a baking sheet.

2 Place the flour in a bowl and rub in the butter. Stir in the sugar, salt and yeast. Make a well in the centre, add the milk and mix to form a soft dough.

3 Turn out on to an unfloured work surface and knead (page 8) for about 10 minutes until smooth. Divide the dough into six pieces. Shape into rolls, place on the baking sheet and flatten with the heel of your hand to make baps about 8 cm (3¼ inches) across. Cover and prove (page 8) in a warm place until doubled in size.

4 Preheat the oven to Gas Mark 6/200°C/400°F

5 Bake the baps for 12–14 minutes until light and golden. Cool on a wire rack.

6 To serve, use a sharp knife to split open horizontally at an angle, leaving a hinge. Spread with clotted cream and spoon in some jam. Dust lightly with icing sugar.

Ginger Sultana Bun Loaf

Makes: *1 loaf* **Preparation time:** *30 minutes + proving + 35 minutes baking*
Freezing: *recommended before glazing*

This subtly flavoured milk bread is delicious on its own, lightly buttered, or toasted the next day and spread with honey.

450 g (1 lb) strong white bread flour
25 g (1 oz) butter
25 g (1 oz) muscovado sugar
1 teaspoon salt
1 teaspoon fast action dried yeast
300 ml (½ pint) warm semi-skimmed milk
80 g (3 oz) sultanas
40 g (1½ oz) stem ginger, finely chopped
finely grated zest of 1 orange
stem ginger syrup, to glaze

Variation: Try finely chopped dried pear instead of sultanas.

1 Grease a 900 g (2 lb) loaf tin.

2 Put the flour in a large mixing bowl and rub in the butter. Stir in the sugar, salt and yeast and mix to a soft dough with the milk.

3 Turn out on to an unfloured work surface and knead (page 8) for about 10 minutes until the dough is soft and smooth. Work the sultanas, chopped ginger and orange zest into the dough.

4 Shape and place in the prepared tin. Cover and prove (page 8) in a warm place until doubled in size.

5 Preheat the oven to Gas Mark 6/200°C/400°F.

6 Bake for about 35 minutes. Turn out on to a wire rack, brush with ginger syrup and leave to cool.

Malt Loaf

Makes: *1 loaf* **Preparation time:** *20 minutes + proving + 40–45 minutes baking*
Freezing: *recommended*

This bread does tend to take quite a while to prove as the malt inhibits its rising. It keeps very well for a few days.

225 g (8 oz) plain all purpose white flour
25 g (1 oz) muscovado sugar
½ teaspoon salt
¾ teaspoon fast action dried yeast
80 g (3 oz) sultanas
150 ml (¼ pint) warm semi-skimmed milk
2 tablespoons malt extract
1 tablespoon treacle
25 g (1 oz) butter, melted

Tip: This loaf has a natural matt appearance. For a shiny top, brush with clear, runny honey when you take the bread out of the oven.

1 Grease a 450 g (1 lb) loaf tin.

2 Combine the flour, sugar, salt, yeast and sultanas in a mixing bowl. Make a well in the centre and add the milk, malt extract, treacle and melted butter. With a wooden spoon, beat the mixture for a couple of minutes until smooth.

3 Pour the mixture into the prepared tin, cover and prove (page 8) in a warm place until it almost comes to the top of the tin. Preheat the oven to Gas Mark 6/200°C/400°F.

4 Bake the loaf for 40–45 minutes. Turn out and cool on a wire rack.

Trail Mix Loaf

Makes: *1 loaf* **Preparation time:** *20 minutes + proving + 30 minutes baking*
Freezing: *recommended*

Make sure you choose a luxury muesli for this recipe, packed with fruit, nuts and seeds.

175 g (6 oz) strong wholemeal bread flour

175 g (6 oz) strong white bread flour

115 g (4 oz) luxury muesli, plus extra for sprinkling

80 g (3 oz) mixed nuts, dried fruits and seeds

1 teaspoon salt

1½ teaspoons fast action dried yeast

2 tablespoons sunflower oil

2 tablespoons runny honey

250 ml (9 fl oz) warm semi-skimmed milk, plus a little extra to glaze

Tips: Sprinkle the top of the dough liberally with the muesli. Any that falls to the bottom of the tin will stick to the edges as the dough rises, resulting in a lovely, tasty outer crust.

Try using rolled oats as a base for your own muesli: cranberries and pumpkin seeds provide colour, dates and dried apricots work well, roasted hazel and brazil nuts are delicious and linseeds, sunflower and sesame seeds add flavour and crunch.

1 Grease a 900 g (2 lb) loaf tin.

2 Combine the two flours, muesli, mixed nuts, fruit and seeds, salt and yeast in a mixing bowl. Make a well in the centre and add the oil, honey and milk. Mix to a soft dough.

3 Turn out on to an unfloured work surface and knead (page 8) for 7–8 minutes until smooth. Shape into an oblong and place in the prepared tin. Brush with milk and sprinkle liberally with muesli. Cover and prove (page 8) in a warm place until doubled in size.

4 Preheat the oven to Gas Mark 7/220°C/425°F.

5 Bake on one shelf below the middle for 30 minutes. Turn out of the tin and cool on a wire rack.

Apple, Honey and Oat Buns

Makes: *12 buns* **Preparation time:** *25 minutes + proving + 12–15 minutes baking*
Freezing: *recommended*

My children loved these appley buns so much it was a surprise any kept until the next day! These are delicious served warm.

350 g (12 oz) strong white bread flour

50 g (2 oz) medium oatmeal

¾ teaspoon salt

1 teaspoon fast action dried yeast

1 teaspoon mixed spice

40 g (1½ oz) dried apple rings, snipped

50 g (2 oz) sultanas

50 g (2 oz) butter, softened

2 tablespoons runny honey, plus extra to glaze

225 ml (8 fl oz) cloudy apple juice

Tips: Try topping these with glacé icing instead of the honey glaze.

These are baked in a muffin tray but could easily be shaped into rolls and cooked on a baking sheet.

1 Combine the flour, oatmeal, salt, yeast, mixed spice, snipped apple rings and sultanas in a bowl. Make a well in the centre and add the butter, honey and apple juice. Mix to a soft dough.

2 Turn out on to an unfloured work surface and knead (page 8) for about 10 minutes until smooth. Cover and prove (page 8) in a warm place until doubled in size.

3 Preheat the oven to Gas Mark 7/220°C/425°F. Grease the holes of a muffin tray.

4 Divide the dough into 12 pieces. Shape each into a ball and place in a hole of the prepared tray. Cover and prove until doubled in size.

5 Bake for 12–15 minutes until the buns are golden. Transfer to a cooling rack and brush at once with honey.

Currant Buns

Makes: *14 buns* **Preparation time:** *30 minutes + proving + 10–12 minutes baking*
Freezing: *Recommended before glazing*

These simple buns literally gleam once brushed with their sugary glaze, making them irresistible.

450 g (1 lb) strong white bread flour
25 g (1 oz) butter
25 g (1 oz) caster sugar
1 teaspoon salt
1 teaspoon fast action dried yeast
300 ml (½ pint) warm semi-skimmed milk
125 g (4 oz) currants
For the glaze:
1 tablespoon granulated sugar
1 tablespoon milk
1 tablespoon water

1 Lightly grease a baking sheet.

2 Place the flour in a large mixing bowl and rub in the butter. Stir in the sugar, salt and yeast and mix to a soft dough with the milk.

3 Turn out on to an unfloured work surface and knead (page 8) for about 10 minutes until smooth. Knead in the currants until evenly distributed.

4 Divide the dough into 14 pieces and shape into rolls. Place well apart on the baking sheet, cover and prove (page 8) in a warm place until doubled in size.

5 Preheat the oven to Gas Mark 7/220°C/425°F. Bake the buns for 10–12 minutes.

6 Prepare the sugar glaze by dissolving the sugar in the milk and water. Boil for 1 minute and then leave to cool. Transfer the buns to a wire rack and brush with the glaze while still hot. Allow to cool.

Illustrated on page 77

Lemon Brioche

Makes: *8 brioche* **Preparation time:** *40 minutes + proving + 15–20 minutes baking*
Freezing: *recommended*

Make these in individual fluted brioche tins, if you have them.

225 g (8 oz) strong white bread flour
25 g (1 oz) caster sugar
¼ teaspoon salt
grated zest of 1 lemon
50 g (2 oz) unsalted butter, softened
2 medium eggs, beaten
8 teaspoons luxury lemon curd
1 egg yolk, beaten
1 tablespoon water
For the yeast batter:
2 teaspoons dried yeast (not fast action)
1 teaspoon sugar
3 tablespoons warm semi-skimmed milk
25 g (1 oz) strong white bread flour

1 Make the yeast batter. Sprinkle the yeast and sugar over the milk and leave for 5 minutes. Stir in the flour to make a paste and leave in a warm place for 15–20 minutes until frothy.

2 Grease eight holes of a muffin tin or line each with a 13 cm (5 inch) square of baking parchment.

3 In a bowl, combine the flour, sugar, salt and lemon zest. Make a well in the centre and add the softened butter, eggs and yeast batter. Mix to a soft dough.

4 Turn out on to an unfloured work surface and knead (page 8) for about 10 minutes until smooth. Place in an oiled polythene bag and leave to prove (page 8) in a warm place until doubled in size.

5 Knead the dough. Cut off one quarter and place back in the oiled bag. Divide the remaining dough into eight pieces and flatten each into a disc in the palm of your hand. Place a teaspoon of lemon curd in the centre, pull up the edges and seal. Place, seam down, in the prepared muffin holes.

6 Divide the remaining dough into eight and roll each piece into a ball. Slightly elongate each to make a pear shape. Make an indent in the middle of each lemon curd-filled ball. Dip the pointed end of the small balls into the beaten egg yolk and press on top of the larger balls. Cover and prove again. Preheat the oven to Gas Mark 5/190°C/375°F.

7 Brush with the remaining egg yolk mixed with water and bake for 15–20 minutes. Cool on a wire rack.

Variation: For a chocolate brioche, use a cube of chocolate instead of the lemon curd or work chocolate drops into the dough itself.

Tip: This bread is more fragile than a standard loaf, so care needs to be taken when brushing with the glaze to ensure that air is not knocked out of the dough.

Swiss Mountain Buns

Makes: *20 buns* **Preparation time:** *30 minutes + proving + 10–12 minutes baking*
Freezing: *recommended*

Our eldest daughter Susie bought me a bar of Toblerone when I was writing this book, and so the idea for this recipe was born. The rest of the family are now keen to try out a variation using Mars Bars or Rolos!

450 g (1 lb) strong white bread flour
50 g (2 oz) unsalted butter
50 g (2 oz) caster sugar
1 teaspoon salt
1 teaspoon fast action dried yeast
300 ml (½ pint) warm semi-skimmed milk
200 g bar Toblerone
milk, for brushing
sifted icing sugar, for dusting

1 Place the flour in a large mixing bowl and rub in the butter. Stir in the sugar, salt and yeast and mix to a soft dough with the milk.

2 Turn out on to an unfloured work surface and knead (page 8) for about 10 minutes until smooth. Cover and prove (page 8) in a warm place until doubled in size.

3 Lightly grease two baking sheets.

4 Break the Toblerone into triangles and cut each triangle in half. Divide the dough into 20 pieces. Keeping the rest covered, take one piece of dough at a time and flatten to a disc in your hand. Place a piece of Toblerone in the centre and pinch up the edges to seal. Roll

into a ball between the palms of your hands. Repeat with the remaining dough, placing the balls well apart on the baking sheets. Cover and prove again.

5 Preheat the oven to Gas Mark 6/200°C/400°F.

6 Lightly brush the buns with milk. Chop any remaining Toblerone and sprinkle over the tops. Bake for 10–12 minutes before removing and cooling on a wire rack. Dust thickly with icing sugar to resemble mountain peaks!

Tip: These buns are at their best while still warm as the chocolate will still be melted. Do take care not to burn yourself on the filling when you bite into them though.

Rocky Moon Buns

Makes: *16 buns* **Preparation time:** *30 minutes + proving + 10–12 minutes baking*
Freezing: *Recommended*

These buns were created after our daughter Beth watched
Dr Who. They look quite startling but are a great way to
encourage children to make their own bread, especially as no
shaping is required.

450 g (1 lb) strong white bread flour
50 g (2 oz) unsalted butter
50 g (2 oz) caster sugar
1 teaspoon salt
1 teaspoon fast action dried yeast
300 ml (½ pint) warm semi-skimmed milk
115 g (4 oz) fudge, cut into small cubes
80 g (3 oz) chocolate-coated raisins or
　　peanuts, Smarties, M&Ms or chocolate
　　buttons
50 g (2 oz) coloured mini marshmallows

Tip: The basic dough is the same as for
Swiss Mountain Buns, so why not make up a
batch and split it to make half of each recipe.

1 Place the flour in a large mixing bowl and rub
in the butter. Stir in the sugar, salt and yeast
and mix to a soft dough with the milk.

2 Turn out on to an unfloured work surface and
knead (page 8) for about 10 minutes until
smooth. Cover and prove (page 8) in a warm
place until doubled in size.

3 Either line two baking sheets with parchment
paper (not greaseproof paper as the fudge
and marshmallows will stick to it), or cut out
16 squares of paper and use these to line
large muffin tins.

4 Work the fudge, sweets and marshmallows
into the dough. Divide into 16 equal pieces
and place just as they are on the baking
sheets or in the muffin tins. Cover and prove
again until doubled in size.

5 Preheat the oven to Gas Mark 6/200°C/400°F.

6 Bake the buns for 10–12 minutes. Cool on a
wire rack.

Date and Orange Cake

Makes: *1 loaf* **Preparation time:** *15 minutes + proving + 45 minutes baking*
Freezing: *recommended*

This has more of a cake texture than bread and is made by beating the mixture rather than kneading.

175 g (6 oz) strong white bread flour
50 g (2 oz) unsalted butter
25 g (1 oz) light muscovado sugar
¼ teaspoon salt
¾ teaspoon fast action dried yeast
¼ teaspoon ground cinnamon
80 g (3 oz) plump dried dates, chopped
grated zest and juice of 1 orange
4 tablespoons warm semi-skimmed milk
1 medium egg, beaten
1–2 tablespoons chopped walnuts
2 teaspoons apricot jam, warmed

1 Grease and base line a 450 g (1 lb) loaf tin.

2 Place the flour in a bowl and rub in the butter. Stir in the sugar, salt, yeast, cinnamon and chopped dates. Make a well in the centre and add the orange zest and juice, milk and egg. Using a wooden spoon, beat well for about 2 minutes to give a smooth batter.

3 Pour the mixture into the prepared tin and level the surface. Cover and prove (page 8) in a warm place until the mixture has risen three quarters of the way up the tin. Preheat the oven to Gas Mark 6/200°C/400°F.

4 Sprinkle the walnuts over the top of the cake and bake for about 45 minutes. To see if the cake is cooked, insert a skewer into the centre. If it comes out clean, the cake is ready.

5 Remove the cake from the tin, brush with warmed jam and cool on a wire rack.

Swedish Tea Ring

Serves: *8* **Preparation time:** *40 minutes + proving + 15–20 minutes baking*
Freezing: *recommended before icing*

This variation on the traditional Swedish recipe contains orange.

225 g (8 oz) strong white bread flour
25 g (1 oz) unsalted butter
25 g (1 oz) caster sugar
½ teaspoon salt
1 teaspoon fast action dried yeast
grated zest of 1 orange
75 ml (3 fl oz) warm semi-skimmed milk
1 medium egg, beaten
50 g (2 oz) muscovado sugar
1½ teaspoons ground cinnamon
15 g (½ oz) unsalted butter, melted and cooled
For the icing:
80 g (3 oz) icing sugar
1 tablespoon orange juice
roughly grated zest of 1 orange

1 Lightly grease a baking sheet.

2 Place the flour in a bowl and rub in the butter. Stir in the sugar, salt, yeast and orange zest. Make a well in the centre, add the milk and egg and mix to a soft dough.

3 Turn out on to an unfloured work surface and knead (page 8) for about 10 minutes until smooth. Place in an oiled polythene bag and prove (page 8) in a warm place until doubled in size. Combine the sugar and cinnamon in a bowl.

4 On a lightly floured surface, roll out the dough to 38 x 23 cm (15 x 9 inches). Brush the melted butter over the surface, making sure that you go right to the edges. Spread the cinnamon sugar over the top to within 1 cm (½ inch) of the edge.

5 Roll the dough up tightly from the long edge, sealing the edge well. Place on the baking sheet, making sure that the join is underneath. Shape the dough into a ring and tuck the ends into each other.

6 Using sharp scissors, cut almost through to the middle of the dough at 4 cm (1½ inch) intervals. Take each section and twist firmly on to its side so that the cinnamon and sugar swirls are visible. Cover and prove again.

7 Preheat the oven to Gas Mark 6/200°C/400°F. Bake the ring for 15–20 minutes until golden, then cool on a wire rack.

8 Sieve the icing sugar into a bowl. Make a well in the centre and gradually stir in the orange juice. Drizzle over the top of the ring and scatter with orange zest to decorate.

Chocolate, Cherry and Coconut Cake

Makes: *1 cake* **Preparation time:** *35 minutes + proving + 20–25 minutes baking*
Freezing: *recommended*

Sharp dried cherries combine beautifully with dark chocolate and coconut to give a bread that is really more of a cake since it is finished with a thick drizzling of melted chocolate and dusted with icing sugar. This is lovely in the morning with coffee or for afternoon tea.

225 g (8 oz) strong white bread flour
25 g (1 oz) caster sugar
½ teaspoon salt
¾ teaspoon fast action dried yeast
50 g (2 oz) dried and sweetened sour cherries
25 g (1 oz) desiccated coconut
grated zest of ½ orange
1 medium egg, beaten
**50 g (2 oz) creamed coconut dissolved in
    125 ml (4 fl oz) boiling water and cooled to
    hand-hot temperature**
**50 g (2 oz) good quality dark chocolate,
    roughly chopped**
1 egg, beaten, to glaze
For decoration:
25 g (1 oz) dark chocolate, melted
sifted icing sugar, for dusting

1   Combine the flour, sugar, salt, yeast, cherries, desiccated coconut and orange zest in a mixing bowl. Make a well in the centre and add the egg and dissolved creamed coconut. Mix to a soft dough.

2   Turn out on to an unfloured work surface and knead (page 8) for 10 minutes until smooth. Cover and prove (page 8) in a warm place until doubled in size.

3   Lightly grease a baking sheet. Preheat the oven to Gas Mark 6/200°C/400°F.

4   Knead the chocolate into the dough until evenly incorporated. Leave to relax for 10 minutes before dividing the dough into two 35 cm (14 inch) strands. Join at one end with a little water if necessary, then plait or twist together. Tuck the ends under and place on the baking sheet. Glaze with beaten egg, cover and prove again.

5   Bake for 20–25 minutes. Cool on a wire rack. To decorate, drizzle the chocolate over the top of the bread and dust thickly with icing sugar.

Apricot and Almond Streusels

Makes: *8 streusels* **Preparation time:** *40 minutes + proving + 10–15 minutes baking*
Freezing: *not recommended*

Think of these tartlets as a simpler form of Danish pastries with a lower fat content. They are best eaten warm from the oven.

225 g (8 oz) strong white bread flour
25 g (1 oz) unsalted butter
25 g (1 oz) caster sugar
½ teaspoon salt
¾ teaspoon fast action dried yeast
6 tablespoons warm semi-skimmed milk
1 medium egg, beaten
¼ teaspoon vanilla essence
115 g (4 oz) white marzipan
410 g can apricot halves in syrup, drained, or 8
   fresh apricots, halved
1 egg, beaten, to glaze
sifted icing sugar, for dusting
For the topping:
1 tablespoon butter
2 tablespoons plain flour
1 tablespoon caster sugar
1 tablespoon flaked almonds
¹/₈ teaspoon ground cinnamon

1 Place the flour in a bowl and rub in the butter. Stir in the sugar, salt and yeast. Make a well in the centre, add the milk, egg and vanilla essence and mix to a soft dough.

2 Turn out on to an unfloured work surface and knead (page 8) for about 10 minutes, until smooth. Cover and prove (page 8) in a warm place until doubled in size. Grease two baking sheets.

3 For the topping, rub the butter into the flour and stir in the sugar, almonds and cinnamon.

4 Divide the dough into eight pieces and form into discs in your hands. Place well apart on the baking sheets and push out into 10 cm (4 inch) circles. Prick all over with a fork.

5 Divide the marzipan into eight and scatter pieces evenly over the circles. Put two apricot halves in the centre of each. Brush the edges with beaten egg and scatter over the topping. Cover and prove again until doubled in size. Preheat the oven to Gas Mark 6/200°C/400°F.

6 Bake the streusels for 10–15 minutes, then transfer to a wire rack. Dust with icing sugar and serve warm.

Tip: Substitute the apricots with plums for a change.

Blueberry Savarin

Makes: *1 savarin* **Preparation time:** *40 minutes + proving + 20 minutes baking*
Freezing: *not recommended*

Although savarins seem to have gone out of popularity, blueberries have never enjoyed such good press. This recipe combines the two to create a lovely summer pudding.

80 g (3 oz) unsalted butter
150 g (5 oz) strong white bread flour
1 tablespoon caster sugar
¼ teaspoon salt
50 g (2 oz) dried and sweetened blueberries
For the starter batter:
2 teaspoons dried yeast (not fast action)
1 teaspoon sugar
6 tablespoons warm semi-skimmed milk
25 g (1 oz) strong white bread flour
For the syrup:
80 g (3 oz) sugar
150 ml (¼ pint) water
2 tablespoons rum
1 tablespoon lemon juice
300 g (10½ oz) fresh blueberries

1 To make the starter batter, sprinkle the yeast and sugar on to the milk and leave for 5 minutes. Stir in the flour and put in a warm place for 20 minutes to froth. (Make sure you use a large enough bowl.)

2 Generously butter a 20 cm (8 inch) savarin tin and place on a baking tray.

3 In another bowl, rub the butter into the flour. Stir through the sugar, salt and dried blueberries. Make a well in the centre and gradually stir in the yeast batter. Beat for 2–3 minutes until smooth. Pour the mixture into the prepared tin, cover and prove (page 8) in a warm place for about 30 minutes, or until the batter almost reaches the top of the tin.

4 Meanwhile, make the syrup. Dissolve the sugar in the water, bring to the boil and simmer for 8–10 minutes until syrupy. Cool slightly before stirring in the rum and lemon juice and fresh blueberries. Preheat the oven to Gas Mark 6/200°C/400°F.

5 Bake the savarin for 20 minutes until golden and set. Cool slightly before running a knife around the edges. Leave to cool in the tin for another 10 minutes, then turn out on to a serving plate or tray.

6 While the savarin is still warm, prick it all over with a fork or skewer. Slowly pour over the syrup and blueberries and leave to soak in thoroughly.

Tips: This is actually better if made the day before so that the rum has a chance to soak right through the savarin.

Dried yeast works better in the starter batter than the fast action type.

Plum Custard Cake

Makes: *1 cake* **Preparation time:** *55 minutes + proving + 55 minutes baking*
Freezing: *not recommended*

This is definitely for comfort eating! Do not worry if the cake rises unevenly, it is part of the home-made appeal.

350 g (12 oz) strong white bread flour
40 g (1½ oz) unsalted butter
25 g (1 oz) caster sugar
½ teaspoon salt
1 teaspoon fast action dried yeast
1 medium egg, beaten
150–175 ml (5–6 fl oz) warm semi-skimmed
 milk
6 ripe plums, de-stoned and thinly sliced
80 g (3 oz) caster sugar
½ teaspoon ground cinnamon
sifted icing sugar, for dusting
For the custard:
600 ml (1 pint) semi-skimmed milk
½ teaspoon vanilla extract
115 g (4 oz) caster sugar
2 medium eggs, plus 2 egg yolks
25 g (1 oz) plain flour

1 Place the flour in a bowl and rub in the butter. Add the sugar, salt and yeast, then make a well in the centre and stir in the egg and milk to make a soft dough. Turn out on to an unfloured work surface and knead (page 8) for 10 minutes until smooth. Cover and prove (page 8) in a warm place until doubled in size.

2 For the custard, warm the milk and vanilla to just below boiling. Meanwhile, whisk the sugar and eggs until light and slightly thickened. Fold in the flour. Pour the hot milk on to the egg mixture, whisking all the time. Return to the pan and continue whisking until the mixture comes to the boil. Simmer for 1 minute before transferring to a bowl to cool. Cover with buttered paper to prevent a skin forming.

3 Line a 20 cm (8 inch) springform or loose bottomed cake tin with a double thickness of baking parchment, ensuring that it extends 10 cm (4 inches) above the rim of the tin.

4 Divide the dough into three. Using floured hands, press or roll out each piece into a 20 cm (8 inch) circle. Place one in the base of the prepared tin. Spoon a third of the cooled custard over the top. (It doesn't matter if this is still warm). Scatter one third of the sliced plums over. Combine the sugar and cinnamon and sprinkle one third of this over the plums. Repeat twice more.

5 Cover and prove for about 45 minutes, or until risen about 5 cm (2 inches) above the tin. Preheat the oven to Gas Mark 6/200°C/400°F.

6 Bake for 55 minutes or until risen and set. Do not worry if some of the plums become charred. Allow to cool in the tin for 15 minutes. Dust with icing sugar to serve.

Caramelised Apple Tart

Makes: *1 tart* **Preparation time:** *45 minutes + rolling + resting + proving + 25–30 minutes baking*
Freezing: *not recommended*

Serve this as a pudding, or warm it through and have with coffee.

225 g (8 oz) strong white bread flour
1 tablespoon sugar
¼ teaspoon salt
¾ teaspoon fast action dried yeast
25 g (1 oz) unsalted butter, softened
1 medium egg, beaten
90 ml (3 fl oz) warm semi-skimmed milk
115 g (4 oz) white marzipan
sifted icing sugar, for dusting
For the topping:
50 g (2 oz) unsalted butter
115 g (4 oz) caster sugar
6 dessert apples, peeled, cored and sliced into
   eighths

1 Combine the flour, sugar, salt and yeast in a
   mixing bowl. Make a well in the centre and
   add the butter, egg and milk. Mix to a soft
   dough.

2 Turn out on to an unfloured work surface and
   knead (page 8) for 8–10 minutes until smooth.
   Cover and allow to rest for 10 minutes.

3 On a lightly floured surface, roll the dough
   into a 28 x 18 cm (11 x 7 inches) rectangle.
   Roll out the marzipan to 13 x 10 cm (5 x 4
   inches) and place in the middle of the dough.
   Fold each side of the dough over and seal by
   pressing down with the rolling pin. Roll out
   to roughly 30 x 13 cm (12 x 5 inches). Fold
   the top half down and the bottom up. Seal
   as before and repeat once more. Cover and

leave to rest at room temperature for
10 minutes.

4 Repeat the rolling and folding twice, allow the
   dough to rest and then repeat twice more.
   Allow the dough to rest for a further
   10 minutes.

5 Either roll out or push the dough into a
   greased 28 cm (11 inch) flan ring. Place this
   on a baking tray and cover. Leave to prove
   (page 8) in a warm place for 45 minutes.

6 Meanwhile, make the topping. Melt the butter
   in a pan large enough to take the apples in a
   single layer. Sprinkle on the sugar and then
   scatter the apples evenly over the top. Bubble
   over a medium heat for 20 minutes until
   golden. Cool. Preheat the oven to Gas
   Mark 6/200°C/400°F.

7 Use a fork to transfer apple slices on to the
   dough. Add a little of the syrup – too much
   will make the dough soggy. Bake for 25–30
   minutes until golden. Allow to rest in the tin for
   10 minutes before transferring to a wire rack.
   Serve warm, dusted with icing sugar.

Tip: Any leftover apple syrup makes a lovely
sauce for bananas or ice cream.

Celebration Time

Bread making, with or without yeast, dates back centuries. Bread is found around the world and plays a part in many religions and faiths, often having a central role in cultural festivals and sacred rituals. Many of the recipes in this chapter are a labour of love, with great symbolic significance attached. They are often made only once a year, specifically for an important occasion or feast when the whole family gathers together.

Glacé Fruit and Nut Wreath, pages 124–125

Chollah

Makes: *1 loaf* **Preparation time:** *30 minutes + proving + 30 minutes baking*
Freezing: *recommended*

Chollah (or Challah) is a Jewish bread, traditionally eaten on the Sabbath. Made with milk, eggs, sugar and butter, it is quite rich. Any left-overs make a delicious bread and butter pudding.

350 g (12 oz) strong white bread flour
¾ teaspoon salt
40 g (1½ oz) unsalted butter
25 g (1 oz) sugar
1 teaspoon fast action dried yeast
2 medium eggs, beaten
125 ml (4 fl oz) warm semi-skimmed milk
1 egg, beaten, to glaze
½ teaspoon poppy seeds, for sprinkling

1 Place the flour and salt in a large mixing bowl and rub in the butter. Stir in the sugar and yeast. Make a well in the centre and add the beaten eggs and milk. Mix to a soft dough.

2 Turn out on to an unfloured surface and knead (page 8) for 10 minutes, until smooth. Place in an oiled polythene bag and leave in a warm place to prove (page 8) until doubled in size.

3 Lightly grease a baking sheet.

4 Divide the dough into three and, without knocking back, roll out using your fingertips into three strands, each measuring 35 cm (14 inches) long. Join the strands together at one end and seal with beaten egg. Plait the strands, seal with more beaten egg and place on the baking sheet. Tuck the ends under to plump up the shape, brush with beaten egg and cover. Leave in a warm place to prove until doubled in size.

5 Preheat the oven to Gas Mark 6/200°C/400°F.

6 Brush the plait again with beaten egg and sprinkle with poppy seeds. Bake one rung below the centre of the oven for 30 minutes. Cool on a wire rack.

Hot Cross Buns

Makes: *12 buns* **Preparation time:** *35 minutes + proving + 20 minutes baking*
Freezing: *recommended*

Traditionally eaten on Good Friday, these are best served toasted or warmed, split and buttered.

350 g (12 oz) strong white bread flour
50 g (2 oz) caster sugar
1 teaspoon salt
2 teaspoons mixed spice
1 teaspoon cinnamon
115 g (4 oz) currants, sultanas or raisins
50 g (2 oz) mixed peel
50 g (2 oz) unsalted butter, softened
1 medium egg, beaten
For the yeast batter:
1 tablespoon dried yeast (not fast action)
1 teaspoon sugar
225 ml (8 fl oz) warm semi-skimmed milk
115 g (4 oz) strong white bread flour
For the crosses:
4 tablespoons plain flour
3 tablespoons water
For the glaze:
2 tablespoons sugar
4 tablespoons semi-skimmed milk

1 First, make the yeast batter. Sprinkle the yeast and sugar on to the milk and leave for 5 minutes to let the yeast dissolve. Stir in the flour to make a paste. Place in a warm place for 15–20 minutes until frothy.

2 Combine the flour, sugar, salt, spices, fruit and peel in a large bowl. Make a well in the centre and add the butter, egg and yeast batter. Gradually draw in the dry ingredients and mix to a soft dough.

3 Turn out on to an unfloured surface and knead (page 8) for 8–10 minutes until smooth. Cover and leave to prove (page 8) in a warm place until doubled in size.

4 Grease a baking sheet.

5 Knock back (page 9) the dough. Divide into 12 equal pieces and roll each into a round. Arrange them in four well-spaced lines on the baking sheet. Cover and prove. Preheat the oven to Gas Mark 7/220°C/425°F.

6 Blend together the flour and water for the crosses to make a smooth paste. Spoon into an icing bag fitted with a small plain nozzle and pipe crosses on the buns.

7 Bake for 10 minutes, reduce the temperature to Gas Mark 5/190°C/375°F and bake for a further 8–10 minutes.

8 For the glaze, dissolve the sugar in the milk and simmer for 1 minute until syrupy. Leave to cool.

9 Remove the buns from the oven and, while still hot, brush with glaze to give a shiny finish. Transfer to a wire rack to cool.

Tsoureki (Greek Easter Bread)

Makes: *8 breads* **Preparation time:** *35 minutes + proving + 15–20 minutes baking*
Freezing: *recommended*

These Greek Easter breads are made from a plaited brioche-like dough. Traditionally, the eggs were dyed red to symbolise the blood of christ.

450 g (1 lb) strong white bread flour
2 tablespoons caster sugar
1 teaspoon salt
1½ teaspoons fast action dried yeast
grated zest of 1 orange
grated zest of 1 lemon
50 g (2 oz) unsalted butter, softened
2 medium eggs, beaten
150 ml (6 fl oz) warm semi-skimmed milk
8 medium eggs
For the topping:
1 egg yolk
1 tablespoon water
slivered almonds or sesame seeds, for
    sprinkling

1 Combine the flour, sugar, salt, yeast and orange and lemon zests in a large mixing bowl. Make a well in the centre and add the butter, beaten eggs and milk. Mix to a soft dough, gradually incorporating the dry ingredients.

2 Turn out on to an unfloured surface and knead (page 8) for 8–10 minutes until smooth. Place in an oiled polythene bag and leave to prove (page 8) in a warm place until doubled in size.

3 Grease two baking sheets.

4 Divide the dough into eight pieces. Take one piece, keeping the rest in the oiled bag to prevent it drying out. Cut this piece into three and, using your fingertips, roll out each third to 25 cm (10 inches). Plait these pieces together, joining the ends to form a ring. Transfer to a baking sheet and place an egg in the centre. Repeat with the remaining pieces of dough.

5 Cover both trays and prove until doubled in size. Preheat the oven to Gas Mark 6/ 200°C/400°F.

6 Beat the egg yolk with the water and brush the breads with the egg glaze, avoiding touching the eggs themselves. Sprinkle with slivered almonds or sesame seeds. Bake for 15–20 minutes until golden. Transfer to a cooling rack and serve warm or cold.

Tips: To avoid the eggs cracking, make sure that they are cushioned on the dough rather than being in direct contact with the baking sheet.

Pretty Cotswold blue eggs are used here, but you can use the more widely available brown speckled eggs and decorate them using non-toxic felt pens.

Irish Barmbrack

Makes: *1 loaf*
Preparation time: *overnight soaking + 40 minutes + proving + 55–60 minutes baking*
Freezing: *recommended*

This is a traditional Irish bread – barm meaning yeast and brack meaning bread. It is popular around Halloween and steeped in tradition. Various favours can be baked in the loaf, such as a gold ring. Superstition says that the lucky recipient will be married within a year.

400 g (14 oz) strong white bread flour
50 g (2 oz) caster sugar
½ teaspoon salt
1¼ teaspoons mixed spice
80 g (3 oz) butter, softened
1 medium egg, beaten
For the overnight soaking:
175 g (6 oz) raisins
175 g (6 oz) sultanas
115 g (4 oz) candied peel, cut small
600 ml (1 pint) strong, hot tea
For the yeast mixture:
1½ teaspoons dried yeast (not fast action)
1 teaspoon sugar
175 ml (6 fl oz) warm semi-skimmed milk
For the glaze:
1 egg
1 tablespoon water

1 The night before you want to make the bread, place the dried fruit in a bowl and pour over the tea. Stir, then cover with a tea towel and leave overnight to plump up the fruit. The following morning, strain the fruit through a sieve, pressing down gently with the back of a wooden spoon to remove as much excess moisture as possible.

2 Make the yeast mixture. Sprinkle the yeast and sugar on to the warm milk and stir. Leave in a warm place for 15–20 minutes until the mixture is frothy and the yeast has dissolved.

3 In a large mixing bowl, combine the flour, sugar, salt and spice. Make a well in the centre and add the softened butter, egg and yeast mixture. Mix to a soft dough. The mixture will probably be a little dry, so add a little of the soaked fruits to moisten if necessary.

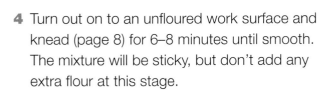

4 Turn out on to an unfloured work surface and knead (page 8) for 6–8 minutes until smooth. The mixture will be sticky, but don't add any extra flour at this stage.

5 Gradually work in the soaked fruit, scraping the dough off the work surface as you go. It does become very sticky at this stage, so work quickly to incorporate all the fruit and then put the dough into a large oiled bowl. Cover and leave to prove (page 8) in a warm place. This will take up to 2 hours.

6 Line a 20 cm (8 inch) springform cake tin with baking parchment.

7 Beat the fruited dough mixture with a wooden spoon for 2–3 minutes, just to knock the air out. Spoon into the prepared tin and level the surface. Cover and prove again for 1½–2 hours.

8 Preheat the oven to Gas Mark 6/200°C/400°F.

9 Beat the egg with the water and use to brush the barmbrack. Bake for 55–60 minutes, covering the top with baking parchment after 15 minutes. Remove from the oven and leave in the tin for at least 15 minutes before turning out on to a wire rack to cool.

Tip: This is delicious thinly sliced and buttered.

Pulla

Makes: *1 loaf* **Preparation time:** *30 minutes + proving + 30–35 minutes baking*
Freezing: *recommended*

This is a speciality Finnish bread that is served as a braided strand or in a ring, as here.

350 g (12 oz) strong white bread flour
40 g (1½ oz) caster sugar
¾ teaspoons salt
1¼ teaspoons fast action dried yeast
1¼ teaspoons freshly crushed cardamom
   (about 28 pods)
grated zest of 1 orange
40 g (1½ oz) unsalted butter, softened
1 medium egg, beaten
175 ml (6 fl oz) warm semi-skimmed milk
For the glaze:
1 egg yolk
1 tablespoon water

1 Combine the flour, sugar, salt, yeast, crushed cardamons and orange zest in a bowl. Make a well in the centre and add the butter, egg and milk. Gradually incorporate the dry ingredients, mixing to a soft dough.

2 Turn out on to an unfloured work surface and knead (page 8) for about 10 minutes. This is quite a sticky dough, so keep going without adding any flour. Then, at the end, wash and dry your hands. Flour them and work the dough into a smooth ball. Place in an oiled bag and leave to prove (page 8) in a warm place until doubled in size.

3 Grease a baking sheet.

4 Without knocking back, cut the dough into three even pieces. Using your fingertips, roll these out into 50 cm (20 inch) strands and plait these together, linking the ends into each other to form a ring.

5 Place on the prepared baking sheet, cover and prove again.

6 Preheat the oven to Gas Mark 5/190°C/375°F.

7 Beat the egg yolk with the water and brush the ring with the egg glaze. Bake for 30–35 minutes, covering with baking parchment after 15–20 minutes if the loaf is browning too much. Transfer to a wire rack to cool.

Tip: Extracting cardamon seeds from their pods is rather a labour of love, but essential to the flavour of this bread. Probably the easiest way is to pound a few at a time in a pestle and mortar, just to break open the pods. Make sure all the green husks are removed and then crush the seeds to a coarse powder.

Mincemeat Plait

Makes: *1 plait* **Preparation time:** *30 minutes + proving + 25 minutes baking*
Freezing: *recommended prior to icing*

It is always useful to have something slightly different to produce at Christmas time. This plait makes a stunning alternative to mince pies. Make it in advance and freeze (minus the icing sugar), ready to warm up when needed.

225 g (8 oz) strong white bread flour
25 g (1 oz) butter
25 g (1 oz) caster sugar
½ teaspoon salt
¾ teaspoon fast action dried yeast
finely grated zest of 1 orange
1 medium egg, beaten
90 ml (3 fl oz) warm semi-skimmed milk
225 g (8 oz) good quality mincemeat
For the topping:
1 egg, beaten, for brushing
25 g (1 oz) flaked almonds
icing sugar, for dusting

1 Place the flour in a bowl and rub in the butter. Stir in the sugar, salt, yeast and orange zest. Make a well in the centre and add the egg and milk. Mix to a soft dough.

2 Turn out on to an unfloured work surface and knead (page 8) for about 10 minutes until smooth. Cover and leave to prove (page 8) in a warm place until doubled in size.

3 Grease a baking sheet.

4 Do not knock back the dough, but roll out to 30 x 23 cm (12 x 9 inches) on a lightly floured surface.

5 Spread the mincemeat down the centre of the dough in a band about 7 cm (3 inches) wide. Be sure to leave a gap of 2.5 cm (1 inch) at each end. Now take a sharp knife and make angled cuts on each side from the mincemeat to the edge at about 5 cm (2 inch) intervals. Brush the dough edges with egg and fold over the top and bottom pieces of dough on to the mincemeat band. Then, starting from the top, fold a strip from one side over the mincemeat, and then a strip from the other side. Repeat, making a plait shape, until all the strips have been incorporated.

6 Carefully transfer to the prepared baking sheet. Cover and prove.

7 Preheat the oven to Gas Mark 6/200°C/400°F.

8 Gently brush the plait with the beaten egg and scatter flaked almonds liberally over the top. Bake for 25 minutes, covering with a piece of parchment paper after 15 minutes.

9 Transfer to a cooling rack and serve warm, dusted with icing sugar.

Stollen

Makes: *1 loaf* **Preparation time:** *40 minutes + soaking overnight + proving + 30 minutes baking*
Freezing: *recommended*

Unlike most other home-made breads, Stollen tastes better if you leave it for a day or two before eating to allow the different flavours time to develop and fuse together. Stollen is a German bread, traditionally served at Christmas time.

50 g (2 oz) dried cranberries
50 g (2 oz) sultanas
25 g (1 oz) candied peel, chopped
3 tablespoons rum
225 g (8 oz) strong white bread flour
25 g (1 oz) unsalted butter
25 g (1 oz) caster sugar
½ teaspoon salt
1 teaspoon fast action dried yeast
40 g (1½ oz) pistachio nuts
grated zest of 1 lemon
6 tablespoons warm semi-skimmed milk
1 medium egg, beaten
15 g (½ oz) melted butter, for brushing
175 g (6 oz) white or gold marzipan
icing sugar, for dusting

1 Place the dried fruit and candied peel in a small bowl, pour over the rum, stir well, cover and leave to marinate overnight.

2 The next day, place the flour in a bowl and rub in the butter. Mix in the sugar, salt, yeast, pistachio nuts and lemon zest. Make a well in the centre and add the milk and egg. Mix to a soft dough.

3 Turn out on to an unfloured work surface and knead (page 8) for about 10 minutes until smooth. Strain any liquid off the marinated fruit and, using floured hands, knead the fruit into the dough. Place in an oiled polythene bag and prove (page 8) until doubled in size.

4 Grease a baking sheet. Using your hands, roll out the marzipan into a 23 cm (9 inch) sausage shape.

5 Lightly flour the work surface and, without knocking back the dough, roll it out to a 23 cm (9 inch) circle. Brush it all over with the melted butter and lay the marzipan down the centre. Fold both sides of the dough over to wrap up the marzipan and press down lightly to seal. Place on the baking sheet, cover and prove until doubled in size.

6 Preheat the oven to Gas Mark 6/200°C/400°F.

7 Brush the stollen with melted butter and bake for 30 minutes. Allow to cool on a wire rack before dusting thickly with sifted icing sugar.

Glacé Fruit and Nut Wreath

Makes: *1 wreath* **Preparation time:** *35 minutes + proving + 20 minutes baking*
Freezing: *recommended prior to icing*

This makes a lovely centrepiece at Christmas time. The nuts take on an almost praline-like flavour as they caramelise with the butter and sugar filling. The recipe list looks daunting, but it is really not as bad as it looks at first glance!

175 g (6 oz) strong white bread flour
25 g (1 oz) caster sugar
¼ teaspoon salt
25 g (1 oz) unsalted butter, softened
1 medium egg, beaten
For the starter batter:
1½ teaspoons dried yeast (not fast action)
½ teaspoon sugar
90 ml (3 fl oz) warm semi-skimmed milk
50 g (2 oz) strong white bread flour
For the filling:
50 g (2 oz) unsalted butter, softened
25 g (1 oz) ground almonds
25 g (1 oz) caster sugar
grated zest of 1 lemon
¼ teaspoon vanilla essence
115 g (4 oz) glacé cherries, chopped
50 g (2 oz) mixed peel
80 g (3 oz) mixed nuts (pecans, brazils, hazelnuts and flaked almonds), chopped and toasted
For the icing:
80 g (3 oz) icing sugar, sifted
1 tablespoon lemon juice

1 Begin by making the starter batter. Sprinkle the yeast and sugar over the milk. Leave for 5 minutes, then stir and mix in the flour. Leave in a warm place for 20 minutes or until the mixture is frothy.

2 In a bowl, combine the flour, sugar and salt. Make a well in the centre and add the butter, egg and starter batter. Stir these together, gradually incorporating the dry ingredients until you have a soft dough.

3 Turn out on to an unfloured work surface and knead (page 8) for about 10 minutes until smooth. Place in an oiled polythene bag and leave to prove (page 8) in a warm place until doubled in size.

4 Meanwhile, make the filling. Beat together the butter, ground almonds, sugar, lemon zest and vanilla essence to a smooth paste. Then work in the cherries and mixed peel. Grease a large baking tray.

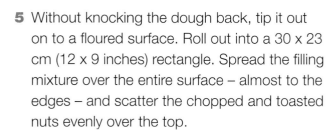

5 Without knocking the dough back, tip it out on to a floured surface. Roll out into a 30 x 23 cm (12 x 9 inches) rectangle. Spread the filling mixture over the entire surface – almost to the edges – and scatter the chopped and toasted nuts evenly over the top.

6 Roll the dough up tightly from the long edge and pinch together to seal. Remove any trace of flour from the work surface and, using your fingers, roll out the dough into a sausage shape, keeping going until it measures 60 cm (24 inches) in length.

7 Take a sharp knife and cut through the middle of the sausage down the entire length. Turn the two pieces so that the filling is facing upwards. Place one end of each strand on the baking tray, and then plait the pieces together, bending them round in a circle. Weave in the ends to form a perfect ring. Cover and prove until doubled in size. Preheat the oven to Gas Mark 6/200°C/400°F.

8 Bake the ring for 20 minutes, covering half way through with baking parchment if it is browning too much. Transfer to a wire rack to cool.

9 In a small bowl, blend the icing sugar to a smooth paste with the lemon juice. Drizzle over the wreath.

Tip: Nuts brown best in the oven. They'll only take 5–10 minutes at a medium temperature, but do keep an eye on them as they can easily burn.

Illustrated on page 113

Panettone

Makes: *1 loaf* **Preparation time:** *25 minutes + proving + 35–45 minutes baking*
Freezing: *recommended*

An Italian bread, traditionally made at Christmas time, Panettone has a distinctive shape. Since it is rich in eggs, sugar and butter, it will take longer to prove than other breads, so don't be tempted to bake it before it has fully risen. Any leftovers make a wonderful base for bread and butter pudding.

400 g (14 oz) strong white bread flour
50 g (2 oz) caster sugar
½ teaspoon salt
1½ teaspoons fast action dried yeast
finely grated zest of 1 lemon
80 g (3 oz) raisins
80 g (3 oz) candied peel, fined chopped
80g (3 oz) unsalted butter, melted, plus extra
**   for brushing**
2 medium eggs, beaten
125 ml (4 fl oz) warm semi-skimmed milk
1 teaspoon vanilla extract

1 Combine the flour, sugar, salt, yeast and lemon zest in a bowl. Stir in the raisins and candied peel. Make a well in the centre and add the butter, eggs, milk and vanilla extract. Mix to a soft dough.

2 Turn out on to an unfloured work surface and knead (page 8) for 10 minutes until smooth. Cover and leave to prove (page 8) in a warm place until doubled in size. (This could take about 2 hours.)

3 Line a 15 cm (6 inch) spring clip or loose bottomed cake tin with a double thickness of baking parchment. Make sure that the paper is 5 cm (2 inches) higher than the tin.

4 Knead the dough again and form into a round. Place in the tin, cover and leave to prove until the dough rises almost to the top of the lining paper (about 1½ hours).

5 Preheat the oven to Gas Mark 6/200°C/400°F. Set the shelf to one rung below the middle.

6 Bake for 35–45 minutes, covering with buttered paper after 15 minutes to prevent it from over browning.

7 Leave the Panettone in the tin for 5–10 minutes before turning out on to a wire rack to cool. The base should sound hollow when tapped. Brush the top with melted butter while still warm.

Tip: Dust the Panettone with sifted icing sugar to give it a Christmasy feel!

Scandinavian Julekage

Makes: *1 loaf* **Preparation time:** *30 minutes + proving + 35–45 minutes baking*
Freezing: *recommended*

Julekage is traditionally served in Scandinavian countries at Christmas. Candied fruit, such as cherries and pineapple, are incorporated into a dough enriched with butter and eggs to give brightly coloured 'jewels' of red, orange and yellow.

450 g (1 lb) strong white bread flour
50 g (2 oz) caster sugar
¾ teaspoon salt
1½ teaspoons fast action dried yeast
½ teaspoon freshly ground cardamom (seeds from 13–14 pods)
grated zest of 1 lemon
115 g (4 oz) dried sweetened tropical fruit (pineapple, papaya, mango and melon)
50 g (2 oz) glacé cherries, roughly chopped
50 g (2 oz) mixed peel
80 g (3 oz) unsalted butter, melted
2 medium eggs, beaten
150 ml (¼ pint) warm semi-skimmed milk
For the icing:
50 g (2 oz) icing sugar
2½ teaspoons boiling water

1 Combine the flour, sugar, salt, yeast, cardamon and lemon zest in a bowl. Stir in the tropical fruit, cherries and mixed peel and make a well in the centre. Add the butter, eggs and milk and mix to a soft dough.

2 Turn out on to an unfloured work surface and knead (page 8) for 10 minutes until smooth. Cover and leave to prove (page 8) in a warm place until doubled in size.

3 Line a 20 cm (8 inch) spring clip cake tin with a double thickness of baking parchment so that it extends 5 cm (2 inches) beyond the rim.

4 Knead the dough again and form into a round. Place in the tin, cover and prove until the dough expands to fill the tin and almost reaches the top.

5 Preheat the oven to Gas Mark 6/200°C/400°F.

6 Bake for 35–45 minutes, covering with buttered paper after 15 minutes to prevent it from over browning.

7 Leave in the tin for 5–10 minutes before turning out on to a wire rack. The bottom should sound hollow when tapped.

8 While the bread is still warm, blend the icing sugar and water together. Drizzle the icing backwards and forwards across the top of the bread to decorate.

Tip: This bread will take a long time to prove, up to 2 hours for the first rising and almost as long for the second. Be patient as it is well worth the result. Because of the added butter it keeps for longer than most breads.

Yeast Free, Gluten Free or Wheat Free

For those who are unable to tolerate the main ingredients in bread – notably wheat, the gluten found in it and yeast – this chapter offers some alternative suggestions. Wheat and gluten free flour is available. It is made up of a variety of different flours blended in a combination to ensure an end product that balances the various attributes of each, whether it is valued for its colour, flavour or water absorbency. Typical flours that might be used include tapioca, potato and rice, together with a gluten improver.

Peshwari Mini Naans, page 140

Cornbread with Parmesan and Sun-dried Tomatoes

Serves: *8* **Preparation time:** *20 minutes + 20–25 minutes baking*
Freezing: *recommended*

Rustle up this delicious bread in no time at all and serve warm from the oven as an ideal accompaniment to soup or a casserole. Cornbread is best eaten fresh on the day it is made. If the bread has been frozen, defrost, wrap in foil and reheat before serving.

150 g (5 oz) cornmeal or polenta
150 g (5 oz) plain flour
1 tablespoon baking powder
1 tablespoon caster sugar
½ teaspoon salt
50 g (2 oz) Parmesan, grated
15 g (½ oz) fresh basil leaves, torn
generous grinding of black pepper
250 g carton buttermilk
80 g (3 oz) drained semi-dried tomatoes in oil, snipped
2 medium eggs, beaten
2 tablespoons extra virgin olive oil

1 Grease and base line a shallow baking tin measuring 25 x 15 cm (10 x 6 inches). Preheat the oven to Gas Mark 6/200°C/400°F.

2 In a large bowl, combine the cornmeal, flour, baking powder, sugar and salt. Stir in the Parmesan and basil leaves and season with pepper.

3 Make a well in the centre of the dry ingredients and add the buttermilk, tomatoes, eggs and oil. Mix quickly to just combine, spoon into the prepared tin and level the surface.

4 Bake in the oven for 20–25 minutes.

5 Turn out on to a wire rack and leave to cool slightly. When ready to serve, cut into eight pieces.

Yeast Free Bread

Fig and Rosemary Damper

Makes: *1 loaf* **Preparation time:** *25 minutes + 30–35 minutes baking*
Freezing: *recommended*

Damper is an Australian bread – a staple for campers. Traditionally, pieces of dough are cooked over the dying embers of the camp fire. This is a more luxurious version, flavoured with sweet dried figs, walnuts and rosemary. It is great served anytime, and hovers between a sweet and savoury bread.

350 g (12 oz) self-raising flour
80 g (3 oz) butter
½ teaspoon salt
80 g (3 oz) dried soft figs, chopped
40 g (1½ oz) walnuts, chopped, plus extra for the topping
2 teaspoons fresh rosemary, chopped, plus extra for the topping
1 tablespoon runny honey
175 ml (6 fl oz) semi-skimmed milk, plus extra to glaze

1 Preheat the oven to Gas Mark 7/220°C/425°F. Grease a baking sheet.

2 Place the flour in a bowl and rub in the butter. Mix in the salt, figs, walnuts and rosemary. Add the honey and milk and mix to a soft dough.

3 Turn out on to a floured work surface and work lightly to make a smooth ball of dough.

4 Transfer to the baking sheet and press down to make an 18 cm (7 inch) circle. Score the top into eight sections. Brush with some milk and sprinkle with walnuts and a little chopped rosemary.

5 Bake for 10 minutes, then reduce the temperature to Gas Mark 4/180°C/350°F. Bake for a further 20–25 minutes or until the loaf is golden and sounds hollow when tapped on the bottom.

6 Transfer to a wire rack to cool.

Yeast Free Bread

Potato Farls

Makes: *4 breads* **Preparation time:** *30 minutes + cooling + 6–8 minutes cooking*
Freezing: *not recommended*

Farls are a form of Irish soda bread, cooked on a griddle or skillet. They are at their best made with freshly cooked potato and are great for brunch, topped with an egg and crispy dry cured bacon.

**300 g (10 oz) floury potatoes, peeled and
 chopped**
1 tablespoon butter
1 medium egg, beaten
115 g (4 oz) plain all-purpose white flour
¼ teaspoon bicarbonate of soda
¼ teaspoon salt
2 teaspoons sunflower oil

1 Place the potatoes in a saucepan, cover with water and bring to the boil. Simmer for 15–20 minutes until tender. Drain well.

2 Add the butter to the potatoes and mash until smooth. Allow to cool – just warm is fine.

3 Beat the egg into the potato mixture. Sift together the flour, bicarbonate of soda and salt and stir into the potato.

4 Flour a work surface well. Tip out the farl mixture and, with heavily floured hands, pat into a 20 cm (8 inch) circle, 5 mm (¼ inch) thick. Alternatively, roll out with a rolling pin. Using a sharp knife, cut into quarters.

5 Heat a 23 cm (9 inch) griddle pan or skillet over a fairly low heat.

6 Pour the oil on to the griddle pan and allow to heat for 30 seconds. Carefully transfer the farls to the griddle, arranging in a single layer. Cook for 3–4 minutes, until puffy and golden. Turn over and cook for a further 3–4 minutes on the other side. Serve at once.

Yeast Free Bread

Mushroom and Taleggio Scone Based Pizzas

Makes: *2 pizzas* **Preparation time:** *30 minutes + 12–15 minutes baking*
Freezing: *not recommended*

These pizzas are made with a scone base, rather than bread dough. Customise with your favourite toppings or add grated Parmesan or dried herbs to the scone base mixture.

2 tablespoons butter
3 large flat field mushrooms, approximately 175 g (6 oz), sliced
1 garlic clove, sliced
400 g can chopped tomatoes
1 teaspoon tomato purée
¼ teaspoon dried mixed herbs
salt, freshly ground black pepper and a pinch of sugar
4 teaspoons extra virgin olive oil
25 g (1 oz) baby spinach leaves, washed and dried
115 g (4 oz) Taleggio or Comté cheese, thinly sliced
For the scone base:
350 g (12 oz) self-raising white flour
¼ teaspoon salt
good pinch of cayenne pepper
50 g (2 oz) butter
approximately 200 ml (7 fl oz) semi-skimmed milk

1 Preheat the oven to Gas Mark 8/230°C/450°F. Grease two baking sheets.

2 Melt the butter in a pan, add the mushrooms and garlic and fry for 3–4 minutes until the mushrooms have re-absorbed their liquid. Leave to cool.

3 Pour the tomatoes into a sieve and drain well. Stir the tomato purée, herbs, seasoning and a pinch of sugar into the tomato pulp.

4 Make the scone base. Place the flour, salt and cayenne pepper in a bowl and rub in the butter. Make a well in the centre and gradually blend in enough milk to make a soft dough.

5 Turn out on to a lightly floured work surface and work gently until smooth. Divide into two. Form each into a round and roll out into 25 cm (10 inch) circles. Place one on each baking sheet.

6 Brush the top of the scones with a little oil, reserving the rest for finishing off. Spread the tomato mixture to the edges. Scatter the spinach leaves over the top, then the cooked mushrooms followed by the cheese. Drizzle a little oil over each pizza.

7 Bake towards the top of the oven for 12–15 minutes until the crusts are golden and the cheese is bubbling. Serve at once.

Yeast Free Bread

Bacon and Cheddar Loaf

Makes: *1 loaf* **Preparation time:** *25 minutes + 35–45 minutes baking*
Freezing: *not recommended*

Gluten and wheat free flour often contains potato flour, which works exceptionally well with bacon and cheese. Spring onions, softened in the bacon fat, gives this bread plenty of flavour. Before baking, score the dough into sections so that, once baked, people can help themselves by breaking off a piece.

80–115 g (3–4 oz) dry cured smoked streaky bacon, finely snipped

1 bunch of spring onions, thinly sliced

225 g (8 oz) wheat and gluten free plain white flour

1 tablespoon wheat and gluten free baking powder

1 teaspoon dry English mustard powder

¼ teaspoon salt

good pinch of cayenne pepper

80 g (3 oz) mature Cheddar cheese, finely grated

175 ml (6 fl oz) semi-skimmed milk, plus a little extra for brushing

1 Fry the bacon in a non-stick pan until it crisps up and is tinged brown. Reduce the heat and add the spring onions. Cook for 1–2 minutes to soften, remove from the heat and leave to cool.

2 Preheat the oven to Gas Mark 5/190°C/375°F. Grease a baking sheet.

3 In a mixing bowl, sift together the flour, baking powder, mustard powder, salt and cayenne pepper. Stir in most of the cheese and the cooled bacon and onion mixture. Make a well in the centre and add the milk. Mix to a soft dough.

4 Turn out on to a lightly floured work surface and work gently to just bring the dough together in a ball.

5 Place on the baking sheet and flatten slightly. Score the top into 6–8 segments. Brush with milk and scatter with the remaining cheese.

6 Bake for 35–45 minutes until golden. Cool on a wire rack.

Yeast, Wheat and Gluten Free Bread

Apricot, Cardamom and Green Tea Teabread

Makes: *1 loaf* **Preparation time:** *25 minutes + overnight soaking + 1¼ hours baking*
Freezing: *recommended*

This teabread is made with yogurt, giving it a fairly dense, almost pudding-like texture. It is also very moist as the apricots are soaked overnight in hot tea. A fruit or flower tea of your choice gives the loaf an aromatic scent.

225 g (8 oz) semi-dried apricots, finely chopped
300 ml (½ pint) strong, hot green tea with jasmine
175 g (6 oz) plain flour
115 g (4 oz) fine wholemeal flour
2 teaspoons baking powder
115 g (4 oz) unsalted butter
115 g (4 oz) caster sugar
40 g (1½ oz) pistachios
1 tablespoon cardamom seeds, husks removed and ground
150 ml (¼ pint) natural yogurt
1 medium egg, beaten
For the topping:
1–2 tablespoons apricot jam, sieved and warmed
2 semi-dried apricots, finely chopped
a handful of pistachios, finely chopped

1 Place the apricots in a bowl, pour over the hot tea, cover and soak overnight to plump up.

2 Preheat the oven to Gas Mark 4/180°C/350°F. Grease and line a 900 g (2 lb) loaf tin.

3 Combine the flours and baking powder in a bowl and rub in the butter. Stir in the sugar, pistachios and ground cardamom. Make a well in the centre and add the soaked apricots, yogurt and egg. Mix the ingredients just enough to combine and spoon into the prepared tin.

4 Bake in the oven for about 1¼ hours, covering the top with foil after an hour. Test to see if the bread is done by inserting a skewer, which should come out clean.

5 Remove from the oven and leave in the tin for 15 minutes before turning out on to a wire rack to cool.

6 Brush with a little warmed apricot jam and sprinkle with the chopped apricots and pistachios. Brush again lightly with apricot jam.

Tip: This teabread is best kept in the fridge because of its yogurt content.

Yeast Free Bread

Basic Wheat and Gluten Free White Bread

Makes: *1 loaf* **Preparation time:** *30 minutes + proving + 25–30 minutes baking*
Freezing: *recommended*

It is useful to have a plain loaf for everyday eating. This recipe makes use of potato and rice flours, which are available from larger supermarkets and health food shops. Xanthan gum is a gluten replacer that can also be found in health food shops or on the Internet.

225 g (8 oz) rice flour (a blend of white and brown)
50 g (2 oz) potato flour
50 g (2 oz) ground almonds
1 tablespoon sugar
½ teaspoon salt
1½ teaspoons fast action dried yeast
1 tablespoon xanthan gum
½ teaspoon bicarbonate of soda
2 medium eggs, beaten
1 teaspoon cider vinegar
5 tablespoons sunflower oil
250 ml (9 fl oz) warm semi-skimmed milk

1 Grease a 900 g (2 lb) loaf tin.

2 Combine the flours in a mixing bowl with the ground almonds, sugar, salt, yeast, xanthan gum and bicarbonate of soda. Make a well in the centre and add the beaten eggs, vinegar, oil and milk. Mix until smooth. The mixture will be quite stiff, but continue beating as best you can for 3–4 minutes.

3 Spoon the mixture into the prepared tin and level the surface. Cover and leave to prove (page 8) in a warm place until doubled in size (about 1–1¼ hours).

4 Preheat the oven to Gas Mark 7/220°C/425°F.

5 Bake in the preheated oven for 25–30 minutes until golden.

6 Remove from the tin and leave to cool on a wire rack.

Tip: Beating by hand is quite hard work, so use a mixer if you have one!

Wheat and Gluten Free Bread

Fennel Seed Flatbreads

Makes: *3 flatbreads* **Preparation time:** *20 minutes + proving + 12–15 minutes baking*
Freezing: *not recommended*

Flatbreads are wonderful for mopping up the juices of a casserole or curry. They are best eaten warm, soon after baking, otherwise they become rather dry. If you are not particularly keen on fennel, try another seed, such as sesame or caraway, or a sprinkling of dried herbs instead.

300 g (10 oz) wheat and gluten free white bread flour
1 teaspoon sugar
½ teaspoon salt
1 teaspoon fast action dried yeast
2 tablespoons olive oil
1 medium egg, beaten
175 ml (6 fl oz) warm water
For the topping:
milk, for brushing
¾ teaspoon fennel seeds

1 Combine the flour, sugar, salt and yeast in a bowl. Make a well in the centre and add the oil, egg and water. Stir the mixture with a wooden spoon until it all comes together.

2 Oil a bowl and transfer the dough into it. Cover and leave in a warm place to prove (page 8) for 1 hour.

3 Grease two or three baking sheets.

4 With well-floured hands, divide the dough into three. On a floured surface, roll out each piece into a 18 cm (7 inch) circle approximately 5 mm (¼ inch) thick. Space well apart on the baking sheets. Cover and prove for 30 minutes until slightly puffy.

5 Preheat the oven to Gas Mark 7/220°C/425°F.

6 Brush the circles with a little milk and sprinkle with the fennel seeds, pressing them down lightly. Bake for 12–15 minutes until beginning to colour.

7 Transfer to a wire rack and serve warm.

Wheat and Gluten Free Bread

Peshwari Mini Naans

Makes: *12 naans* **Preparation time:** *20 minutes + proving + 12 minutes grilling*
Freezing: *recommended*

These little flat breads are filled with coconut and sultanas, giving them a surprising, delicious sweetness. Serve as an accompaniment to spicy stews or make up mini ones and use as a base for canapés.

450 g (1 lb) wheat and gluten free white bread flour
2 teaspoons sugar
½ teaspoon salt
1½ teaspoons fast action dried yeast
1 teaspoon wheat and gluten free baking powder
1 teaspoon black onion seeds
2 tablespoons chopped fresh coriander
4 tablespoons natural yogurt
1 medium egg, beaten
25 g (1 oz) butter, melted, plus extra for brushing
200–225 ml (7–8 fl oz) hand-hot water
For the filling:
40 g (1½ oz) desiccated coconut
3 tablespoons sultanas

1 Combine the flour, sugar, salt, yeast, baking powder, onion seeds and coriander in a bowl. Make a well in the centre and add the yogurt, egg, butter and water. Mix to a soft dough.

2 Turn out on to a lightly floured work surface and form into a smooth ball. (This flour does not require kneading.) Place in an oiled bowl, cover and leave to prove (page 8) in a warm place for about 1 hour.

3 Grease two baking sheets.

4 Lightly knead (page 8) the dough just to knock out the air. Divide into 12 equal pieces. Using well-floured hands, shape each into a 10 cm (4 inch) disc.

5 Mix together the coconut and sultanas. Place a little of the filling mixture in the middle of a circle of dough. Fold the dough over to form a semicircle and press the edges to seal. (You don't need any water.) Pat the dough out to form an oval shape about 10 cm (4 inches) long and 5 mm (¼ inch) thick. Place on the baking sheet and repeat with the remaining discs. Cover and leave to prove until puffy.

6 Preheat the grill to its highest setting and grill the breads for 3 minutes on each side.

7 Serve brushed with melted butter.

Tip: Wheat and gluten free products do tend to dry out quickly, so eat on the day of baking.

Wheat and Gluten Free Bread

Banana and Chocolate Drop Cake

Makes: *1 loaf* **Preparation time:** *20 minutes + proving + 40–45 minutes baking*
Freezing: *recommended*

This bread is more like a cake. It keeps very well so you may want to double the quantities and freeze half.

225 g (8 oz) wheat and gluten free white
   bread flour
50 g (2 oz) muscovado sugar
¼ teaspoon salt
¾ teaspoon fast action dried yeast
50 g (2 oz) milk chocolate drops
50 g (2 oz) unsalted butter, melted
1 ripe banana, mashed
125 ml (4 fl oz) warm semi-skimmed milk
1 medium egg, beaten
¼ teaspoon vanilla essence
For the glaze:
2 tablespoons granulated sugar
4 tablespoons water

1 Grease and base line a 450 g (1 lb) loaf tin.

2 Combine the flour, sugar, salt, yeast, and chocolate drops in a bowl. Make a well in the middle and add the melted butter, mashed banana, milk, egg and vanilla essence. Beat with a wooden spoon until smooth.

3 Spoon the mixture into the prepared tin and level the surface, making a slight indent in the centre. Cover and leave to prove (page 8) in a warm place until doubled in size.

4 Preheat the oven to Gas Mark 6/200°C/400°F.

5 Make the glaze by dissolving the sugar in the water in a pan. Bring to the boil and simmer for 1 minute. Allow to cool.

6 Bake the loaf for 40–45 minutes. Remove from the oven and run a knife around the edge of the loaf. Leave in the tin for 5 minutes before turning out on to a wire rack.

7 Brush with the sugar glaze while still warm. Leave to cool.

Wheat and Gluten Free Bread

White Spelt 'Daisy' Rolls

Makes: *10 rolls* **Preparation time:** *15 minutes + proving + 12–15 minutes baking*
Freezing: *recommended*

This recipe is in this chapter because spelt is a 'true' cereal, not a modified one. Some people who are unable to tolerate wheat may therefore be able to eat spelt. White spelt flour is available from good health food shops, but it is expensive, as quite an intensive milling process is necessary to extract all the bran and wheat germ from the grain. The result is a creamy, cakey flour.

450 g (1 lb) white spelt flour
25 g (1 oz) butter
115 g (4 oz) barley flakes
1 teaspoon sugar
1 teaspoon salt
1 teaspoon fast action dried yeast
300 ml (½ pint) hand-hot water

1 Place the flour in a bowl and rub in the butter. Stir in the barley flakes, sugar, salt and yeast. Make a well in the centre and add the water to make a soft dough.

2 Turn out on to an unfloured work surface and knead (page 8) for 4–5 minutes only. Cover and leave in a warm place to prove (page 8) until doubled in size.

3 Grease two baking sheets.

4 Divide the dough into 10 pieces. Form each into a ball, flatten slightly then make five cuts with scissors, almost through to the centre, so that you have a 'daisy' effect. Place well apart on the baking sheets, cover and prove until doubled in size.

5 Preheat the oven to Gas Mark 7/220°C/425°F.

6 Bake the rolls for 12–15 minutes until golden. Cool on a wire rack.

Tips: Spelt flour has a more delicate gluten structure than wheat, so only requires 4–5 minutes kneading and does not take so long to prove.

The barley flakes give this bread a lovely crunchy, slightly chewy texture. They do, however, contain some gluten, so if you are worried about this omit them.

Cakes

Introduction

Cakes are enjoyed by everyone – from a toddler's first sponge finger clasped in a fist to a sophisticated gateau to celebrate a milestone birthday. The label of 'naughty but nice' only adds to their appeal!

One of the joys of cake making is that, come a wet afternoon, the chances are that you will be able to find all the ingredients necessary to make a tea time treat in your kitchen cupboards. There is, after all, a certain satisfaction in being able to eat the product of your labours. And children love to launch their cooking career with individual fairy cakes topped with colourful sprinklings and scatterings of some brightly coloured sugar decoration.

Undoubtedly life would go on without cake, but how enriched it is by them. Cakes are one of life's pleasures, and the core reason is that they are made for sharing, and the enjoyment of baking is reciprocated in the pleasure of their consumption – be it with family or friends.

Methods of Cake Making

While each recipe provides a detailed method, it is useful to have a general understanding of the way in which cakes are categorised – namely according to the technique by which they are made. There are five basic methods: creaming, all-in-one, rubbing in, whisking and melting.

CREAMING

This is probably the best-known and most widely used method. It involves beating butter and/or margarine with sugar until the mixture becomes paler in colour and lighter in texture. By doing this, the sugar starts to break down and become amalgamated with the fat. The next stage is to gradually add eggs, beating well after each addition to prevent curdling. The flour is then folded in using a metal spoon and a cutting, rather than beating, action to maintain the incorporated air.

Cakes made by this method include Victoria sandwich cakes, Madeira cake, some fruit cakes and many everyday cakes.

ALL-IN-ONE

This is a variation on the creaming method and became popular with the introduction of soft margarine, the consistency of which ensured that the fat could be quickly distributed into the cake batter. This method, as the term suggests, involves putting all the ingredients for the cake into a bowl. They are then beaten for a couple of minutes to thoroughly combine to a smooth batter. This is quicker than the traditional creaming method, cutting out the various stages involved. As with all cake making, but particularly more so here, it is important that all the ingredients are at room temperature so that they will blend easily without curdling.

When making a cake by the all-in-one method it is necessary to add a small amount of baking powder, even though self-raising flour is used. This is necessary since the short beating time does not

allow for sufficient air to be incorporated. It is equally important not to beat the mixture for longer than 2 minutes as, instead of a light, spongy cake, the texture will be close.

RUBBING IN

This type of cake starts in a similar way to making shortcrust pastry or crumble topping. Using either your hands or a food processor, cold fat straight from the fridge is rubbed into the flour until the mixture resembles fine breadcrumbs. Sugar is then stirred through, a well is made in the centre and the remaining ingredients are beaten in with a wooden spoon.

Cakes made by this method use half the amount of fat to the weight of flour, so are lower in calories. Tea breads and some fruit loaves are based on this method.

WHISKING

This type of cake uses eggs as the prime raising agent. Sufficient air needs to be incorporated using an electric whisk so that the eggs are able to form the structure of the cake. The eggs and sugar are whisked together for 7–10 minutes until they increase in volume and are light and foamy. To judge whether the mixture is thick enough, lift the beaters. If a trail of batter stays on the surface of the mixture for a few seconds, then it is ready. Whisking over a pan of hot water will encourage the sugar to melt and speed up the process. Half the flour at a time is then sifted over the mixture and folded in very carefully. Plain flour is normally used, but self-raising flour can be substituted if you prefer to have a safeguard!

Swiss rolls and Genoese sponges are both made using this method, which produces very light cakes with an open texture and often a low fat content. Since fatless sponges do tend to be rather dry, an option is to make a Genoese-style sponge, which has added melted fat. This both improves the cake's keeping qualities and gives it a better flavour and texture.

MELTING

Cakes made by the melting method use block fat, taken straight from the fridge. Often they are made in one pan, which is a bonus on the washing up front! The fat is warmed with sugar and sometimes syrup and treacle. It should not be boiled as this will alter the flavour. Once this mixture has cooled, the dry ingredients and egg are beaten in using a wooden spoon.

Gingerbread and some fruit cakes are made following this method.

Basic Ingredients for Cake Making

I always think of cakes as an 'add on item' – more of a treat than a basic necessity. It therefore follows that you should use the best quality ingredients possible. Listed below are some of the most commonly used ingredients.

BAKING POWDER AND BICARBONATE OF SODA
These are added to help the cake to rise. They may be used together or on their own.

BUTTER One of the basic ingredients of cake making and often used in preference to margarine for its flavour. Unsalted butter is often used in European recipes and many types of icing. It is important that butter be at room temperature if it is to be creamed or used in the all-in-one method. Butter can be softened most effectively in a microwave – watch it carefully as it melts quickly and will continue to heat through even when the microwave has been turned off.

CHOCOLATE Added to cakes in either block form or as cocoa. Cocoa powder (not sweetened drinking chocolate) should be dissolved first if it is not going to be cooked. Mix it with boiling water in order to eliminate its raw flavour. Plain, milk or white chocolate are available, as are chocolate chips/drops. The strength of the chocolate will vary according to the percentage of cocoa it contains. Generally, the higher the proportion of cocoa, the more expensive it will be. Plain (dark) chocolate is the most successful for cake making as it gives the best flavour. Unless stated otherwise, the recipes in this book use 50% cocoa solids plain chocolate.

Chocolate can be temperamental and requires handling with care. Melt in a bowl over a pan of hot (not boiling) water or, if using a microwave, remove before it is fully melted as the heat generated means that it will continue to melt. Try not to stir the chocolate more than necessary. Over working or heating results in grainy chocolate or the solids may separate from the fat. Chocolate gives a lovely gloss to icings but bear in mind that this will dull if it is refrigerated.

DRIED FRUIT There is a wealth of various dried fruit available, from currants, raisins, sultanas, apricots, dates and prunes to mango, pineapple, papaya and melon, not to forget cranberries and blueberries. Some of these have been sweetened, forming a halfway house between dried and candied fruit. Glacé cherries, mixed peel and candied peel are also widely used. With apricots, dates and prunes, do check on the packet that they are 'no need to soak' or 'ready to eat'. These can be used without the need to plump them up first and are more succulent.

EGGS All the recipes in this book use large (size 1) eggs. Eggs should be stored in the fridge but used at room temperature.

EXTRACTS, FLAVOURINGS AND FLOWER WATERS Extracts are made by distilling essential oils. Only a small amount needs be added. Flavours are synthetically made, and consequently cheaper, but do not impart such an authentic flavour. Flower waters, made by mixing an essential oil and distilled water, are very popular in Middle Eastern and Indian cooking. They are delicate flavour waters that are excellent used in syrups to drizzle over cakes and for flavouring icings.

FLOURS Flour really only needs to be sifted if being used for whisked sponges or when being incorporated with other ingredients as well – such as raising agents, spices or cocoa.

Self-raising is the most widely used flour in cake making. It has the correct proportion of raising agents already added to ensure a consistent rise.

Plain flour is used in whisked sponges, which rely on air rather than a raising agent for their volume. Additionally it is often used in conjunction with either baking powder or bicarbonate of soda to achieve a different texture or crumb.

Wholemeal flour – either plain or self-raising – will give a more crumbly result to cakes.

MARGARINE Soft margarine is mostly used throughout this book. To ensure that it is at room temperature, remove the margarine from the fridge about 30 minutes before needed, depending on the air temperature. I often use half margarine and half butter in recipes – butter for its flavour and margarine because of the lightness it gives the sponge. Sunflower or vegetable-based margarines are preferable since they are high in polyunsaturated fat.

Hard margarine is useful for fruit cakes and gingerbreads where the recipe requires the fat to re-set when the cake cools in order to give a firm, more supportive structure.

NUTS Nuts can be added to cakes chopped, flaked or ground. They are also widely used for decoration. In some recipes, ground almonds replace flour. I would always recommend toasting nuts prior to adding them to a cake as this heightens their flavour. Place on a lipped baking sheet in a medium hot oven for 6–8 minutes (macadamias will take less), but do keep a close eye on them as they turn from golden to burnt surprisingly quickly!

OIL This is used more in baking in America – recipes such as carrot cake and muffins use oil in preference to butter or margarine. A light, tasteless oil such as sunflower, corn, vegetable or rapeseed should be used. Avoid olive oil, which is heavy and has a strong flavour.

SUGAR Almost all cakes rely on sugar to sweeten them.

Caster sugar is the most widely used since it has fairly fine granules. Unrefined golden caster is also available.

Brown sugars vary in colour from light to dark. The darker the colour, the higher the molasses content. Light sugars are good for imparting a butterscotch flavour, whereas the darker ones work well in fruit cakes and with syrup and treacle, giving a denser texture to the cake. They will be labelled as soft light brown sugar or soft dark brown sugar. Muscovado is an unrefined raw cane sugar, available in both light and dark varieties.

Vanilla sugar can be found in some shops but is easily made by storing sugar in an airtight jar with a vanilla pod. This naturally flavours the sugar. The vanilla pod lasts for a long time so can be re-used several times – simply top up the jar with more sugar.

Demerara sugar is similar in grain size to granulated sugar and is a good choice for sprinkling over a cake before it is baked to give a rustic looking, crunchy topping.

Icing sugar is a powdered sugar ideal for making icing. It needs to be sieved before use. Unrefined icing sugar is also available and is good for fudge and coffee icings. Icing sugar can be used for the simplest of finishes by dusting over the top of a cake.

Honey, golden syrup, black treacle and maple syrup are usually used in conjunction with sugar as they are quite dense.

Helpful Tips

PREHEATING THE OVEN

Always preheat the oven. Too cold an oven and the cake will not rise properly; too hot and it will rise too quickly, only to collapse with an over-brown crust. The middle shelf should be used for all cakes unless otherwise stated. Place the cake centrally on the shelf – ovens are often hotter towards the sides, which results in uneven browning. It may be necessary to rotate the tins round for the last 5 minutes of cooking if more than one tin is in the oven, such as when making a sandwich cake.

It is important to bake the cake as soon as possible after the ingredients have been mixed together as the raising agents will start to react.

TIN SIZE

Always use the correct size. Too small and the cake is likely to be peaked and cracked on the surface. Too large and it will be a disappointing height and most likely dry from having been cooked for longer than necessary. The tin sizes in this book for round tins refer to the diameter across the top of the tin.

PREPARING THE TIN

TYPE OF TIN Non-stick cake tins are good when it comes to releasing the cake after baking. However, even these require greasing and lining. Silicone 'tins' are a very good alternative; they do not require greasing and release the cake very well. Spring form cake tins are good when making a deep round cake, as the easy release catch on the side helps with removing the cake from the tin. Cake tins with a loose bottomed base will also help you to turn out the cake with minimal damage. Individual muffin/bun trays are also available.

LINING PAPER Greaseproof paper is good for lining both the base and sides of a tin. It does need to be brushed with a thin layer of fat to repel the batter. Non-stick baking parchment acts in the same way, but does not require greasing unless you are making a fatless sponge. Alternatively, use silicone liners. These can be cut to size and are reusable – simply wash with soapy water and dry flat. You can also buy pre-cut liners that will line the base and sides of your tin.

Cakes with a short cooking time only require their base to be lined. Those cooked for over an hour often need to be fully lined. Fruit cakes cooked at a low temperature for a long period are best protected with a double layer of lining paper and then the whole tin wrapped around with a double thickness of brown paper, tied with string. This helps prevent the outside from drying out before the centre is fully cooked.

Soft margarine, melted butter or vegetable fat are all suitable for greasing, spread in a thin layer to provide a non-stick surface. Flavourless oil can be used but tends to leave a residue on the tin that is difficult to remove.

LINING THE TIN For loaf tins, I would recommend buying pre-shaped non-stick paper liners. These are very effective, save time and eliminate the need for greasing. Alternatively, grease the tin then estimate how much greaseproof paper you will need to cover the base and sides. Place the paper in the tin and snip from the edge to each corner. Overlap the edges so that the paper sits neatly in the base. Use paper clips to hold the edges together and lightly grease.

Sandwich tins only need to be base lined. Lightly grease the tin then place it on a piece of greaseproof paper and, using the tin as a guide, draw around it. Cut the circle out, place into the base of the tin and grease.

For deep round or square tins, place on greaseproof paper and draw around the base. Do this a second time and cut out two shapes. Measure a length of paper that will circle the outside of the tin once with a 5 cm (2 inch) overlap. Fold so that you have a double thickness and the paper extends 5 cm (2 inches) above the top of the tin. Make a fold 2.5 cm (1 inch) along the long edge of the paper. Snip through to the fold at regular intervals. Lightly grease the inside of the tin and place one shape of paper in the base. Grease one side of the long strip and position in the tin so that the ungreased side is against the tin and the frayed cut edge is on the base. The ends around the side should overlap. Finally, place the remaining paper shape on the base and grease.

For Christmas or heavy fruit cakes, make a collar as above, but with brown parcel paper and position on the outside of the tin. Secure with string.

Use baking parchment for swiss roll or tray bake tins. Lightly grease the tin then cut out a piece of paper approximately 5 cm (2 inches) larger than the tin. Place in the tin and cut through to the base at each corner. Overlap the snipped edges and secure at the top corners with paper clips.

WEIGHING INGREDIENTS

Cake making is not an exact science, but it does require ingredients to be used in the correct ratios. Use either metric or imperial measurements; never combine the two.

LEVELLING THE SURFACE

It is worth taking a little care when transferring cake batters to their tins. Liquid mixtures will find their own level. For stiffer batters it is necessary to smooth the surface. Make a slight hollow or dip in the middle to help ensure a level surface when cooked. When dividing the mixture into two or more tins, try to do so as evenly as possible, both for the sake of appearances and to ensure equal cooking times.

NO PEEPING!

On no account be tempted to open the oven before the recommended cooking time is up, particularly during the first 10–15 minutes. The cake will collapse if you do, as it will not have had time to set. However, for cakes with a long cooking time it may be necessary to cover the top with foil or greaseproof paper to prevent further browning after 45 minutes or so.

IS IT DONE YET?

There are two basic methods for testing to see if the cake is cooked. First, use your eyes and fingertips. The cake should look risen and be golden brown in colour. It should have shrunk away slightly from the edges of the tin. When you lightly press the top of the cake it should spring back. This method is used for sponges and small cakes.

Second, for larger, deep cakes and fruit cakes, it is necessary to use a skewer. This should be carefully inserted into the centre of the cake. If it comes out clean then the cake is done. If there is some cake batter on it then the cake needs to be returned to the oven for further cooking, perhaps another 5–10 minutes before being re-tested.

For both methods, do not remove the cake from the oven until you are sure that it is cooked. Open the oven door and, using oven gloves, slightly pull out the shelf with the cake on in order to test.

STRAIGHT FROM THE OVEN

Even a well-baked cake is still quite unstable when it is taken out of the oven. Leave it in its tin for 5–10 minutes for creamed cakes and sponges and about 30 minutes for larger, denser cakes. Some cakes, particularly those containing fresh fruit, should be left in their tins until completely cold.

When removing the cake from its tin it is important to take time and care. Very carefully run a round ended knife around the edge of the tin or ease the cake away using your fingertips. Turn the cake out onto a wire rack and remove the lining paper. If you do not wish the surface to be marked by the cooling rack, then turn the cake out onto a clean tea towel and then revert onto the cooling rack so that the top is uppermost.

Common Faults and Remedies

STORING AND FREEZING

Fruit cakes with a high fruit content will keep for a few weeks in an airtight container, whereas most sponge cakes are at their best for up to 4 days. Fatless sponges should be eaten as soon as possible. Any cake containing cream or other dairy products should be kept refrigerated. Wrap cakes up as soon as they have cooled. Cakes without icing should be wrapped in greaseproof paper or foil and then kept in a polythene bag or airtight tin. Iced cakes have a fragile finish so should be stored in an airtight container that will not stick to their icing.

It is best to freeze cakes un-iced where possible. Freezing often dulls the icing or alters the effectiveness of the decorations. Wrap un-iced cakes in greaseproof paper and then a polythene bag to protect them from freezer burn. If freezing un-iced sandwich cakes, place a sheet of greaseproof paper or baking parchment between the layers.

If the cake has been iced then open freezing is recommended, after which the cake will need to be placed in a polythene bag and sealed. Remove the cake from the bag before you defrost it, otherwise the icing might stick to the bag.

ELECTRICAL EQUIPMENT

Using a machine for cake making certainly speeds up the process. Whether using a hand-held or free-standing type, start the mixer on the slowest speed until the ingredients are blended and then increase to fast. It is important to scrape the sides down at intervals to ensure that all the ingredients are thoroughly mixed.

THE MIXTURE CURDLES
The ingredients were not all at room temperature to start with.
The egg was added too quickly, without sufficient beating between additions (if this happens add a tablespoon of the measured flour and beat in the egg more slowly).

THE CAKE PEAKS IN THE MIDDLE AND CRACKS
The tin used was too small.
The oven temperature was too high.
The cake was baked on too high a shelf in the oven.

THE CAKE IS SUNKEN
The cake was undercooked.
The oven was too cool, so the cake never rose.
The oven was too hot, so the cake appeared done on the outside but was not cooked in the centre.
Too much raising agent was used, which caused the cake to over-rise and then deflate.
The oven door was opened during cooking.

THE TEXTURE IS TOO CLOSE/
THE CAKE DID NOT RISE
Insufficient raising agent was used.
Not enough air was incorporated during mixing.
The mixture was too sloppy.
There was excessive beating in of the flour or of the mixture in general.
The oven was too cool.

THE CAKE IS DRY AND CRUMBLY
The cake was baked for too long.
Excessive raising agent was added.
There was not enough fat.
The mixture was too stiff.

THE FRUIT SANK TO THE BOTTOM OF THE CAKE
The syrup was not rinsed off glacé fruit.
The cake mixture was too liquid and not able to hold the fruit.
Self-raising flour was used instead of plain, so that the sponge rose but left the fruit behind.
The oven door was opened during baking.

Sponge Cakes

This chapter contains recipes for those essential cakes that form the basis of a cook's repertoire! From sandwich cakes to sponges, Madeira cake to gingerbread, there are many delicious everyday cakes to try. Some draw on influences from other countries, such as American Passion Cake and Latin American Milk Ring. Others are a variation on an old favourite, such as Coffee Battenburg. There are also several different Victoria sandwich variations.

Coffee Sandwich Cake, page 16

Traditional Victoria Sandwich

Serves: *8*   **Preparation and baking time:** *20 minutes + 25 minutes baking + cooling*
Freezing: *recommended prior to filling*

As its name suggests, this cake was popular in the reign of Queen Victoria and it remains so today – a testament to its simplicity and taste. For the best results, use a mixture of margarine and butter.

**175 g (6 oz) half each of softened butter
and soft margarine**
175 g (6 oz) caster sugar
¼ teaspoon vanilla extract
3 eggs, beaten
175 g (6 oz) self-raising flour
TO FINISH:
3 tablespoons raspberry conserve
caster sugar, for dusting

1 Grease and base line two 18 cm (7 inch) sandwich tins. Preheat the oven to Gas Mark 4/180°C/350°F.

2 In a mixing bowl, cream together the butter, margarine, sugar and vanilla extract until pale and fluffy. Gradually beat in the eggs a little at a time, beating well after each addition. If the mixture curdles, add a spoonful of the flour.

3 Using a large metal spoon, fold in the flour using a cutting action, so as not to knock out any of the incorporated air.

4 Divide the mixture between the tins and level the surfaces. Then make a slight dip in the centre of each. Bake for about 25 minutes until the sponges have risen and are golden and springy to the touch.

5 Remove from the oven and leave in the tins for 5 minutes. Then very carefully run a knife around the edge of the tins or ease the sponges away from the sides using your fingertips. Turn out onto a wire rack to cool.

6 Once cooled, spread the conserve evenly over one of the sponges. Place the other on top and press down lightly to join the two. Dust with caster sugar and serve.

Tip: When removing the cakes from their tins, turn them out onto a tea towel or oven glove, peel off the lining paper and then put them base side down onto the cooling rack. This will stop the top from being marked by the cooling rack.

All-in-one Victoria Sandwich

Serves: *8* **Preparation and baking time:** *15 minutes + 25 minutes baking + cooling*
Freezing: *recommended prior to filling*

This cake is slightly different to a traditional Victoria sandwich. First, it is necessary to add a little baking powder to help the cake rise. Second, it is important to use soft margarine or softened butter that blends easily.

**175 g (6 oz) half each of softened butter
and soft margarine**
175 g (6 oz) caster sugar
175 g (6 oz) self-raising flour
½ teaspoon baking powder
3 eggs
¼ teaspoon vanilla extract
TO FINISH:
3 tablespoons raspberry conserve
caster sugar, for dusting

1 Grease and base line two 18 cm (7 inch) sandwich tins. Preheat the oven to Gas Mark 4/180°C/350°F.

2 Place the butter, margarine and sugar in a mixing bowl. In a separate bowl, sift together the flour and baking powder. Add to the fat and sugar with the eggs and vanilla extract.

3 Using an electric whisk, begin with it on slow to mix the ingredients and then increase to fast and beat for 2 minutes, stopping to scrape down the mixture halfway through.

4 Divide the batter equally between the tins and smooth the surfaces, making a slight dent in the centre of each. Bake for about 25 minutes or until the cakes are risen, golden and springy. Remove from the oven and leave in the tins for 5 minutes to allow the cakes to settle.

5 Either run a knife very carefully around the edge of the tin to loosen the cake or, using your fingertips, gently draw the sponge away from the edge. Place on a wire rack to cool.

6 Once cooled, spread one of the sponges with conserve. Place the other on top and press down lightly. Dust the surface with caster sugar.

Tip: As with nearly all cakes, the ingredients should all be at room temperature. Soft margarine has a low melting point, so it should only be taken out of the fridge half an hour before needed, perhaps even less in the summer months or if your kitchen is exceptionally warm.

Coffee Sandwich Cake

Serves: *8*   **Preparation and baking time:** *25 minutes + 25 minutes baking + cooling*
Freezing: *recommended, although the icing does tend to go shiny*

Soft brown sugar gives this cake a softer crumb with a slight butterscotch flavour. If making for a special occasion, you may wish to use half margarine and half softened butter for the sponge and a coffee Crème au Beurre icing (page 39) in the middle and on top.

175 g (6 oz) soft margarine
175 g (6 oz) soft light brown sugar
175 g (6 oz) self-raising flour
½ teaspoon baking powder
3 eggs
2 teaspoons instant coffee granules dissolved
 in 1 tablespoon boiling water
8 walnut or pecan halves, to decorate
FOR THE COFFEE BUTTER CREAM:
40 g (1½ oz) butter, softened
80 g (3 oz) icing sugar, sifted
1 teaspoon instant coffee granules dissolved
 in 2 teaspoons boiling water
FOR THE COFFEE GLACÉ ICING:
115 g (4 oz) icing sugar, sifted
1½ teaspoons instant coffee granules
 dissolved in 1 tablespoon hot water

1 Grease and base line two 18 cm (7 inch) sandwich tins. Preheat the oven to Gas Mark 4/180°C/350°F.

2 Place the margarine and sugar in a mixing bowl. Sift the flour and baking powder together and add to the bowl with the eggs. Whisk the ingredients together for 2 minutes only, stopping halfway through and scraping the mixture down to ensure that all the ingredients are evenly combined. Add the dissolved coffee and beat in for just 5 seconds to incorporate.

3 Divide the batter equally between the tins. Smooth the surface and make a slight dent in the centre of each. Bake for about 25 minutes until the sponges are risen, golden and just firm to the touch.

4 Remove from the oven and leave in the tins for 5 minutes before turning out onto a wire rack to cool.

5 For the butter cream, beat the butter until smooth. Gradually beat in the icing sugar and then the dissolved coffee. Spread the cream over one of the sponges and place the other on top. Press down lightly.

6 For the glacé icing, place the icing sugar in a small bowl and make a well in the centre. Gradually mix in enough dissolved coffee to give a smooth, coating consistency. Spoon onto the cake and spread it almost to the edges. Decorate with the walnuts or pecans.

Photo on page 13

Chocolate Sandwich Cake

Serves: *8* **Preparation and baking time:** *25 minutes + 25 minutes baking + cooling*
Freezing: *recommended before filling and icing*

Margarine makes this cake light, and the cocoa masks the
fact that butter is not used.

175 g (6 oz) soft margarine
175 g (6 oz) light soft brown sugar
160 g (5½ oz) self-raising flour
2 tablespoons cocoa powder
¾ teaspoon baking powder
3 eggs
¼ teaspoon vanilla extract
FOR THE CHOCOLATE ICING:
50 g (2 oz) dark chocolate
15 g (½ oz) butter
2 tablespoons milk
TO FINISH:
3 tablespoons apricot conserve
chocolate curls or crumbled Flake bar

1 Grease and base line two 18 cm (7 inch)
sandwich tins. Preheat the oven to Gas
Mark 4/180°C/350°F.

2 Place the margarine and sugar in a mixing
bowl. Sift in the flour, cocoa and baking
powder. Add the eggs and vanilla extract.
Whisk the ingredients together for 2 minutes
only, scraping the mixture down halfway
through to ensure that all the ingredients are
evenly combined.

3 Divide the batter between the prepared tins.
Smooth the surface and make a slight dent in
the centre of each. Bake for about 25 minutes
until the surface is springy to the touch.

4 Remove from the oven and leave in the tins
for 5 minutes before running a knife around
the edges and turning the cakes out onto a
wire rack to cool.

5 Once cooled, spread one of the sponges
with conserve. Place the other on top and
press down lightly.

6 For the icing, place all the ingredients in
a bowl over a pan of hot water. Leave
them to melt, stirring occasionally. Once
melted, remove from the heat and stir until
smooth then allow to cool to a spreadable
consistency. Using a palette knife, smooth
the icing over the surface of the cake and
decorate with chocolate curls or a crumbled
Flake. Leave the icing to set before serving.

Tip: Jam does not freeze well. If you wish to
freeze a finished cake, then either fill and top
with Butter Cream (page 39), or make up double
the quantity of chocolate icing and use half
for the filling.

Whisked Fatless Sponge Cake

Serves: *8* **Preparation and baking time:** *25 minutes + 20 minutes baking + cooling*
Freezing: *not recommended*

One of the all-time classics! Choose a dark, full-bodied conserve (such as blackcurrant or bramble) for flavour and maximum colour. Alternatively, omit the cream and use fresh fruit with a reduced sugar jam to make a cake low in calories.

115 g (4 oz) caster sugar
3 eggs
½ teaspoon vanilla extract
80 g (3 oz) plain flour
1 tablespoon just-boiled water
icing sugar, for dusting
FOR THE FILLING:
3 tablespoons conserve
150 ml (5 fl oz) double cream

1 Grease and line two 18 cm (7 inch) sandwich tins with non-stick baking parchment. Preheat the oven to Gas Mark 4/180°C/350°F.

2 Place the sugar, eggs and vanilla extract in a large bowl over a pan of hot, but not boiling, water, making sure that the bowl does not touch the water. Using an electric hand whisk, beat for about 10 minutes until the mixture becomes foamy and thickens. It should leave a trail on the surface if you lift the beaters. Remove the bowl from the pan.

3 Sift half the flour over the top and very gently fold into the mixture, taking care not to knock out any of the air. Repeat with the remaining flour then fold in the water.

4 Divide the mixture between the prepared tins and gently shake, if necessary, to ensure that the mixture reaches the edges of the tins.

5 Bake for 20 minutes until the sponges are risen and golden. Remove from the oven and leave in the tins for 5 minutes before turning out onto a wire rack to cool.

6 Once cooled, spread the conserve over one of the sponges. Whip the cream until it holds its shape and smooth over the jam. Place the remaining sponge on top.

7 Dust lightly with sifted icing sugar and serve as soon as possible as fatless sponges do tend to dry out quickly.

Tip: It is best to line the whole tin as these sponges are quite tricky to turn out. Alternatively, line the bases and then grease the edges and dust with a coating of equal parts flour and caster sugar.

St Clements Sandwich Cake

Serves: *8* **Preparation time:** *25 minutes + 25 minutes baking + cooling*
Freezing: *recommended before icing*

Using half butter and half margarine gives a good flavour and creates a light textured cake. If you prefer, use just one type of fruit to make a lemon or orange cake.

**175 g (6 oz) half each of softened butter
  and soft margarine**
175 g (6 oz) caster sugar
175 g (6 oz) self-raising flour
½ teaspoon baking powder
3 eggs
grated zest of 1 orange and 1 lemon
FOR THE BUTTER ICING:
40 g (1½ oz) softened butter
80 g (3 oz) icing sugar, sifted
1–2 teaspoons lemon juice
FOR THE GLACÉ ICING:
115 g (4 oz) icing sugar, sifted
3–4 teaspoons orange juice

1 Grease and base line two 18 cm (7 inch) sandwich tins. Preheat the oven to Gas Mark 4/180°C/350°F.

2 Place the butter, margarine and sugar in a mixing bowl. Sift the flour and baking powder together and add to the bowl with the eggs and orange and lemon zests. Whisk with an electric beater on slow to begin with, and then increase to fast. Beat for no more that 2 minutes, scraping down the mixture halfway through.

3 Divide the mixture between the prepared tins, smooth the surfaces and make a slight indent in the centre of each. Bake for about 25 minutes until risen, golden and springy to the touch.

4 Remove from the oven and leave in the tins for 5 minutes before turning out onto a wire rack to cool.

5 For the butter icing, cream the butter until smooth. Gradually beat in the icing sugar and lemon juice to flavour. Spread this over one of the sandwich cakes. Lay the other on top and press down gently to join the two.

6 For the glacé icing, place the icing sugar in a small bowl. Make a well in the centre and gradually mix in enough orange juice to give a smooth paste. Spoon over the cake and, using a round-ended knife, spread the icing to the edges.

Tip: This quantity of cake mixture can also be used to make a tray bake. Use a 28 x 18 cm (11 x 7 inch) tin and finish with a glacé icing made with 225 g (8 oz) icing sugar. Decorate with Citrus Julienne Strips (page 142), finely grated orange zest or ready bought sugar decorations.

Lemon Curd Sandwich Sponge

Serves: *6* **Preparation and baking time:** *25 minutes + 20 minutes baking + cooling*
Freezing: *recommended*

This cake will not rise significantly but you will still get a beautifully light result, zinging with citrus flavour.

40 g (1½ oz) butter
100 g (3½ oz) caster sugar
3 eggs, separated
grated zest and juice of 1 lemon
30 g (1¼ oz) plain flour
25 g (1 oz) fine semolina
20 g (¾ oz) ground almonds
icing sugar, for dusting
FOR THE FILLING:
2 tablespoons lemon curd
40 g (1½ oz) softened butter
80 g (3 oz) icing sugar, sifted
1 teaspoon lemon juice

1 Grease and base line two 18 cm (7 inch) sandwich tins. Dust with equal parts flour and caster sugar. Preheat the oven to Gas Mark 4/ 180°C/350°F.

2 Melt the butter and cool slightly.

3 Whisk together the sugar, egg yolks and lemon zest until light and mousse like.

4 Combine the flour, semolina and ground almonds in a bowl. Fold into the egg mixture with 1 tablespoon of lemon juice. Stiffly whisk the egg whites and fold into the mixture.

5 Divide the mixture equally between the prepared tins and shake gently to level the surfaces. Bake for 20 minutes until golden and set.

6 Remove from the oven and leave to cool in the tins for 5 minutes before turning out onto a wire rack to cool.

7 Spread one of the cakes with the lemon curd. Beat the butter until smooth then gradually add the icing sugar. Stir in the lemon juice and spread the icing over the other sponge. Sandwich the two cakes together and finish with a dusting of sieved icing sugar.

Tip: Greasing the baking tins and dusting them with a combination of flour and caster sugar gives the sides a lovely golden colour and crunchy crumb.

Genoese Sponge

Serves: _8_ **Preparation and baking time:** _20 minutes + 25–30 minutes baking + cooling_
Freezing: _recommended_

Genoese cake is essentially a Swiss roll sponge but with added melted butter. This makes it less dry while retaining the classic lightness. Fill with fresh fruit and whipped cream and dust the surface lightly with icing sugar for a simple, versatile cake.

50 g (2 oz) butter
65 g (2½ oz) plain flour
15 g (½ oz) cornflour
3 eggs
80 g (3 oz) caster sugar
½ teaspoon vanilla extract

1 Grease and base line two 18 cm (7 inch) sandwich tins with baking parchment. Preheat the oven to Gas Mark 4/180°C/350°F.

2 Melt the butter and leave to cool – it should remain liquid. Combine the flour and cornflour.

3 In a large bowl set over hot water, whisk together the eggs, sugar and vanilla extract for about 10 minutes, until pale, thick and mousse like. Remove the mixture from the heat.

4 Sift half the flours over the surface of the egg mixture and drizzle half the melted butter around the edge of the bowl. Very carefully, so as not to knock out any of the air, fold in the ingredients. Repeat with the remaining flour and butter.

5 Divide the mixture equally between the prepared tins, shaking to level the surfaces. Bake for 25–30 minutes until risen, golden and springy to the touch. Remove from the oven and allow to rest in the tins for 10 minutes before turning out onto a wire rack to cool. Fill or use as required.

Madeira Cake

Serves: *8* **Preparation and baking time:** *20 minutes + 1 hour baking + cooling*
Freezing: *recommended*

Originally Madeira cake was served mid-morning with a glass of Madeira, hence its name.

175 g (6 oz) softened butter
175 g (6 oz) caster sugar
grated zest of 1 lemon
3 eggs, beaten
115 g (4 oz) plain flour
115 g (4 oz) self-raising flour
1–2 tablespoons milk
1 piece candied lemon peel, thinly sliced

1 Grease and line an 18 cm (7 inch) deep, round cake tin. Preheat the oven to Gas Mark 4/180°C/350°F.

2 Cream together the butter, sugar and lemon zest until light and fluffy. Gradually beat in the eggs a little at a time. If the mixture shows signs of curdling, add a spoonful of the flour.

3 Mix the flours together and carefully fold in. Add a little milk if necessary to give a soft dropping consistency.

4 Spoon the mixture into the prepared tin and level the surface. Bake for 20 minutes then half draw the shelf out of the oven. Place the piece of peel on top of the cake and bake for about another 40 minutes. Test with a skewer to see if the cake is cooked.

5 Remove from the oven and leave in the tin for 10 minutes before turning out onto a wire rack to cool.

Tip: Half a teaspoon of vanilla extract can be used to replace the lemon zest if preferred.

Latin American Milk Ring

Serves: *16*   **Preparation and baking time:** *30 minutes + 35 minutes baking + cooling + soaking*
Freezing: *recommended*

With origins in Latin America, this cake is steeped in three types of milk (hence it is sometimes called 'Tres Leches Cake'), covered in whipped cream and finished with jewel-like pieces of tropical fruit.

225 g (8 oz) self-raising flour
1 teaspoon baking powder
175 g (6 oz) caster sugar
150 g (5 oz) butter or margarine
2 eggs
½ teaspoon vanilla extract
a pinch of salt
2 tablespoons evaporated milk
FOR THE TRES LECHE:
150 ml (¼ pint) condensed milk
125 ml (4 fl oz) evaporated milk
90 ml (3 fl oz) double cream
TO FINISH:
300 ml (½ pint) double cream
2 tablespoons icing sugar
¼ teaspoon vanilla extract
50 g (2 oz) dried sweetened tropical fruit
(pineapple, papaya, mango, melon),
finely chopped

1 Grease and flour a 20 cm (8 inch) savarin tin or ring mould. Preheat the oven to Gas Mark 4/180°C/350°F.

2 Place all the cake ingredients except the evaporated milk in a bowl and beat for a couple of minutes, scraping down the mixture halfway through. Fold in the evaporated milk.

3 Spoon the mixture into the prepared tin, level the surface and bake for about 35 minutes or until the cake is risen and golden and an inserted skewer comes out cleanly.

4 Remove from the oven and leave in the tin for 10 minutes before turning out onto a wire rack to cool slightly.

5 Wash and thoroughly dry the savarin tin.

6 Stir the three milks together to thoroughly blend. Return the cake to the savarin tin and stand the tin on a large plate. Prick the top of the cake well with a skewer. Very slowly drizzle the milks over the surface, allowing time for them to sink in. You may need to wait for a couple of minutes for each spoonful to be absorbed before adding some more.

7 Leave for 30 minutes to ensure that all the milk has been absorbed and then carefully turn the cake out onto a serving plate.

8 Whip the cream, icing sugar and vanilla extract to soft peaks and spread over the entire ring. Stud with the chopped fruit. Refrigerate for a few hours or overnight before serving.

Coffee Battenburg

Serves: *8* **Preparation and baking time:** *45 minutes + 25 minutes baking + cooling*
Freezing: *not recommended*

Few cakes are more distinguished than Battenburg, with its pink and white chequered squares. Here, I have used a coffee sponge instead, which is complemented by the apricot jam and marzipan.

**115 g (4 oz) half each of softened butter and
    soft margarine**
115 g (4 oz) caster sugar, plus extra for dusting
2 eggs, beaten
115 g (4 oz) self-raising flour
**1 tablespoon instant coffee granules dissolved
    in 1 tablespoon boiling water**
a few drops of vanilla extract
1 tablespoon milk
225 g (8 oz) white almond paste
2 tablespoons apricot jam, sieved and warmed

1 Grease and line an 18 cm (7 inch) deep square cake tin. To divide the tin into two, use a pleat of greased foil or greaseproof paper. Preheat the oven to Gas Mark 4/180°C/350°F.

2 Beat the butter and margarine with the sugar until pale and fluffy. Gradually whisk in the eggs, then fold in the flour.

3 Divide the cake mixture between two bowls. Fold the dissolved coffee into one half and the vanilla extract and enough milk to give a soft dropping consistency into the other.

4 Spoon each mixture into one half of the prepared tin and smooth the surfaces, making a slight dip in the centre of each. Bake for about 25 minutes until risen and spongy to the touch. Remove from the oven, turn out onto a wire rack and leave to cool.

5 Roll out the almond paste on a surface dusted with caster sugar, into a 30 x 18 cm (12 x 7 inch) rectangle. Lightly brush warmed jam over the surface.

6 Trim all the edges of the cakes and cut in half lengthways. Lay a piece of cake across the short edge of the rectangle. Brush the side facing the long edge of marzipan with jam. Nudge a different coloured piece of sponge up next to it, and brush both tops with jam. Repeat with the remaining two slices, stacking them on top of the other pieces so that alternate colours sit on top of each other. Give the cake a squeeze to stick the pieces together and make a uniform shape.

7 Tightly roll the cake up in the marzipan, taking extra care at the corners to make sure that the cake keeps its shape and that there aren't any gaps between the marzipan and sponge. Seal the edges together, and place the cake, seam side down, on a serving plate.

8 Taking a sharp knife, score a diamond pattern on the top and crimp the long edges with your fingers. Leave to stand for 1–2 hours to firm up.

Hazelnut and Lemon Cake

Serves: *12–16* **Preparation and baking time:** *30 minutes + 40–45 minutes baking + cooling*
Freezing: *recommended*

Ground almonds are often used in cakes, but other nuts, such as hazelnuts, work equally well. It is best to roast the nuts before grinding as this brings out their full flavour.

175 g (6 oz) shelled hazelnuts, without skins
3 eggs, separated
225 g (8 oz) golden caster sugar
finely grated zest and juice of 1 lemon
1 teaspoon vanilla extract
225 g (8 oz) self-raising flour
1 teaspoon baking powder
a pinch of salt
115 g (4 oz) unsalted butter, melted and cooled

1 Grease and base line a 23 cm (9 inch) deep round cake tin. Preheat the oven to Gas Mark 3/170°C/320°F.

2 Place the hazelnuts on a baking tray with a lip and roast in the oven for 10–15 minutes, until golden. Grind to a rough powder, similar in appearance to ground almonds. (Take care not to over process as they will turn oily.)

3 Using an electric whisk, cream together the egg yolks, sugar, lemon zest and vanilla extract for about 2 minutes. The mixture will look grainy.

4 Add the flour, baking powder, salt, ground nuts and butter. Do not worry that the mixture looks more like a biscuit dough at this stage.

5 Clean and dry the electric beaters well, then stiffly whisk the egg whites until they form peaks. Fold one tablespoon into the cake mixture. Once this is incorporated, add the remainder. Fold in the lemon juice to give a soft dropping consistency.

6 Transfer the mixture to the prepared tin and smooth the surface, making a slight dip in the centre. Bake for 40–45 minutes until risen, firm to the touch and a beautiful golden colour. Remove from the oven and leave in the tin for 10 minutes before transferring to a wire rack to cool.

Tip: If you like your cakes iced, make up some lemon Glacé Icing (page 64) using 80 g (3 oz) icing sugar, and drizzle this over the cooled cake.

Hummingbird Cake

Serves: *16* **Preparation and baking time:** *30 minutes + 25–30 minutes baking + cooling + chilling*
Freezing: *not recommended*

This cake is as beautiful as its name sounds. Almost pure white in colour, the cream cheese frosting makes it equally suitable for a pudding gateau.

220 g can of pineapple slices in natural juice
250 g (9 oz) self-raising flour
1 teaspoon baking powder
225 g (8 oz) caster sugar
a pinch of salt
2 very ripe bananas, peeled and mashed
150 ml (¼ pint) sunflower or vegetable oil
80 g (3 oz) chopped pecans, toasted
3 eggs, beaten
1 teaspoon vanilla extract
FOR THE ICING:
50 g (2 oz) softened butter
175 g (6 oz) cream cheese
275 g (9½ oz) icing sugar, sifted
1 teaspoon lemon juice
a few drops of vanilla extract
50 g (2 oz) coconut flakes

1 Grease and base line two 20 cm (8 inch) sandwich tins. Preheat the oven to Gas Mark 4/180°C/350°F.

2 Drain the pineapple slices and reserve the juice. Purée the pineapple in a food processor, or chop as finely as you can so that it resembles crushed pineapple.

3 Combine the flour, baking powder, sugar and salt in a large mixing bowl. Make a well in the centre. Add the pineapple to the well with 4 tablespoons of pineapple juice, the mashed bananas, oil, pecans, eggs and vanilla extract. Beat with a wooden spoon for about 1 minute until smooth.

4 Divide the batter between the prepared tins. Bake for 25–30 minutes until risen, golden and firm. Remove from the oven and leave to cool in the tin for 10 minutes before turning out onto a wire rack to cool.

5 For the icing, cream the butter until smooth. Beat in the cream cheese and then gradually add the icing sugar. Stir in the lemon juice and vanilla extract to taste.

6 Use one third of the icing to sandwich the cakes together. Spread the remainder over the top and sides to coat completely. Scatter the coconut flakes all over the cake and refrigerate for a couple of hours before serving. This cake needs to be kept in the fridge.

Tip: Coconut flakes (sometimes sold as 'chips' in health food shops) give a stunning feathery-like finish to this cake. If you are unable to find them, use desiccated coconut instead.

Honey, Spice and Orange Cake

Serves: *12–16*   **Preparation and baking time:** *25 minutes + 45 minutes baking + cooling*
Freezing: *recommended*

This cake is lovely on its own, drizzled with honey while still warm to intensify its flavour.

115 g (4 oz) butter
115 g (4 oz) runny honey,
   plus 3–4 tablespoons for drizzling
80 g (3 oz) golden caster sugar
grated zest and juice of 1 orange
2 eggs, beaten
225 g (8 oz) self-raising flour
1 teaspoon bicarbonate of soda
1 teaspoon cinnamon
1 teaspoon mixed spice
½ teaspoon ground ginger
50 g (2 oz) candied peel, finely chopped

1 Grease and line an 18 cm (7 inch) deep square cake tin. Preheat the oven to Gas Mark 3/ 170°C/320°F.

2 Cream together the butter, honey, sugar and orange zest until light and fluffy. Gradually beat in the eggs.

3 Sift together the flour, bicarbonate of soda, cinnamon, mixed spice and ginger. Fold these into the egg mixture with the candied peel and orange juice.

4 Spoon the mixture into the prepared tin and level the surface, creating a slight dip in the middle. Bake for 45 minutes until risen and golden and an inserted skewer comes out cleanly.

5 Remove from the oven and, while the cake is still in the tin and warm, prick holes all over the top with a skewer. Drizzle honey evenly over the surface. Leave in the tin for 15 minutes before transferring to a wire rack to cool.

Tip: If you like your cakes iced, reserve a tablespoon of orange juice from the cake and use this to make up some Glacé Icing (page 64) with 175 g (6 oz) sifted icing sugar. Finish with a sprinkling of very finely chopped orange candied peel.

Passion Cake

Serves: *12–14* **Preparation and baking time:** *30 minutes + 45 minutes baking + cooling*
Freezing: *recommended*

This cake, also known as carrot cake, traditionally has a cream cheese frosting. Here I have used a vanilla butter cream icing topped with orange zest, which gives a remarkably similar result with the added advantage that it does not need to be kept in the fridge.

225 g (8 oz) wholemeal self-raising flour

1 teaspoon baking powder

1 teaspoon bicarbonate of soda

2 teaspoons mixed spice

a pinch of salt

175 g (6 oz) soft light brown muscovado sugar

1 ripe banana, mashed

175 g (6 oz) carrots, finely grated

80 g (3 oz) walnut pieces

50 g (2 oz) raisins

50 g (2 oz) desiccated coconut

150 ml (¼ pint) sunflower or vegetable oil

3 eggs, beaten

1 teaspoon vanilla extract

FOR THE ICING:

80 g (3 oz) softened butter

175 g (6 oz) icing sugar, sieved

a few drops of vanilla extract

1 tablespoon orange juice

grated zest of 1 orange

12 walnut halves (approximately 25 g/1 oz)

1 Grease and base line an 18 cm (7 inch) deep square cake tin. Preheat the oven to Gas Mark 4/180°C/350°F.

2 Combine the flour, baking powder, bicarbonate of soda, spice and salt in a mixing bowl. Rub in the sugar.

3 Make a well in the centre and stir in the banana, carrots, walnuts, raisins, coconut, oil, eggs and vanilla extract. Beat well to just combine the ingredients.

4 Pour the mixture into the prepared tin and make a slight hollow in the centre. Bake for about 45 minutes until firm and golden. Test with a skewer. Remove from the oven and leave in the tin for 10 minutes before transferring to a wire rack to cool.

5 For the icing, cream the butter until smooth. Gradually beat in the icing sugar, then add the vanilla extract and orange juice. Split the cake in half horizontally. Use half the icing to sandwich the cake back together and spread the remainder over the top. Sprinkle the orange zest over the top and finish with the walnut halves.

Butterscotch Walnut Cake

Makes: *12 portions*   **Preparation and baking time:** *25 minutes + 30–35 minutes baking + cooling*
Freezing: *recommended*

This cake is quick to make and has the added bonus of using only one pan, thus saving on the washing up!

80 g (3 oz) chopped walnuts, plus 25 g (1 oz)
   for sprinkling
175 g (6 oz) butter
250 g (9 oz) soft light brown sugar
3 eggs, beaten
1 teaspoon vanilla extract
175 g (6 oz) self-raising flour

1 Grease and base line a shallow 28 x 18 cm (11 x 7 inch) baking tin. Preheat the oven to Gas Mark 4/180°C/350°F.

2 Place 80 g (3 oz) walnuts on a baking tray and brown in the oven for 6–8 minutes.

3 In a medium-sized saucepan, slowly melt the butter and sugar together, without boiling, until the sugar has dissolved. Remove from the heat and allow to cool for 5–10 minutes.

4 Gradually add the eggs, beating well with a wooden spoon after each addition. Stir in the vanilla extract. Add the flour all at once and beat the mixture to a smooth batter. Mix in the toasted walnuts.

5 Pour the mixture into the prepared tin and sprinkle the remaining untoasted walnuts evenly over the surface. Bake for 30–35 minutes, until the cake is just set and springy to the touch.

6 Remove from the oven and leave in the tin for 10 minutes before transferring to a wire rack to cool completely. Cut into 12 squares.

Orange and Almond Slices

Makes: *12 portions*   **Preparation and baking time:** *20 minutes + 30–35 minutes baking + cooling*
Freezing: *recommended*

This makes a good packed lunch or picnic standby as it has no icing to stick to the wrapping and make a mess. Using icing sugar in the cake mix gives it a softer crumb.

175 g (6 oz) half each of softened butter and
    soft margarine
175 g (6 oz) icing sugar, sifted
grated zest and juice of 1 orange
3 eggs, beaten
115 g (4 oz) self-raising flour
½ teaspoon baking powder
50 g (2 oz) ground almonds
15 g (½ oz) flaked almonds
icing sugar, for dusting

1 Grease and base line a shallow 28 x 18 cm (11 x 7 inch) tin. Preheat the oven to Gas Mark 4/180°C/350°F.

2 Cream together the butter, margarine, icing sugar and orange zest for a couple of minutes until light and fluffy. Gradually add the eggs, beating well after each addition. If the mixture shows signs of curdling then add a spoonful of the flour.

3 Combine the flour, baking powder and ground almonds. Fold into the cake mixture and add enough orange juice to make a soft, dropping consistency.

4 Spoon the mixture into the prepared tin and level the surface, making a slight hollow in the centre. Scatter the flaked almonds evenly over the top. Bake for 30–35 minutes until risen, golden and springy to the touch.

5 Remove from the oven and leave in the tin for 10 minutes before turning out onto a wire rack to cool. Dust lightly with icing sugar and cut into 12 slices.

Gingerbread

Serves: *16–20* **Preparation and baking time:** *35 minutes + 1–1¼ hours baking + cooling*
Freezing: *recommended but keeps well anyway*

Gingerbread received its name as it was traditionally served more as bread – thinly sliced and buttered. It tastes best after being wrapped in layers of greaseproof paper and foil for a few days.

175 g (6 oz) black treacle
175 g (6 oz) golden syrup
175 g (6 oz) dark brown muscovado sugar
175 g (6 oz) butter
350 g (12 oz) plain flour
¾ teaspoon bicarbonate of soda
1 tablespoon ground ginger
1 teaspoon mixed spice
150 ml (¼ pint) milk
1 egg, beaten
4 pieces stem ginger, finely chopped

1 Grease and line a 20 cm (8 inch) deep square cake tin. Preheat the oven to Gas Mark 3/ 170°C/320°F.

2 Place the treacle, syrup, sugar and butter in a pan. Heat very gently, stirring occasionally, until the sugar has dissolved and the butter melted. Remove from the heat.

3 In a large mixing bowl, sift together the flour, bicarbonate of soda, ginger and spice. Make a well in the centre.

4 Blend the milk into the sugary syrup and test the mixture. It should be no more than tepid. If it is too hot, leave it to cool for a little longer.

5 Gradually pour the syrup mixture into the flour with the egg and chopped ginger, beating continuously with a wooden spoon. You should now have a smooth, shiny batter with a delicious spicy aroma.

6 Pour the mixture into the prepared tin and bake for 1–1¼ hours until risen and a skewer comes out clean when inserted. Remove from the oven and leave in the tin for 1 hour before removing the paper and cooling on a wire rack.

7 Wrap in a sheet of fresh greaseproof paper and then foil. Store in an airtight container for at least 2 days before eating. This helps the cake to moisten and take on its classic chewy texture.

Parkin

Makes: *12–16 portions* **Preparation and baking time:** *30 minutes + 1–1¼ hours baking + cooling*
Freezing: *recommended but keeps well anyway*

Parkin is a traditional Yorkshire cake, similar to gingerbread but with the addition of oatmeal. It is best stored for a week before eating to achieve its wonderful texture.

115 g (4 oz) golden syrup
115 g (4 oz) treacle
80 g (3 oz) butter
80 g (3 oz) dark soft brown sugar
115 g (4 oz) self-raising flour
1 teaspoon bicarbonate of soda
2 teaspoons ground ginger
½ teaspoon cinnamon
a pinch of salt
225 g (8 oz) medium oatmeal
1 egg
2 tablespoons milk

1 Line an 18 cm (7 inch) deep square cake tin with baking parchment. Preheat the oven to Gas Mark 2/150°C/300°F.

2 Without allowing them to boil, melt the syrup, treacle, butter and sugar in a pan over a low heat. Remove from the heat and allow to cool slightly.

3 Sift the flour, bicarbonate of soda, spices and salt into a bowl. Stir in the oatmeal. Make a well in the centre and, using a wooden spoon, gradually beat in the syrup, egg and milk.

4 Pour the mixture into the prepared tin and bake for 1–1¼ hours until firm to the touch. Remove from the oven and leave to cool in the tin. Do not worry if the cake sinks slightly in the middle.

5 Wrap the cake in a sheet of fresh baking parchment and then foil. Store in an airtight container for a week before cutting.

Sticky Toffee Cake

Makes: *18 portions*   **Preparation and baking time:** *40 minutes + 35 minutes baking + cooling*
Freezing: *recommended*

Every year, my mother makes sticky toffee pudding as a special Boxing Day treat for her grandsons. Adapted into cake form, this is delicious all year round!

225 g (8 oz) dried dates
300 ml (½ pint) water
1 teaspoon bicarbonate of soda
175 g (6 oz) light soft brown sugar
115 g (4 oz) butter or margarine
1 teaspoon vanilla extract
2 eggs, beaten
175 g (6 oz) self-raising flour
FOR THE TOFFEE ICING:
6 tablespoons double cream
80 g (3 oz) light soft brown sugar
25 g (1 oz) butter
25 g (1 oz) natural golden icing sugar, sifted

1 Grease and base line a shallow 28 x 18 cm (11 x 7 inch) tin. Preheat the oven to Gas Mark 4/180°C/350°F.

2 Snip each date roughly into three pieces. Place in a small pan with the water, bring to the boil and boil, uncovered, for about 10 minutes, until the water is absorbed and the dates softened. Remove from the heat, stir in the bicarbonate of soda and leave to cool.

3 Cream together the sugar, butter or margarine and vanilla extract. Gradually beat in the eggs, then fold in the dates and then the flour.

4 Spoon the mixture into the prepared tin, level the surface and make a slight dip in the centre. Bake for about 35 minutes until risen and just set. You may need to cover the cake for the last 10 minutes as the dates are liable to burn.

5 Remove from the oven and leave in the tin for 15 minutes before turning out onto a wire rack to cool.

6 For the icing, gently heat the cream, sugar and butter together in a small pan until the sugar dissolves. Bring to the boil and cook, uncovered, for 4 minutes until golden. Do not stir. You will need to watch the mixture and take it off the heat if it darkens too much. Leave to cool.

7 When the icing is cold, beat in the icing sugar until smooth. Using a wetted palette knife, spread it over the cake to give a decorative finish. Leave to set before cutting into 18 rectangles.

Marmalade Cake

Serves: *12*   **Preparation and baking time:** *50 minutes + 30–35 minutes baking + cooling*
Freezing: *recommended before icing*

Marmalade gives this cake an underlying sharp taste, set off by the zingy lemon icing and candied orange peel.

**175 g (6 oz) half each of softened butter
and soft margarine**
175 g (6 oz) golden caster sugar
grated zest of 1 lemon
grated zest of 1 orange
4 tablespoons marmalade
2 eggs, beaten
225 g (8 oz) self-raising flour
3 tablespoons orange juice
FOR DECORATION:
peel of ½ orange
2 tablespoons granulated sugar
75 ml (3 fl oz) water
225 g (8 oz) icing sugar
juice of 1 lemon

1   Grease and base line a shallow 28 x 18 cm (11 x 7 inch) baking tin. Preheat the oven to Gas Mark 4/180°C/350°F.

2   Place the butter, margarine, sugar and lemon and orange zest in a bowl. Beat for a couple of minutes, until light and fluffy. Add the marmalade and then gradually beat in the eggs. Fold in the flour and enough orange juice to make a soft dropping consistency.

3   Spoon the batter into the prepared tin and level the surface, making a slight hollow in the middle. Bake for 30–35 minutes until risen, golden and just firm to the touch. Remove from the oven and leave in the tin for 10 minutes before transferring to a wire rack to cool.

4   Pare the peel from the orange and trim away any white pith. Roughly chop the peel into small pieces. In a small pan, dissolve the sugar in the water. Add the orange peel and bring to the boil. Simmer for 5–10 minutes or until the peel is candied. Discard the syrup and set the peel aside to cool.

5   Sieve the icing sugar into a bowl and add enough lemon juice to make a smooth paste. Add a little water if necessary.

6   Pour the lemon icing over the cake and spread to cover evenly. Mark out 12 sections and pile a small heap of candied orange peel onto each section. Leave the icing to set completely before cutting into pieces.

Butter Cream

Makes: *enough to fill and top an 18–20 cm (7–8 inch) round cake*
Preparation time: *5 minutes*
Freezing: *recommended*

This is probably the most widely used and versatile icing – use it to sandwich a cake together or spread over the top. It is also ideal for piping.

80 g (3 oz) softened butter
175 g (6 oz) icing sugar, sieved
¼ teaspoon vanilla extract
1 tablespoon milk or recently boiled water

1 Cream the butter until smooth, then gradually beat in the icing sugar. Flavour with vanilla extract.

2 Depending on the consistency, add a little milk or boiled water to make the icing spreadable.

Variations

Chocolate Beat in 80 g (3 oz) melted plain chocolate with the vanilla extract. Alternatively, dissolve 2 tablespoons cocoa in 2 tablespoons boiling water. Cool and add with the vanilla extract.

Coffee Dissolve 2 teaspoons of instant coffee granules in 1 tablespoon of boiling water. Cool before adding and omit vanilla extract.

Mocha Dissolve 1½ teaspoons of cocoa powder and 1½ teaspoons of instant coffee powder in 1 tablespoon boiling water. Cool before adding and omit vanilla extract.

Citrus Omit the vanilla extract. Instead of hot water use freshly squeezed lemon or orange juice.

Crème au Beurre

Makes: *enough to fill and top an 18 cm (7 inch) sandwich cake*
Preparation time: *15 minutes*
Freezing: *recommended*

This very rich French icing is a classy alternative to butter cream. It makes a lovely glossy, light icing and goes well with sponge cakes, dessert cakes and meringues.

80 g (3 oz) caster sugar
4 tablespoons water
2 egg yolks
175 g (6 oz) unsalted butter, softened

1 In a small saucepan, dissolve the sugar in the water without boiling. Then, bring the syrup to the boil and cook steadily until it reaches the soft ball stage (120°C/240°F on a sugar thermometer).

2 Whisk the egg yolks with an electric whisk and pour the syrup onto them in a thin, steady stream, beating all the time.

3 Continue whisking for about 5 minutes until the mixture cools and forms a thick mousse.

4 In another bowl, beat the butter until smooth. Gradually beat in the yolk mixture to give a light, glossy icing.

5 If desired, flavour as for Butter Cream (left) with citrus zest, coffee or melted chocolate.

Muffins and Cup Cakes

Most cake mixtures can be baked in individual cases instead of one large tin. Muffins are usually slightly larger and tend not to be iced; cup cakes generally do seem to be iced and invariably warrant a decorative finishing touch. Both, complete with their own paper cases, are ideal for popping into lunch boxes or serving at a picnic or party. By virtue of their size they are also universally loved by children – whether they are helping with the making or the eating of them!

Pineapple and Coconut Cup Cakes, page 58

Banana Banoffee Muffins

Makes: *10 muffins* **Preparation time:** *20 minutes + 20–25 minutes baking + cooling*
Freezing: *recommended*

We often eat these moreish muffins as a pudding. The toffee will sink to the bottom during cooking, but not before it has flavoured the cake mixture on its way down! These are delicious warm or cold.

225 g (8 oz) plain flour
1½ teaspoons baking powder
½ teaspoon bicarbonate of soda
150 g (5 oz) golden caster sugar
2 medium ripened bananas, mashed
2 eggs, beaten
4 tablespoons sour cream
½ teaspoon vanilla extract
80 g (3 oz) butter, melted and cooled
10 teaspoons Dulce De Leche or
caramel toffee

1 Line a deep bun tin or muffin tray with 10 paper cases. Preheat the oven to Gas Mark 5/190°C/375°F.

2 Sift the flour, baking powder and bicarbonate of soda into a bowl. Stir in the sugar.

3 Make a well in the centre of the dry ingredients and add the bananas, eggs, sour cream, vanilla extract and butter. Fold in until just amalgamated.

4 Spoon the mixture into the muffin cases. Place a teaspoonful of caramel toffee on the centre of each muffin.

5 Bake for 20–25 minutes until risen, golden and just firm to the touch. Transfer to a wire rack to cool.

Carrot and Orange Muffins

Makes: *10 muffins*   **Preparation time:** *25 minutes + 25–30 minutes baking + cooling*
Freezing: *recommended before icing*

These muffins are better than most when it comes to incorporating healthy ingredients – wholemeal flour, sunflower margarine, natural yogurt and carrots.

225 g (8 oz) wholemeal flour
2 teaspoons baking powder
½ teaspoon bicarbonate of soda
115 g (4 oz) golden caster sugar
150 g (5 oz) carrots, finely grated
80 g (3 oz) sunflower margarine,
    melted and cooled
250 ml (8 fl oz) natural bio yogurt
1 egg, beaten
grated zest of 1 orange
½ teaspoon vanilla extract
FOR THE ICING:
115 g (4 oz) icing sugar, sifted
1 tablespoon orange juice

1 Line a deep bun tin or muffin tray with
   10 paper cases. Preheat the oven to
   Gas Mark 4/180°C/350°F.

2 Combine the flour, baking powder and
   bicarbonate of soda in a mixing bowl.
   Stir in the sugar.

3 Make a well in the centre of the dry ingredients
   and add the carrots, margarine, yogurt, egg,
   orange zest and vanilla extract. Fold together
   quickly, just sufficiently to combine all the
   ingredients.

4 Divide the mixture between the paper cases
   and bake for 25–30 minutes until risen and
   set. Transfer to a wire rack to cool.

5 For the icing, place the icing sugar in a small
   bowl. Make a well in the centre and blend
   in enough orange juice to make a smooth,
   spreadable consistency. Spoon over the
   muffins and leave for about 30 minutes to
   allow the icing to set.

Lemon Zucchini Muffins

Makes: *10 muffins*   **Preparation time:** *20 minutes + 30 minutes baking + cooling*
Freezing: *recommended*

I have used the American name for courgettes in the hope that those wary of courgettes in baking will give this a go. This is a lovely throw together summer recipe. The courgette speckles the crumb with a pretty fresh greenness and adds moistness to boot.

½ **teaspoon bicarbonate of soda**
250 ml (8 fl oz) buttermilk
225 g (8 oz) plain flour
2 teaspoons baking powder
150 g (5 oz) caster sugar
1 medium courgette
   (approximately 300 g/10 oz), finely grated
90 ml (3 fl oz) sunflower oil
1 egg, beaten
grated zest of 1 lemon
½ **teaspoon vanilla extract**

1 Place 10 paper muffin cases in a deep bun tin or muffin tray. Preheat the oven to Gas Mark 4/180°C/350°F.

2 Stir the bicarbonate of soda into the buttermilk and set to one side.

3 Combine the flour, baking powder and sugar in a large bowl. Make a well in the centre.

4 Add the grated courgette, oil, egg, lemon zest, vanilla extract and buttermilk mixture. Fold in quickly until all the ingredients are just combined.

5 Divide the mixture between the paper cases and bake for about 30 minutes or until the muffins are puffy and just firm to the touch. Cool on a wire rack.

Tip: Make sure that you use a fine grater for the courgettes, as they should blend into the mixture.

Raspberry and White Chocolate Muffins

Makes: *10–12 muffins* **Preparation time:** *20 minutes + 30 minutes baking + cooling*
Freezing: *not recommended*

These moreish cakes can also be served as a pudding. Make them when fresh raspberries are in season or substitute other fruit such as blueberries – just omit the white chocolate.

225 g (8 oz) plain flour
2 teaspoons baking powder
½ teaspoon bicarbonate of soda
115 g (4 oz) caster sugar
80 g (3 oz) butter or margarine,
   melted and cooled
80 g (3 oz) white chocolate, roughly chopped
225 ml (8 fl oz) natural bio yogurt
1 egg, beaten
½ teaspoon vanilla extract
175 g (6 oz) raspberries

1 Line a deep bun tin or muffin tray with
  10–12 paper muffin cases. Preheat the oven
  to Gas Mark 4/180°C/350°F.

2 In a large bowl, sift together the flour, baking
  powder, bicarbonate of soda and sugar. Make
  a well in the centre.

3 Add the butter or margarine, chocolate,
  yogurt, egg and vanilla extract. Using a
  metal spoon, quickly fold the ingredients
  together until they are just combined. Add the
  raspberries and mix gently, taking care not to
  break them up.

4 Divide the mixture evenly between the muffin
  cases. Bake for about 30 minutes or until
  risen, golden and springy. Transfer to a wire
  rack to cool.

Tip: These are delicious warm or cold.

Cranberry and Seed Brunch Muffins

Makes: *10 muffins*   **Preparation time:** *20 minutes + 20–25 minutes baking + cooling*
Freezing: *recommended*

These are incredibly quick to make and just perfect for setting you up for the day ahead.

25 g (1 oz) pumpkin seeds,
   plus extra for sprinkling
25 g (1 oz) sunflower seeds,
   plus extra for sprinkling
225 g (8 oz) plain flour
2 teaspoons baking powder
½ teaspoon bicarbonate of soda
2 teaspoons poppy seeds
½ teaspoon cinnamon
115 g (4 oz) Demerara sugar,
   plus 2 teaspoons for sprinkling
80 g (3 oz) dried cranberries
250 ml (8 fl oz) natural bio yogurt
75 ml (3 fl oz) sunflower oil
1 egg, beaten

1 Line a deep bun tin or muffin tray with 10 paper muffin cases. Preheat the oven to Gas Mark 5/190°C/375°F.

2 Place the pumpkin and sunflower seeds on a baking tray and toast them in the oven for 5–6 minutes. Remove and leave to cool.

3 In a large mixing bowl, combine the flour, baking powder, bicarbonate of soda, poppy seeds, cinnamon and sugar. Mix in the cranberries and toasted seeds.

4 Make a well in the centre of the dry ingredients and pour in the yogurt, oil and egg. Fold the wet ingredients in quickly until just incorporated.

5 Divide the mixture between the paper cases. Sprinkle with a few extra seeds and a little Demerara sugar and bake for 20–25 minutes until risen and golden. Leave to cool on a wire rack.

Cardamom Friands

Makes: *10 cakes*   **Preparation time:** *20 minutes + 20 minutes baking + cooling*
Freezing: *recommended*

Originally from France, these are very popular in Australia and are
a cross between a macaroon and a cake. They are traditionally baked
in an oval container, but bun or muffin trays work equally well.

175 g (6 oz) unsalted butter
5 egg whites
225 g (8 oz) icing sugar
65 g (2½ oz) plain flour
115 g (4 oz) ground almonds
grated zest of 1 lemon
6 cardamom pods, seeds removed and
  crushed in a pestle and mortar

1 Melt the butter and use some of it to
generously grease 10 holes in a deep bun
tin or muffin tray. Allow the remainder to
cool slightly. Preheat the oven to Gas
Mark 6/200°C/400°F.

2 Place the egg whites in a bowl and, using
a fork or balloon whisk, beat for about
30 seconds until frothy.

3 Mix the icing sugar and flour together and
sieve over the egg whites. Fold in. Stir in the
almonds, lemon zest and cardamom.

4 Add the remaining butter and combine to
make a smooth batter. Pour this into the
prepared bun tin so that the mixture three
quarters fills each hole.

5 Bake for 20 minutes until risen, golden
and just firm to the touch. Leave in the tin
for 5 minutes before carefully transferring
to a wire rack to cool.

Tip: I have flavoured these with cardamom,
but, alternatively, omit the cardamom and try
topping each cake with 4–5 blueberries or
raspberries before baking and finishing with
a sprinkling of icing sugar.

Vanilla Cakes with Hazelnut Chocolate

Makes: *14 cakes*   **Preparation time:** *25 minutes + 20 minutes baking + cooling*
Freezing: *recommended prior to icing*

These are fun cakes to make with children. They are simple but effective, and they love the secret 'button' of hazelnut chocolate inside.

115 g (4 oz) softened butter
115 g (4 oz) caster sugar
½ teaspoon vanilla extract
2 eggs, beaten
115 g (4 oz) self-raising flour
1 tablespoon milk
7 teaspoons chocolate and hazelnut spread
FOR THE ICING:
4 tablespoons chocolate and hazelnut spread
60 g (2 oz) milk chocolate
2 teaspoons butter

1 Place 14 paper cake cases on a baking tray. Preheat the oven to Gas Mark 4/180°C/350°F.

2 Cream together the butter, sugar and vanilla extract. Gradually beat in the eggs. Fold in the flour and add enough milk to make a soft dropping consistency.

3 Using half the mixture, put a scant teaspoonful into each paper case. Make a slight indent in the centre and place half a teaspoon of chocolate and hazelnut spread in the middle of each. Divide the remaining cake mixture between the cases, spooning it on top of the spread to cover it.

4 Bake for 20 minutes until golden and set. Remove from the oven and leave to cool on a wire rack.

5 For the icing, place the spread, chocolate and butter in a bowl and melt in the microwave or over a pan of hot water. Remove from the heat, stir until smooth and spread a rounded teaspoonful over each cake. Allow the icing to set before serving.

Fudge Cup Cakes

Makes: *14 cakes*   **Preparation time:** *30 minutes + 15–20 minutes baking + cooling*
Freezing: *recommended prior to icing*

These cakes are topped with an extravagant rich icing. You can also add tiny cubes of diced fudge for a delicious finish.

115 g (4 oz) softened butter
115 g (4 oz) soft light brown sugar
½ teaspoon vanilla extract
2 eggs, beaten
115 g (4 oz) self-raising flour
fudge, to decorate (optional)
FOR THE ICING:
80 g (3 oz) soft light brown sugar
40 g (1½ oz) butter
3 tablespoons evaporated milk
125 g (4½ oz) natural golden icing sugar, sifted
1½ tablespoons just boiled water

1 Place 14 paper cake cases on a baking tray.
   Preheat the oven to Gas Mark 4/180°C/350°F.

2 Cream together the butter, sugar and vanilla
   extract. Gradually beat in the eggs, adding a
   tablespoon of the flour if the mixture curdles.
   Fold in the flour.

3 Divide the mixture between the paper cases
   and bake for 15–20 minutes until risen and
   spongy to the touch. Cool on a wire rack.

4 To make the icing, combine the sugar, butter
   and evaporated milk in a small saucepan.
   Heat gently to melt and then bring to the boil
   and bubble for 5 minutes, stirring occasionally,
   until the mixture is golden brown in colour.
   Remove from the heat and stir in the icing
   sugar. If the icing looks too thick, then add
   a little boiling water to make a spreadable
   consistency.

5 Use the icing at once to top the cakes.
   A knife wetted with hot water will help to
   spread it more easily. Decorate with diced
   fudge if wished.

Lamingtons

Makes: *24 portions*   **Preparation time:** *40 minutes + 30 minutes baking + cooling*
Freezing: *recommended*

Australia's famous teatime treat is fun to make, albeit a bit messy! To help to keep the icing and coconut separate, use two different forks to dip the lamingtons at each stage.

175 g (6 oz) caster sugar
150 g (5 oz) softened butter or soft margarine
½ teaspoon vanilla extract
2 eggs, beaten
225 g (8 oz) self-raising flour
a pinch of salt
2 tablespoons milk
175–200 g (6–7 oz) desiccated coconut
FOR THE ICING:
450 g (1 lb) icing sugar
50 g (2 oz) cocoa powder
125 ml (4 fl oz) milk
15 g (½ oz) butter
½ teaspoon vanilla extract

1 Grease and base line a 28 x 18 cm
(11 x 7 inch) shallow baking tin. Preheat the oven to Gas Mark 4/180°C/350°F.

2 Cream together the sugar, butter or margarine and vanilla extract until light and fluffy. Gradually beat in the eggs. Fold in the flour, salt and enough milk to give a soft dropping consistency.

4 Spoon the mixture into the tin, level the surface and bake for 30 minutes or until risen and golden. Allow to cool in the tin for 10 minutes before transferring to a wire rack.

5 Once cool, cut the cake into 24 square or rectangular pieces.

6 For the icing, sift together the icing sugar and cocoa powder. Place the milk, butter and vanilla extract in a bowl over a pan of hot water and stir until the butter has melted. Remove from the heat and, using a wooden spoon, gradually beat the mixture into the sugar and cocoa powder to give a smooth consistency. Place the bowl back over the pan of hot water to keep the icing runny.

7 Place the coconut on a small plate. Take a piece of cake and dip it into the chocolate icing, turning it over with the help of two forks so that it is coated completely. Allow any excess icing to run off, back into the bowl.

8 Roll the cake in the coconut, making sure it is completely coated. Carefully transfer to a plate and repeat with the remaining cakes. Refrigerate for at least an hour to allow the icing to firm up.

Fairy Cakes

Makes: *14 cakes* **Preparation time:** *20–25 minutes + 20 minutes baking + cooling*
Freezing: *recommended*

This basic little cake mixture is a useful standby for making several types of cakes – fairy or cup cakes; queen cakes, which have added sultanas or currants; and butterfly cakes, which have a butter cream centre and are topped with sponge 'wings'.

115 g (4 oz) half each of softened butter and
    soft margarine
115 g (4 oz) caster sugar
¼ teaspoon vanilla extract
2 eggs, beaten
115 g (4 oz) self-raising flour

1 Lay 14 paper cases on a baking tray. Preheat the oven to Gas Mark 4/180°C/350°F.

2 Cream together the butter, margarine, sugar and vanilla extract until light and fluffy. Gradually beat in the eggs, then fold in the flour.

3 Divide the mixture equally between the paper cases, putting a heaped teaspoonful in each. Bake for about 20 minutes until risen, golden and just firm to the touch.

4 Cool on a wire rack and ice as required.

Tip: Use all butter if you prefer and add 1 tablespoon milk or recently boiled water to give a soft dropping consistency.

Queen Cakes

Follow the recipe as for Fairy Cakes but fold in 50 g (2 oz) sultanas or currants with the flour. Chocolate chips are a popular alternative – substitute the dried fruit with milk chocolate chips.

Butterfly Cakes

Follow the recipe as for Fairy Cakes but, once the cakes have cooled, cut out a small circle, about the size of a two pence piece, from the top centre of each cake. Spoon a little Butter Cream (page 39) into the hole. Cut the removed piece of sponge in half and arrange on the butter cream to represent butterfly wings. Dust lightly with sifted icing sugar.

Cup Cake Madeleines

Makes: *14 cakes* **Preparation time:** *25 minutes + 15–20 minutes baking + cooling*
Freezing: *recommended*

This is a modern day version of English madeleines, using paper cases in place of the traditional tin moulds, which few people own these days.

**115 g (4 oz) half each of softened butter
   and soft margarine**
115 g (4 oz) caster sugar
¼ teaspoon vanilla extract
2 eggs, beaten
115 g (4 oz) self-raising flour
1 tablespoon milk
FOR THE TOPPING:
40 g (1½ oz) desiccated coconut
4–5 tablespoons red conserve, sieved
**dried cranberries or dried sweetened
   tropical fruit**

1 Place 14 paper cases on a baking tray.
   Preheat the oven to Gas Mark 5/190°C/375°F.

2 Cream the butter, margarine, sugar and vanilla
   extract together in a bowl until pale and fluffy.
   Gradually beat in the eggs a little at a time.
   If the mixture shows signs of curdling, add a
   spoonful of the flour each time with the egg.
   Fold in the flour and enough milk to give a soft
   dropping consistency.

3 Divide the mixture equally between the paper
   cases and bake for 15–20 minutes until risen
   and golden. Leave to cool on a wire rack.

4 Put the coconut on a small plate or in a bowl.
   Remove the cakes from their paper cases.
   Brush a thin layer of jam around the base
   and sides of a cake and dip into the coconut
   to coat. Repeat with all the cakes. The bare
   sponge, originally the top, is now the bottom
   of the cake.

5 To decorate, arrange three cranberry halves
   in the centre of each cake. Alternatively, cut
   thin strips of dried tropical fruit and arrange
   pieces of papaya and pineapple, or mango
   and melon, over each other in the middle of
   the cake.

Tip: Using conserve in place of jam eliminates
the need for warming, as it is already the right
consistency. For a quicker version, leave the
cup cakes in their cases, spread with jam and
sprinkle with coconut.

Blackberry and Apple Crumble Cakes

Makes: *10 cakes*   **Preparation time:** *20 minutes + 25–30 minutes baking + cooling*
Freezing: *recommended*

These individual cakes are perfect for using up autumn fruits from the hedgerow. Frozen blackberries work equally well – just don't panic when the mixture curdles! These are at their best served still warm from the oven.

115 g (4 oz) softened butter
115 g (4 oz) caster sugar
2 eggs
½ teaspoon vanilla extract
115 g (4 oz) self-raising flour
1 teaspoon baking powder
150g (5 oz) blackberries
1 medium sized Bramley apple,
    peeled and grated
1 tablespoon milk
FOR THE CRUMBLE TOPPING:
20 g (¾ oz) softened butter
25 g (1 oz) self-raising flour
25 g (1 oz) caster sugar
15 g (½ oz) chopped hazelnuts
¼ teaspoon cinnamon

1 Place 10 paper muffin cases in a deep bun tin or muffin tray. Preheat the oven to Gas Mark 4/180°C/350°F.

2 Place the butter, sugar, eggs and vanilla extract in a mixing bowl.

3 Sift the flour together with the baking powder and add to the bowl. Beat together, using an electric hand whisk, for 2 minutes, scraping the mixture down halfway through.

4 Fold in the blackberries and grated apple, and add enough milk, if required, to give a dropping consistency.

5 Divide the mixture equally between the muffin cases.

6 For the topping, rub the butter into the flour. Stir in the sugar, hazelnuts and cinnamon and sprinkle this mixture over the cakes.

7 Bake for 25–30 minutes until golden. Transfer to a wire rack to cool.

Tip: You can place the paper cases on a baking tray instead, but this will make flatter cakes. To help keep their shape, use two cases for each cake.

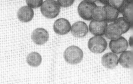

Cappuccino Cup Cakes

Makes: *14 cakes*   **Preparation time:** *25 minutes + 15–20 minutes baking + cooling*
Freezing: *recommended*

These little cup cakes are made with a coffee sponge topped with a white chocolate butter cream icing and finished as you would a cappuccino coffee – with a dusting of cocoa.

115 g (4 oz) soft light brown sugar
115 g (4 oz) softened butter or soft margarine
2 eggs, beaten
115 g (4 oz) self-raising flour
4 teaspoons instant coffee granules dissolved
   in 4 teaspoons just-boiled water
cocoa powder, for dusting
FOR THE ICING:
50 g (2 oz) white chocolate
50 g (2 oz) butter, softened
115 g (4 oz) icing sugar, sifted

1 Place 14 paper cake cases on a baking sheet. Preheat the oven to Gas Mark 4/180°C/350°F.

2 Cream together the sugar and butter or margarine until light and fluffy. Gradually beat in the eggs, adding a tablespoon of the flour if the mixture starts to curdle. Fold in the flour and then the coffee.

3 Divide the mixture between the paper cases and bake for 15–20 minutes until risen and set. Transfer to a wire rack to cool.

4 For the icing, melt the chocolate in a bowl over a pan of hot water. Stir until smooth and leave to cool. Beat the butter until smooth, then gradually beat in the icing sugar. Set the whisk to slow speed and incorporate the melted chocolate.

5 Ice the cakes, spreading the icing right to the edges of the paper cases. Dust each with a little cocoa powder

Pineapple and Coconut Cup Cakes

Makes: *20 cakes*   **Preparation time:** *30 minutes + 20–25 minutes baking + cooling*
Freezing: *recommended before icing*

Dried sweetened pineapple gives an instant and intense flavour to cakes. For an adult version (pina colada cup cakes) add a little rum to the icing.

225 g (8 oz) plain flour
1 teaspoon bicarbonate of soda
150 g (5 oz) caster sugar
115 g (4 oz) half each of softened butter
    and soft margarine
2 eggs
grated zest of 1 lime
50 g (2 oz) dried sweetened pineapple,
    roughly chopped
150 ml (¼ pint) milk
25 g (1 oz) desiccated coconut
FOR THE ICING:
150 g (5 oz) cream cheese
65 g (2½ oz) icing sugar, sifted
1–1½ teaspoons lime juice
TO DECORATE:
dried, sweetened pineapple, diced
coconut flakes

1 Put 20 paper cases on a large baking tray.
   Preheat the oven to Gas Mark 4/180°C/350°F.

2 Place the flour, bicarbonate of soda, sugar,
   butter, margarine, eggs and lime zest in a bowl
   and beat for a couple of minutes, scraping
   down the mixture halfway through. Fold in
   the pineapple with the milk and coconut.

3 Divide the mixture equally between the
   paper cases and bake for 20–25 minutes
   until golden and springy. Leave to cool on
   a wire rack.

4 For the icing, beat the cream cheese and icing
   sugar together until smooth. Add lime juice to
   taste.

5 Spread the icing over the cakes and decorate
   with pineapple cubes and coconut flakes,
   toasted if you wish.

Tip: Coconut flakes (or chips) can be bought from
health food shops and some supermarkets. If you
cannot find them, use desiccated coconut instead.

Photo on page 41

Malted Chocolate Cup Cakes

Makes: *14 cakes* **Preparation time:** *25 minutes + 15–20 minutes baking + cooling*
Freezing: *recommended before adding Maltesers*

Malted milk and chocolate have long been associated with
bedtime drinks. Here they combine to make a teatime treat.

115 g (4 oz) half each of softened butter
   and soft margarine
115 g (4 oz) soft light brown sugar
2 eggs, beaten
100 g (3½ oz) self-raising flour
1 tablespoon cocoa powder
2 tablespoons malted milk powder dissolved
   in 2 tablespoons boiling water
Maltesers, to decorate
FOR THE ICING:
50 g (2 oz) dark chocolate
50 g (2 oz) softened butter
115 g (4 oz) golden icing sugar, sifted
2 tablespoons malted milk dissolved in
   1 tablespoon boiling water

1 Set out 14 paper cases on a baking tray.
Preheat the oven to Gas Mark 4/180°C/350°F.

2 Cream together the butter, margarine and
sugar. Gradually beat in the eggs.

3 Sift together the flour and cocoa powder
and fold in, followed by the dissolved malted
milk powder.

4 Divide the mixture equally between the
paper cases and bake for 15–20 minutes
until spongy to the touch. Leave to cool on
a wire rack.

5 For the icing, melt the chocolate in a bowl
over a pan of hot water and cool slightly. In a
separate bowl, cream the butter and gradually
beat in the icing sugar. Beat the dissolved
malted milk powder into the mixture with the
melted chocolate.

6 Spread the cakes with the icing and decorate
each with a Malteser.

Lemon Poppy Seed Cakes

Makes: *10 cakes*   **Preparation time:** *15 minutes + 25 minutes baking + cooling*
Freezing: *recommended*

Sour cream enriches these cakes, giving them an almost cheesecake-like texture.

115 g (4 oz) softened butter
115 g (4 oz) caster sugar
2 eggs
115 g (4 oz) self-raising flour
1 teaspoon baking powder
grated zest of 1 lemon
1 tablespoon lemon juice
4 tablespoons sour cream
1 tablespoon poppy seeds
icing sugar, for dusting

1 Place 10 paper muffin cases in a deep bun tin or muffin tray. Preheat the oven to Gas Mark 4/180°C/350°F.

2 Place the butter, sugar and eggs in a mixing bowl. Sift the flour together with the baking powder and add to the bowl with the lemon zest. Beat the ingredients together, using an electric hand whisk, for just 2 minutes, scraping the mixture down halfway through. Fold in the lemon juice with the sour cream and poppy seeds to give a soft dropping consistency.

3 Divide the mixture equally between the muffin cases and bake for 25 minutes until risen and golden. Transfer to a wire rack to cool.

4 Dust lightly with a little sifted icing sugar.

Lemon Fondant Cup Cakes

Makes: *22–24 cakes*   **Preparation time:** *25 minutes + 20 minutes baking + cooling*
Freezing: *recommended before icing*

The fondant icing floods right over these cakes to meet the paper cases, so no sponge is visible. Decorate with bought sugar flowers or fresh sugared violas (see Frosted Flowers, page 65). Tiny strands of Citrus Julienne Strips (page 142) also look pretty.

225 g (8 oz) self-raising flour
½ teaspoon baking powder
175 g (6 oz) caster sugar
150 g (5 oz) half each of softened butter
  and soft margarine
2 eggs
finely grated zest of 1 lemon
2 tablespoons lemon juice
4 tablespoons milk
FOR THE ICING:
350 g (12 oz) fondant icing sugar
approximately 3 tablespoons lemon juice
yellow food colouring

1 Divide 24 paper cases between two baking trays. Preheat the oven to Gas Mark 4/ 180°C/350°F.

2 Place all the sponge ingredients, except the milk, in a bowl and beat for a couple of minutes, scraping the mixture down halfway through. Fold in the milk.

3 Divide the mixture between the paper cases. Bake for 20 minutes until risen and just firm to the touch. Remove from the oven and leave to cool on a wire rack.

4 For the icing, sift the icing sugar into a bowl. Make a well in the centre and gradually blend in enough lemon juice to give a coating consistency, adding a few drops of water if required. Tint the icing with yellow food colouring and spoon over the cakes. Leave to set before decorating if wished.

Pink Rose Fondant Fancies

Makes: *16 cakes*   **Preparation time:** *45 minutes + 30–35 minutes baking + cooling*
Freezing: *not recommended*

These are very pretty individual teatime sponges. The fondant icing is a little fiddly but the results are worthwhile. Decorate with piped, pink-tinged vanilla Butter Cream (page 39) and silver balls or Frosted Flowers (page 65).

225 g (8 oz) self-raising flour
½ teaspoon baking powder
175 g (6 oz) caster sugar
150 g (5 oz) half each of softened butter
   and soft margarine
2 eggs
1 teaspoon rose water
4 tablespoons milk
4 tablespoons red jam
FOR THE ICING:
450 g (1 lb) fondant icing sugar
1–2 teaspoons rose water
3–4 tablespoons water
pink food colouring

1 Grease and base line a 20 cm (8 inch) square deep cake tin. Preheat the oven to Gas Mark 4/180°C/350°F.

2 In a large bowl, beat together the flour, baking powder, sugar, butter, margarine, eggs and rose water for a couple of minutes, scraping down halfway through. Fold in the milk.

3 Spoon the mixture into the prepared tin. Make a slight dent in the centre and bake for 30–35 minutes until risen, golden and springy to the touch. Remove from the oven and leave in the tin for 10 minutes before turning out onto a wire rack to cool.

4 Trim the edges of the cake. Cut the sponge in half horizontally and spread one half with the jam. Sandwich the cakes back together. Turn the sponge upside down and cut into 16 cubes.

5 For the icing, sift the icing sugar into a bowl. Add the rose water and enough water to create a consistency similar to thick double cream. Colour with pink food colouring.

6 Taking one square at a time, place on a large fork and hold over a small bowl. Spoon some icing over the surface of the cake, using a knife to spread it over the top and sides. Return each cake to the wire rack and leave to set. Decorate as wished.

Tip: This recipe makes generous-sized cakes. If you prefer more dainty fancies, cut the whole sponge in half horizontally and then follow directions from step 4. You will need double the amount of icing.

Glacé Icing

Makes: *enough to cover an 18–20 cm (7–8 inch) round cake*
Preparation time: *5 minutes*
Freezing: *not recommended*

This seems like one of the simplest icings to make. However, there is an art to achieving the correct consistency – too runny and the cake will be visible through the icing, too thick and it will be difficult to spread.

115 g (4 oz) icing sugar
approximately 1 tablespoon warm water

1 Sift the icing sugar into a small bowl. Make a well in the centre and gradually stir in the water. You may need a little less or a drop or two more.

2 Pour the icing onto the centre of the cake and, using a wetted palette knife, spread almost to the edges. (This allows for the icing to spread slightly further without running down the side.)

Variations

Colouring A plate of small cakes looks lovely in an assortment of colours. Divide the glacé icing between several bowls and add a drop of different food colouring to each.

Lemon/orange Replace the water with lemon or orange juice for a tangy flavour.

Coffee Dissolve 2 teaspoons of instant coffee granules in 1 tablespoon of boiling water and use instead of warm water.

Chocolate Mix 2 teaspoons of cocoa powder with 1 tablespoon of just-boiled water. Stir this into the icing sugar with a few drops of extra water if needed.

Rose water Replace 1 teaspoon of water with rose water. This looks pretty tinged pink with a drop of food colouring.

Tip: If adding decorations, do so as soon as the icing shows signs of beginning to set. Small decorations, such as hundreds and thousands should be sprinkled on straight away before the icing hardens, otherwise they will simply bounce off!

Frosted Flowers

Edible flowers make a delicate, pretty decoration for little teatime cakes or cakes for dessert. Suitable varieties include violets, nasturtiums, rose petals, borage and calendula.

1 egg white
2 teaspoons cold water
fresh edible, non-fleshy flowers
1–2 tablespoons caster sugar

1 Lightly beat the egg white and water together until just frothy and light.

2 Using a paint brush, carefully brush this mixture onto both sides of the flowers, taking care not to damage the petals.

3 Dip into the caster sugar to coat and shake gently to remove any excess. Place the flowers, face side up, on a sheet of baking parchment and leave overnight to dry.

4 Store in an airtight container.

Tip: Make sure that the flowers used have not been sprayed with any pesticides and are at their peak, dry and insect and dirt free. It is useful to leave a little of the stem attached to make handling easier. This can be snipped off when the flowers are to be used.

Ganache

Makes: *enough to fill and top an 18–20 cm (7–8 inch) round cake*
Preparation time: *10 minutes + cooling*
Freezing: *recommended but icing will loose its shine*

Ganache is a soft icing, suitable for topping a cake or sandwiching two cakes together. It has a lovely sheen. No sugar is added, so it has a continental chocolate taste. It can be used once it has cooled slightly and thickened, or cooled completely and whipped to give a thicker icing.

115 g (4 oz) dark chocolate
125 ml (4 fl oz) double cream

1 Place the chocolate and cream in a bowl over a pan of hot (not boiling) water and leave the chocolate to melt, stirring occasionally.

2 Remove the bowl from the heat and stir the icing until smooth.

3 Leave the icing to cool slightly until it reaches a spreadable consistency. Use as required.

Tips: For a thicker and more aerated icing, beat with an electric whisk for 3–5 minutes until paler and lighter.

The quality of the chocolate used will determine how hard the resulting icing will be. A high cocoa content gives a firmer finish. A firmer finish may also be achieved by increasing the ratio of chocolate to cream.

Chocolate Cakes

Such is chocolate's affinity with cake making that it warrants a chapter to itself! Recipes that combine chocolate with nuts, cherries, ginger or orange all feature, with the affinity of the underlying chocolate bringing richness and luxury. Cocoa powder and block chocolate are both used, and few chocolate cakes escape being iced. Those counting the calories should beware!

Devil's Food Cake, page 69

Chocolate Fudge Cake

Serves: *12*   **Preparation time:** *40 minutes + 30–35 minutes baking + cooling*
Freezing: *recommended*

This is great as a basis for a birthday cake. It also works well split into four layers of sponge, sandwiched together and then coated with a double quantity of Chocolate Mousse Icing (page 89).

80 g (3 oz) dark chocolate
2 tablespoons cocoa powder
175 g (6 oz) softened butter or soft margarine
1 teaspoon vanilla extract
175 g (6 oz) soft light brown sugar
3 eggs, separated
175 g (6 oz) self-raising flour
FOR THE CHOCOLATE FUDGE ICING:
225 g (8 oz) plain chocolate
8 tablespoons double cream
225 g (8 oz) icing sugar, sifted
2–3 tablespoons recently boiled water

1 Grease and base line two 18 cm (7 inch) sandwich tins. Preheat the oven to Gas Mark 4/180°C/350°F.

2 Place the chocolate, cocoa powder, butter or margarine and vanilla extract in a bowl and melt over a pan of hot water. Remove from the heat, stir until smooth and allow to cool slightly.

3 Cream together the sugar and egg yolks until light and creamy. Fold in the chocolate mixture, followed by the flour.

4 Stiffly whisk the egg whites until they form soft peaks. Fold one tablespoon into the cake mixture to loosen and then add the remainder.

5 Divide the mixture evenly between the tins. Smooth the surface, leaving a small hollow in the centre of each. Bake for 30–35 minutes until risen and springy to the touch. Remove from the oven and leave in the tins for 10 minutes before turning out onto a wire rack to cool.

6 For the icing, melt the chocolate and cream in a bowl over a pan of hot water. Remove from the heat and gradually beat in the icing sugar. If the mixture becomes too stiff, add enough hot water to make it a spreadable consistency.

7 Use a third of the chocolate fudge icing to sandwich the cakes together. Smooth the remainder over the top and sides.

Devil's Food Cake

Serves: *12* **Preparation time:** *50 minutes + 25–35 minutes baking + cooling*
Freezing: *recommended before icing*

Perhaps this cake should be renamed Devil's 'Fool' Cake, as underneath its seemingly angelic white exterior lies a dark rich chocolate cake. This would make a lovely alternative Christmas cake.

115 g (4 oz) dark chocolate
225 g (8 oz) soft light brown sugar
115 g (4 oz) soft margarine
½ teaspoon vanilla extract
3 eggs, beaten
225 g (8 oz) plain flour
1 teaspoon bicarbonate of soda
pinch of salt
250 ml (8 fl oz) milk
FOR THE ICING:
1 quantity of 7 Minute Frosting or American
  Frosting (page 88)

1 Grease and base line two 20 cm (8 inch) sandwich cake tins. Preheat the oven to Gas Mark 4/180°C/350°F.

2 Melt the chocolate over a pan of hot water. Remove from the heat and leave to cool slightly.

3 Cream together the sugar, margarine and vanilla extract until light and fluffy. Gradually whisk in the eggs then stir in the melted chocolate.

4 Sift together the flour, bicarbonate of soda and salt. Fold this in alternately with the milk to give a smooth batter.

5 Divide the batter between the prepared tins and bake for 25–35 minutes until risen and spongy. Remove from the oven and leave the cakes in the tins for 5 minutes before turning out onto a wire rack to cool.

6 Make up either of the frostings and use one third to sandwich the cakes together. Swirl the remainder over the top and sides of the cake, making soft peaks.

Photo on page 67

Chocolate Beetroot Cake

Serves: *12* **Preparation time:** *30 minutes + 40–45 minutes baking + cooling*
Freezing: *recommended prior to icing*

This is one for the grown ups! It is characteristically bitter, dark and earthy with a colour intensified by the beetroot.

50 g (2 oz) cocoa powder
6 tablespoons boiling water
175 g (6 oz) plain flour
1½ teaspoons baking powder
½ teaspoon bicarbonate of soda
225 g (8 oz) caster sugar
115 g (4 oz) softened butter or soft margarine
3 eggs
5 tablespoons milk
1 teaspoon vanilla extract
225 g (8 oz) beetroot, peeled and finely grated
65 g (2½ oz) chopped walnuts, toasted
80 g (3 oz) dark chocolate, chopped
FOR THE ICING:
125 ml (4 fl oz) double cream
115 g (4 oz) 70% dark chocolate

1 Base line, grease and flour two 20 cm (8 inch) sandwich cake tins. Preheat the oven to Gas Mark 4/180°C/350°F.

2 Place the cocoa powder in a medium-sized mixing bowl, pour over the boiling water and mix to a paste. Allow to cool.

3 Combine the flour, baking powder and bicarbonate of soda and sift into the bowl. Add all the remaining ingredients, except the beetroot, walnuts and chopped chocolate. Blend on slow speed with an electric whisk to combine the ingredients, then increase the speed and beat for a minute to reach a smooth batter. Stir in the beetroot, walnuts and chocolate.

4 Divide the mixture between the tins and bake for 40–45 minutes until risen and an inserted skewer comes out cleanly. The top will probably crack but this is fine. Remove from the oven and leave in the tins for 10 minutes before turning out onto a wire rack to cool.

5 For the icing, melt the cream and chocolate in a bowl over a pan of hot water. Allow to cool slightly and then use half to sandwich the cakes together. Spread the remainder over the top.

Tip: The beetroot doesn't need cooking first if you grate it finely enough. Use the middle gauge of a grater.

Chocato Cake

Serves: *8–10* **Preparation time:** *40 minutes + 55–60 minutes baking + cooling*
Freezing: *recommended*

Potato sounds like a strange ingredient to find in a chocolate cake, but it does result in a cake with a fulfilling texture. It probably originates from frugal times, when cheap potatoes extended the bulk of the cake.

1 teaspoon bicarbonate of soda
125 ml (4 fl oz) buttermilk
1 medium potato (approximately 175–200 g/
6–7 oz), peeled and quartered
175 g (6 oz) caster sugar
150 g (5 oz) butter
3 eggs, beaten
175 g (6 oz) self-raising flour
25 g (1 oz) cocoa powder
a pinch of salt
FOR THE ICING:
115 g (4 oz) dark chocolate
115 g (4 oz) softened butter
225 g (8 oz) icing sugar, sifted
1 tablespoon recently boiled water

1 Line a 20 cm (8 inch) spring form cake tin with baking parchment. Preheat the oven to Gas Mark 4/180°C/350°F.

2 Stir the bicarbonate of soda into the buttermilk and set to one side.

3 Bring a pan of water to the boil and cook the potato for 15–20 minutes until tender. Drain and return to the pan to dry off thoroughly. Place in a bowl and mash or beat until smooth.

4 Add the sugar and butter to the potato and mix until the butter melts and the mixture is smooth. Cool slightly.

5 Gradually beat in the eggs. Sift together the flour, cocoa powder and salt. Turn the electric mixer onto its slowest setting and beat in the dry ingredients, followed by the buttermilk.

6 Pour the mixture into the prepared tin and bake for 55–60 minutes until risen and springy to the touch. Test with a skewer to make sure that it is cooked through. Leave in the tin for 10 minutes before turning out onto a wire rack to cool.

7 For the icing, melt the chocolate in a bowl over a pan of hot water and allow to cool slightly. Cream the butter until smooth, then gradually beat in the icing sugar followed by the melted chocolate and enough water to give a spreadable consistency.

8 Split the cake horizontally into three. Spread a thin layer of icing on two of the sponges and layer the tiers. Use the remaining icing to cover the top and sides.

Dark Chocolate Stem Ginger Cake

Serves: *12* **Preparation time:** *25 minutes + 1 hour baking + cooling*
Freezing: *recommended before icing*

This is a very simple cake to make and a good choice for a beginner. The icing is slightly grainy, which gives a pleasant rough finish.

50 g (2 oz) cocoa powder
6 tablespoons boiling water
175 g (6 oz) plain flour
2 teaspoons baking powder
½ teaspoon bicarbonate of soda
225 g (8 oz) soft dark brown sugar
115 g (4 oz) softened butter or soft margarine
3 eggs
4 tablespoons milk
2 tablespoons stem ginger syrup
4 pieces stem ginger, rinsed,
   dried and finely chopped
FOR THE TOPPING:
115 g (4 oz) dark chocolate
25 g (1 oz) soft dark brown sugar
3 tablespoons stem ginger syrup
1 teaspoon sunflower oil
1 – 2 pieces stem ginger, finely sliced

1　Line a 20 cm (8 inch) spring form cake tin with non-stick baking parchment. Preheat the oven to Gas Mark 4/180°C/350°F.

2　Place the cocoa in a small bowl, add the boiling water and stir to form a smooth paste.

3　In a large bowl, sift together the flour, baking powder and bicarbonate of soda. Add the cocoa mixture then all the remaining ingredients except the chopped stem ginger.

4　Blend with an electric whisk on slow speed to combine, then increase to fast and beat for 1 minute to make a smooth batter. Add the chopped stem ginger.

5　Pour the batter into the prepared tin and shake gently to ensure that it is evenly distributed. Bake for about 1 hour or until a skewer comes out cleanly. Remove from the oven and leave in the tin for 15 minutes before turning out onto a wire rack to cool.

6　For the icing, place all the ingredients, except the sliced stem ginger, in a bowl over a pan of hot water. Heat until the chocolate has melted, stirring often. Do not worry if it is still slightly grainy. Spread over the top of the cake, decorate with the sliced stem ginger and allow the icing to set before serving.

Mocha Swiss Roll

Serves: *8* **Preparation time:** *40 minutes + 7–10 minutes baking + cooling*
Freezing: *not recommended*

Swiss rolls do tend to be rather dry, so here I have used a deliciously rich, buttery mocha filling. Serve at teatime, or replace the filling with cream and fruit and turn it into a dessert.

115 g (4 oz) caster sugar, plus extra for dusting
3 eggs
100 g (3½ oz) plain flour
15 g (½ oz) cocoa powder
1 tablespoon recently boiled water
FOR THE FILLING:
50 g (2 oz) dark chocolate
1 tablespoon instant coffee granules dissolved
  in 1 tablespoon boiling water
50 g (2 oz) softened butter
115 g (4 oz) icing sugar

1 Grease and line a 33 x 23 cm (13 x 9 inch) Swiss roll tin with parchment paper. Preheat the oven to Gas Mark 7/220°C/425°F.

2 Place the sugar and eggs in a large bowl and stand over a pan of hot, but not boiling, water. Using a hand-held electric whisk, beat the mixture until it is thick enough to leave a trail, about 10 minutes. Remove the bowl from the pan.

3 Sift the flour and cocoa powder together. Then sift half over the egg mixture and, using a large metal spoon, very gently fold in the flour using a cutting action. Repeat with the remaining flour, being careful to avoid knocking out any air. Fold in the boiled water.

4 Carefully pour the mixture into the prepared tin and either tilt it so that the mixture reaches the edges or gently smooth it with a knife. Bake for 7–10 minutes until golden and springy to the touch.

5 Meanwhile, sprinkle a sheet of parchment paper, just a little larger than the baking tin, liberally with caster sugar. Cut another piece of paper to the same size.

6 As soon as the roll comes out of the oven, turn it out onto the sugared sheet. Remove the lining paper and trim away the hard edges of the sponge. Place the remaining piece of paper on top of the sponge and roll it up tightly from the short edge. Place on a cooling rack and leave it to cool, still wrapped in the paper.

7 For the filling, melt the chocolate and dissolved coffee in a bowl over a pan of hot water. Allow to cool slightly. In a separate bowl, beat the butter until smooth. Gradually sift in the icing sugar and beat together until fluffy. Mix in the chocolate and coffee to make a smooth icing.

8 Carefully unroll the sponge and discard the centre piece of paper. Spread the mocha filling over the entire surface then re-roll tightly, finishing with the seam underneath. Leave the sugared paper around the roll for about 1 hour before serving.

Prune and Chocolate Orange Cake

Serves: *8*   **Preparation time:** *40 minutes + 25–30 minutes baking + cooling*
Freezing: *recommended*

Use French Agen prunes for this recipe if you can. Simmering them in orange juice gives them a luscious flavour and softness. Serve this cake with coffee or as a dessert.

115 g (4 oz) ready-to-eat prunes
grated zest and juice of 1 orange
115 g (4 oz) soft light brown sugar
50 g (2 oz) soft margarine
2 tablespoons golden syrup
1 egg, beaten
175 g (6 oz) self-raising flour
2 tablespoons cocoa powder
1 teaspoon bicarbonate of soda
150 ml (¼ pint) milk
FOR THE ICING:
175 g (6 oz) Terry's plain chocolate orange
150 ml (5 fl oz) double cream

1 Snip the prunes so that they are just a little larger than sultanas and place in a small pan with the orange juice. Bring to the boil and simmer, uncovered, for about 10 minutes, until the juice has been absorbed. Set aside to cool.

2 Grease and base line two 18 cm (7 inch) sandwich tins. Preheat the oven to Gas Mark 4/180°C/350°F.

3 Cream together the sugar, margarine, golden syrup and orange zest. Gradually beat in the egg.

4 Sift together the flour, cocoa powder and bicarbonate of soda. Set the mixer to slow speed and alternately add the sifted ingredients and milk, mixing to give a smooth batter. Stir in the prunes.

5 Divide the mixture between the prepared tins and bake for 25–30 minutes until the sponge is just firm to the touch. Leave in the tins for 10 minutes before transferring to a wire rack to cool.

6 For the icing, break the chocolate orange into segments. Reserve three of these and place the remainder in a bowl with the cream. Set this over a pan of hot water and leave until the chocolate has melted, stirring occasionally. Remove from the heat and stir until smooth. Leave until the mixture begins to firm up.

7 Use a scant half of the icing to sandwich the cakes together. Pour the remainder over the top of the cake, smoothing evenly over the surface and allowing any excess to run down the sides. Roughly chop the reserved chocolate segments and scatter over the top of the cake. Refrigerate until required.

Sachertorte

Serves: *12*   **Preparation time:** *40 minutes + 35–40 minutes baking + cooling*
Freezing: *not recommended*

This Austrian cake contains ground almonds, which give it an unusually dense texture. Traditionally its name is piped in chocolate across the top.

150 g (5 oz) dark chocolate
115 g (4 oz) caster sugar
115 g (4 oz) soft margarine
4 eggs, separated
115 g (4 oz) ground almonds
50 g (2 oz) self-raising flour
3 tablespoons apricot jam
1 teaspoon lemon juice
FOR THE ICING:
150 g (5 oz) plain chocolate
150 ml (¼ pint) double cream

1 Line a 23 cm (9 inch) sandwich tin with greaseproof paper and grease and flour the tin. Preheat the oven to Gas Mark 4/ 180°C/350°F.

2 Melt the chocolate in a bowl over a pan of hot water. Remove from the heat and cool slightly.

3 Cream together the sugar and margarine until light and fluffy. Beat in the egg yolks. Whisk the whites until stiff.

4 Work quickly to fold the melted chocolate into the sugar and margarine. Combine the almonds and flour and fold these in, followed by the egg whites.

5 Scrape the mixture into the prepared tin and spread to level the surface, leaving a slight dip in the centre. Bake for 35–40 minutes. Remove from the oven and leave in the tin for 10 minutes before turning out onto a wire rack to cool.

6 Sieve the apricot jam and mix in the lemon juice. Place the cake on a serving plate and, using a pastry brush, brush the apricot glaze over the top and sides of the cake.

7 For the icing, melt the chocolate and double cream in a bowl over a pan of hot water. Remove from the heat and stir until smooth, then allow it to cool and thicken slightly. Using a palette knife, spread the icing over the top and sides of the cake. Leave it to set completely.

Tip: The icing will loose its lovely shiny appearance if the cake is refrigerated. Store the cake wrapped in a polythene bag and only ice a couple of hours before serving.

Chocolate Almond Torte with Raspberries

Serves: *12*   **Preparation time:** *25 minutes + 35–40 minutes baking + cooling*
Freezing: *recommended*

This makes a lovely dessert cake that can be baked in advance and assembled just prior to serving. Vary the fruit if you wish, or serve it as an accompaniment and just dust the torte with icing sugar.

115 g (4 oz) plain chocolate
115 g (4 oz) caster sugar
115 g (4 oz) softened butter or soft margarine
3 eggs, separated
50 g (2 oz) ground almonds
50 g (2 oz) self-raising flour
TO FINISH:
150 g (5 oz) fresh raspberries
icing sugar, sifted

1 Base line, grease and flour a 20 cm (8 inch) reasonably deep sandwich cake tin. Preheat the oven to Gas Mark 4/180°C/350°F.

2 Melt the chocolate in a bowl over a pan of hot water. Stir until smooth, then remove from the heat and cool slightly.

3 Cream together the sugar and butter or margarine. Beat in the egg yolks, one at a time, then add the melted chocolate.

4 Combine the almonds and flour and fold into the mixture. Stiffly whisk the egg whites and carefully fold in.

5 Spoon the mixture into the prepared tin and level the surface. Bake for 35–40 minutes until risen and set. Test with a skewer if in doubt – it should come out cleanly. Remove from the oven and leave in the tin for 10 minutes before turning out onto a wire rack to cool.

6 When ready to serve, place the cake on a plate, heap the raspberries into the centre and dust with icing sugar.

Marbled Chocolate Orange Ring Cake

Serves: *10*   **Preparation time:** *30 minutes + 45 minutes baking + cooling*
Freezing: *recommended prior to icing*

This cake has a silky shiny icing and, when cut, reveals swirls of both rich dark brown and golden coloured sponge.

80 g (3 oz) plain chocolate
1 tablespoon milk
½ teaspoon vanilla extract
165 g (6 oz) half each of softened butter and
    soft margarine
165 g (6 oz) caster sugar
3 eggs
175 g (6 oz) self-raising flour
1 teaspoon baking powder
grated zest of 1 orange
1 tablespoon orange juice
FOR THE ICING:
115 g (4 oz) plain chocolate
80 g (3 oz) butter
1 tablespoon orange juice

1 Generously grease and flour a 1.2 litre (2 pint) ring mould or savarin tin. Preheat the oven to Gas Mark 4/180°C/350°F.

2 Gently melt the chocolate, together with the milk and vanilla extract in a bowl over a pan of hot water. Stir until smooth, remove from the heat and leave to cool slightly.

3 Place the butter, margarine, sugar and eggs in a mixing bowl. Sift the flour and baking powder together and add to the bowl. Beat everything together for 2 minutes using an electric hand whisk, scraping the mixture down halfway through.

4 Divide the batter between two bowls. Fold the melted chocolate into one half of the cake mixture and the orange zest and juice into the other.

5 Spoon some of the chocolate cake mixture into the prepared tin, leaving gaps between spoonfuls. Spoon the orange cake mixture into the gaps. Repeat to use up both mixtures. Using a knife, move it through the mixtures in a meandering motion, just enough so that the two colours run into each other.

6 Place the ring mould on a baking tray and bake for about 45 minutes or until a skewer comes out cleanly. Remove from the oven and leave to stand for 5 minutes before turning out onto a wire rack to cool.

7 For the icing, melt all the ingredients together in a bowl over a pan of hot water. Stir to combine and then use straight away, slowly spooning over the cake.

Macadamia and White Chocolate Blondies

Makes: *12 blondies*   **Preparation time:** *20 minutes + 30–40 minutes baking + cooling*
Freezing: *recommended*

'Blondies', as opposed to 'brownies', are equally moreish. Use salted or unsalted macadamia nuts – the former come ready toasted.

50 g (2 oz) white chocolate
175 g (6 oz) caster sugar
150 g (5 oz) self-raising flour
1 teaspoon baking powder
2 eggs
115 g (4 oz) softened butter or soft margarine
1 teaspoon vanilla extract
100 g (3½ oz) macadamia nuts, toasted and
  roughly chopped
100 g (3½ oz) white chocolate chips
icing sugar, for dusting

1 Line a 28 x 18 cm (11 x 7 inch) baking tin with baking parchment. Preheat the oven to Gas Mark 4/ 180°C/350°F.

2 Melt the chocolate in a bowl over a pan of hot water. Remove from the heat and allow to cool slightly.

3 Place the sugar, flour, baking powder, eggs, butter or margarine and vanilla extract in a bowl and beat for a couple of minutes, scraping down the mixture halfway through. Stir in the nuts with the melted chocolate and half the chocolate chips.

4 Pour the mixture into the prepared tin, making a slight indent in the centre. Scatter the remaining chocolate chips over the top and bake for 30–40 minutes until risen, golden and springy to the touch. Remove from the oven and leave in the tin to cool.

5 Sprinkle with sieved icing sugar and cut into 12 squares to serve.

Choc Cherry Brownies

Makes: *18 brownies*　**Preparation time:** *35 minutes + 35–40 minutes baking + cooling*
Freezing: *recommended*

American brownies are loved by all. Here I have added dried sour cherries – the cherries' tartness cuts through the rich sweetness of the cake. Children might prefer these if you use a packet of mini marshmallows instead!

350 g (12 oz) plain chocolate
225 g (8 oz) soft margarine
3 eggs
225 g (8 oz) caster sugar
1 teaspoon vanilla extract
80 g (3 oz) self-raising flour
100 g (3½ oz) dried sour cherries, halved
80 g (3 oz) macadamia nuts, chopped
100 g (3½ oz) plain chocolate chips

1 Break up the chocolate into squares and place in a bowl over a pan of hot, but not boiling water. Add the margarine and leave to melt, stirring occasionally.

2 Grease and line a 30 x 23 cm (12 x 9 inch) shallow baking tin. Preheat the oven to Gas Mark 5/190°C/375°F.

3 Remove the chocolate and margarine from the heat, stir until smooth and allow to cool slightly.

4 Whisk together the eggs, sugar and vanilla extract for 2–3 minutes until pale and mousse like. Mix in the chocolate mixture then fold in the flour, followed by the cherries, nuts and chocolate chips.

5 Pour the mixture into the prepared tin and bake for 35–40 minutes until the crust feels just firm. Allow the cake to cool in the tin and cut into 18 rectangles when cold.

Tip: This amount of chocolate takes quite a little while to melt, so it is probably best to do this first and line the baking tin while you are waiting.

Triple Chocolate Muffins

Makes: *14 muffins*   **Preparation time:** *30 minutes + 20–25 minutes baking + cooling*
Freezing: *recommended*

These are a sight to make even grown-ups' eyes grow wider!
The cakes start off with a dark base, graduate to paler brown
icing and are topped off with delicate white curls.

175 g (6 oz) dark chocolate
175 g (6 oz) margarine
175 g (6 oz) caster sugar
4 eggs, beaten
½ teaspoon vanilla extract
175 g (6 oz) self-raising flour
50 g (2 oz) white chocolate, chilled
FOR THE ICING:
50 g (2 oz) milk chocolate
25 g (1 oz) butter
2 tablespoons milk
115 g (4 oz) icing sugar, sifted

1 Line a deep bun tin or muffin tray with paper
muffin cases. This mixture will actually fill
14 cases, so you'll need to put another two
onto a separate baking sheet. Preheat the
oven to Gas Mark 4/180°C/350°F.

2 Break the dark chocolate up into squares and
place in a bowl with the margarine over a pan
of hot water. Leave it to melt, then stir until
smooth. Remove from the heat and stir in the
sugar. Leave to cool slightly.

3 Using a balloon whisk, beat in the eggs and
vanilla extract. Then fold the flour in with a
large metal spoon.

4 Divide the mixture between the cases, half
filling them. Bake for 20–25 minutes until risen
and springy. Leave to cool on a wire rack.

5 For the icing, melt the milk chocolate, butter
and milk in a bowl over a pan of hot water.
Add the icing sugar and beat until smooth
and glossy. Remove from the heat and leave
to cool.

6 Spread the icing over the muffins. Make curls
from the white chocolate using a vegetable
peeler and scatter liberally over the tops.

Tip: If you don't have two muffin trays, use a
double thickness of paper cases on a baking
sheet. This helps the muffins keep their shape
better.

Chocolate Ganache Butterfly Cakes

Makes: *16 cakes*   **Preparation time:** *30 minutes + 15–20 minutes baking + cooling*
Freezing: *recommended before filling*

Ganache is a mixture of melted chocolate and double cream, whipped to a glossy, spreadable icing. Using milk chocolate, rather than plain, sweetens the icing slightly.

115 g (4 oz) softened butter or soft margarine
115 g (4 oz) soft light brown sugar
2 eggs, beaten
100 g (3½ oz) self-raising flour
15 g (½ oz) cocoa powder
½ teaspoon baking powder
2 tablespoons milk
icing sugar, for dusting
FOR THE GANACHE:
80 g (3 oz) milk chocolate
90 ml (3 fl oz) double cream

1 Place 16 paper cake cases on a baking tray. Preheat the oven to Gas Mark 5/190°C/375°F.

2 Cream together the butter and sugar until light and fluffy. Gradually beat in the eggs.

3 Sift together the flour, cocoa powder and baking powder. Fold into the mixture with enough milk to give a soft, dropping consistency.

4 Divide the mixture between the paper cases and bake for 15–20 minutes until risen and set. Transfer to a wire rack to cool.

5 For the icing, melt the chocolate and cream in a bowl over a pan of hot water. Remove the bowl from the heat and whisk for 2–3 minutes until the icing is shiny and smooth and has thickened to a spreadable consistency.

6 Cut a 2 cm (¾ inch) circle of sponge out of the top centre of each cake and place about a teaspoonful of ganache in each hollow. Cut each circle of sponge in half and arrange the semi-circles on top of the ganache to look like butterfly wings. Dust lightly with icing sugar.

Peanut Butter Chocolate Squares

Makes: *12* **Preparation time:** *30 minutes + 30–35 minutes baking + cooling*
Freezing: *recommended before icing*

These are reminiscent of a well-loved chocolate bar, the sponge being coated with a rich chocolate and peanut topping.

115 g (4 oz) crunchy peanut butter
(no added sugar variety)
115 g (4 oz) soft margarine
175 g (6 oz) soft light brown sugar
3 eggs
1 teaspoon vanilla extract
175 g (6 oz) self-raising flour
1½ teaspoons baking powder
80 g (3 oz) milk chocolate drops
2 tablespoons milk
FOR THE ICING:
80 g (3 oz) milk chocolate
50 g (2 oz) crunchy peanut butter
3 tablespoons milk
115 g (4 oz) icing sugar, sifted

1 Grease and base line a shallow 28 x 18 cm (11 x 7 inch) baking tin. Preheat the oven to Gas Mark 4/180°C/350°F.

2 Place the peanut butter, margarine, sugar, eggs and vanilla extract in a mixing bowl. Sift the flour and baking powder together and add to the bowl. Beat the ingredients together for 2 minutes using an electric hand whisk, scraping the mixture down halfway through. Fold in the chocolate drops and enough milk to give a soft dropping consistency.

3 Spoon the mixture into the tin, smoothing the surface and hollowing out the centre slightly. Bake for 30–35 minutes until risen, set and golden. Remove from the oven and leave in the tin for 5 minutes before turning out onto a wire rack to cool.

4 For the icing, melt the chocolate, peanut butter and milk together in the microwave or in a bowl over a pan of barely simmering water. Stir until smooth, then gradually beat in the icing sugar. Spread the icing over the cake straight away and allow to set before cutting into squares or bars.

Yule Log

Serves: *12*   **Preparation time:** *40 minutes + overnight soaking + 15–20 minutes baking + cooling*
Freezing: *recommended before icing*

Cranberries, sultanas, mixed peel, pistachio nuts and chunks of chocolate adorn this splendid centrepiece.

5 eggs, separated
150 g (5 oz) caster sugar
1 teaspoon vanilla extract
50 g (2 oz) cocoa powder
2 tablespoons recently boiled water
sifted icing sugar, for dusting
FOR THE CHESTNUT CREAM FILLING:
2 tablespoons dried cranberries
2 tablespoons sultanas
1 tablespoon cut mixed peel
2 tablespoons Cointreau, Amaretto,
   rum or brandy
225 g (8 oz) unsweetened chestnut purée
50 g (2 oz) caster sugar
40 g (1½ oz) chocolate chunks
25 g (1 oz) pistachio kernels, chopped
150 ml (5 fl oz) double cream
FOR THE ICING:
90 ml (3 fl oz) double cream
80 g (3 oz) dark chocolate
25 g (1 oz) icing sugar, sifted
FOR THE TOPPING:
1 tablespoon each of dried cranberries,
   chocolate chunks, sultanas and chopped
   pistachio nuts
½ tablespoon cut mixed peel

1 Start the chestnut cream filling the night before. Put the cranberries, sultanas and mixed peel into a small bowl. Pour over the liqueur, stir, cover and leave overnight.

2 The next day, line a 33 x 23 cm (13 x 9 inch) Swiss roll tin with non-stick baking parchment. Preheat the oven to Gas Mark 4/180°C/350°F.

3 For the sponge, beat the egg yolks, sugar and vanilla extract until light and mousse like. Sift in the cocoa and fold in carefully. Stiffly whisk the egg whites and very gently fold these into the mixture. Add the boiled water and fold in.

4 Pour the mixture into the prepared tin and shake to level the surface. Bake for 15–20 minutes until risen and just set. Remove from the oven and leave in the tin to cool.

5 For the filling, place the chestnut purée in a bowl, add the sugar and beat until smooth. Stir the chocolate chunks and pistachios into the soaked fruits and add these to the chestnut mixture. Whisk the cream until it is fairly stiff and fold in.

6 Dust a large piece of baking parchment with icing sugar and turn out the chocolate sponge. Peel away the lining paper. Spread the chestnut cream filling over the surface, right to the edges, and roll up tightly from the long edge, ensuring that the join is underneath. Leaving the paper wrapped around the roll, chill for a couple of hours.

7 For the icing, melt the cream and chocolate in a bowl over a pan of hot water. Stir until smooth, remove from the heat and beat in the sifted icing sugar.

8 Remove the paper from the rolled up sponge. Place it on a serving dish and spread over the icing to cover. Sprinkle with the topping ingredients and chill until set. Dust with icing sugar just prior to serving.

Tip: If you wish to freeze this cake, do bear in mind that alcohol intensifies in flavour when frozen. Ice the log after it has defrosted, otherwise the icing will lose its shine.

Frostings

Here are two different methods for making the same icing. You do not need a sugar thermometer for the 7 Minute Frosting, but it does not produce such a smooth result as the American Frosting.

7 Minute Frosting

Makes: *enough to fill and cover a 20 cm (8 inch) round cake*
Preparation time: *10 minutes*
Freezing: *not recommended*

175 g (6 oz) caster sugar
1 egg white
¼ teaspoon cream of tartar
2 tablespoons water
2 teaspoons golden syrup

1 Place all the ingredients in a large bowl. Set over a pan of hot, but not boiling, water.

2 Using an electric hand-held whisk, beat on full speed for 7 minutes – set the timer to be sure that you whisk for the exact amount of time. The mixture should increase dramatically in volume and form a shiny white icing that can be formed into soft peaks.

American Frosting

Makes: *enough to cover a 20–23 cm (8–9 inch) round cake*
Preparation time: *15 minutes + 10 minutes cooking*
Freezing: *not recommended*

This spectacular white creamy frosting usually covers the whole of a cake and can also be used to sandwich layers together. It is classically used on Devil's Food Cake (page 69), but would work well on Banana Pecan Cake (page 113), Hummingbird Cake (page 28) or Passion Cake (page 30)

1 egg white
a pinch of cream of tartar
225 g (8 oz) granulated sugar
4 tablespoons water

1 Place the egg white and cream of tartar in a medium sized bowl. Whisk until the egg white is stiff.

2 In a small pan, dissolve the sugar in the water, stirring continuously. Bring the syrup to the boil and simmer without stirring until it registers 120°C/240°F on a sugar thermometer. Carefully remove the pan from the heat and wait until the bubbles die down.

3 Taking care, pour the hot syrup onto the egg white in a thin steady stream, whisking continuously. Carry on whisking until the mixture cools slightly and thickens enough to hold its shape.

Tip: This icing is lovely and shiny when first made but does dull when set. If you prefer it glistening, then ice just prior to serving.

Chocolate Fudge Icing

Makes: *enough to fill and top an 18–20 cm (7–8 inch) round cake*
Preparation time: *10 minutes*
Freezing: *not recommended*

115 g (4 oz) plain chocolate
4 tablespoons double cream
115 g (4 oz) icing sugar, sifted
1 tablespoon recently boiled water

1 Place the chocolate and cream in a bowl over a pan of hot, but not boiling, water and leave to melt, stirring occasionally. Remove from the heat and stir until smooth.

2 Gradually beat in the sifted icing sugar. If the icing becomes too stiff, add enough hot water to make a spreadable consistency.

Chocolate Mousse Icing

Makes: *enough to fill and top an 18 cm (7 inch) round cake*
Preparation time: *10 minutes + cooling*
Freezing: *not recommended*

65 g (2½ oz) plain chocolate
40 g (1½ oz) butter
125 ml (4 fl oz) evaporated milk
25 g (1 oz) golden icing sugar, sifted

1 Melt the chocolate, butter and evaporated milk in a bowl over a pan of hot water. Remove from the heat and beat in the icing sugar. Leave to cool – placing the bowl in the fridge will speed this process up.

2 Using an electric hand whisk, beat the icing for 2–3 minutes until thickened and the icing holds its shape. Use as required.

Fruity Cakes

This chapter includes cakes made with fresh and dried fruit. Fruit, particularly if it has a concentrated or tart taste, makes an ideal partner for cakes; apples cook down into the sponge, citrus fruit punctuates the flavour and dried fruit gives bursts of concentrated taste. When using fresh fruit, make sure that it is perfectly ripe to get the best flavour.

Pear and Almond Cake, page 99

Light Fruit Cake

Serves: *10–12*   **Preparation time:** *25 minutes + 1¼ hours baking + cooling*
Freezing: *recommended*

This is a basic, not-too-rich fruit cake and is a useful standby recipe. It's perfect if you need an instant fruit cake.

175 g (6 oz) sunflower margarine
175 g (6 oz) soft light brown sugar
3 eggs, beaten
350 g (12 oz) dried fruit (sultanas, raisins, currants)
80 g (3 oz) chopped nuts (walnuts, brazils, almonds)
115 g (4 oz) plain wholemeal flour
115 g (4 oz) plain flour
1 teaspoon baking powder
1 teaspoon mixed spice
¼ teaspoon freshly grated nutmeg
a pinch of salt
1 tablespoon Demerara sugar, for sprinkling

1 Grease and line a 20 cm (8 inch) spring form cake tin. Preheat the oven to Gas Mark 3/ 170°C/320°F.

2 Cream the margarine and sugar for a couple of minutes. Gradually beat in the eggs, adding a spoonful of the flour if the mixture starts to curdle. Fold in the dried fruit and nuts.

3 Sift together the flours, baking powder, spices and salt. Fold these into the fruit mixture, together with the bran and wheat germ particles remaining in the sieve from the flour.

4 Spoon the mixture into the prepared tin and smooth the surface, creating a slight dip in the centre. Sprinkle the Demerara sugar over the top and bake for about 1¼ hours, until an inserted skewer comes out cleanly.

5 Leave in the tin for 30 minutes before transferring to a wire rack to cool.

Dundee Cake

Serves: 12   Preparation time: *35 minutes + 2–2½ hours baking + cooling*
Freezing: *not required as cake keeps well for up to a month*

This traditional Scottish fruit cake is characterised by its classic decoration of whole almonds.

175 g (6 oz) softened butter

175 g (6 oz) caster sugar

grated zest of either 1 lemon or 1 orange

3 eggs, beaten

225 g (8 oz) plain flour

1 teaspoon baking powder

25 g (1 oz) ground almonds

115 g (4 oz) sultanas

115 g (4 oz) currants

50 g (2 oz) candied peel, chopped

50 g (2 oz) glacé cherries, quartered, rinsed and dried

1–2 tablespoons milk, optional

50 g (2 oz) whole blanched almonds

1 Grease and line an 18 cm (7 inch) round deep cake tin. Preheat the oven to Gas Mark 3/170°C/320°F.

2 Cream together the butter, sugar and citrus zest until light and fluffy. Gradually beat in the eggs, adding a little of the flour if the mixture shows signs of curdling.

3 Sift together the flour and baking powder and fold in using a metal spoon. Fold in the ground almonds, sultanas, currants, candied peel and cherries. Add a little milk to the mixture if it looks dry.

4 Spoon the mixture into the prepared tin and level the surface, making a slight dip in the centre. Arrange the blanched almonds in a petal pattern on the surface. Do not push them in as this will make them sink into the cake on cooking.

5 Bake for 2–2½ hours, covering with greaseproof paper or foil if the top starts to brown too much. Test with a skewer – it should come out cleanly if the cake is cooked. Remove from the oven and leave in the tin for 30 minutes before turning out onto a wire rack to cool.

Tip: Dundee cake is best left for a few days to mature before cutting.

Sultana Cake

Serves: *6–8*   **Preparation time:** *20 minutes + 1¼ hours baking + cooling*
Freezing: *recommended*

This cake is quick and simple to make. It has a more open texture than traditional fruit cake, making it a lighter alternative. Simmering the sultanas first ensures that they are beautifully succulent.

225 g (8 oz) sultanas
115 g (4 oz) butter
115 g (4 oz) soft light brown sugar
2 eggs, beaten
175 g (6 oz) self-raising flour
1 teaspoon mixed spice
½ teaspoon bicarbonate of soda

1 Place the sultanas in a small saucepan with enough water to just cover. Bring to the boil and simmer for 8 minutes.

2 Grease and line a 15 cm (6 inch) round cake tin, ensuring that the greaseproof paper comes 5 cm (2 inches) above the top of the tin. Preheat the oven to Gas Mark 3/ 170°C/320°F.

3 Drain the sultanas, shaking the sieve to remove as much water as possible, and return to the pan. Cut the butter into pieces and add to the sultanas with the sugar. Heat gently, stirring until the butter has melted.

4 Cool the mixture for at least 10 minutes before beating in the eggs using a wooden spoon. It is important to make sure the mixture is cool enough, or the eggs will scramble.

5 Sift together the flour, mixed spice and bicarbonate of soda. Stir into the mixture and pour into the prepared tin.

6 Bake for about 1¼ hours, or until an inserted skewer comes out cleanly. Remove from the oven and leave in the tin for 30 minutes before turning out onto a wire rack to cool.

Cathedral Cake

Serves: *10–12*   **Preparation time:** *10 minutes + 1½–1¾ hours baking + cooling*
Freezing: *not necessary*

This is also sometimes known as Bishop's cake. Thin slices held up to the light reveal the reason for its name – the translucent fruit and nuts create a mosaic effect reminiscent of stained glass windows.

100 g (3½ oz) dried sweetened tropical fruit (melon, papaya, mango, pineapple)
100 g (3½ oz) mixed colour glacé cherries
100 g (3½ oz) jumbo golden raisins and sultanas
100 g (3½ oz) brazil nuts
50 g (2 oz) blanched almonds
50 g (2 oz) macadamia nuts
50 g (2 oz) caster sugar
50 g (2 oz) plain flour
¼ teaspoon baking powder
1 egg, beaten
¼ teaspoon vanilla extract

1 Line a 450 g (1 lb) loaf tin with baking parchment. Preheat the oven to Gas Mark 2/150°C/300°F.

2 Combine the tropical fruit, cherries, raisins and sultanas and all the nuts in a mixing bowl. Combine the sugar, flour and baking powder and sift into the bowl containing the fruit and nuts. Mix everything together.

3 Add the egg and vanilla extract and stir to mix.

4 Spoon into the prepared tin. Wet your hands and then firmly push the mixture down into the tin so that there are no air holes.

5 Bake in the oven for 1½–1¾ hours, or until an inserted skewer comes out cleanly. Remove from the oven and leave to cool in the tin. Slice very thinly to serve.

Tip: Try to find jumbo raisins and golden-coloured sultanas as they will lighten the colour. Mixed glacé cherries (red, green and yellow) are also essential to convey the colours found in a stained glass window.

Apple and Cinnamon Cake

Serves: *10* **Preparation time:** *30 minutes + 55–60 minutes baking + cooling*
Freezing: *recommended*

This cake works equally well served warm as a pudding. Serve it with custard or cream, or natural yogurt if you are feeing virtuous!

225 g (8 oz) self-raising flour
1 level teaspoon baking powder
80 g (3 oz) softened unsalted butter
150 g (5 oz) Demerara sugar
1 large egg, beaten
a few drops of vanilla extract
150 ml (¼ pint milk)
FOR THE TOPPING:
3 eating apples, peeled if wished, cored and
    thinly sliced
25 g (1 oz) unsalted butter, melted and cooled
    slightly
40 g (1½ oz) Demerara sugar

1 teaspoon cinnamon

1 Grease and line a 23 cm (9 inch) spring form cake tin. Preheat the oven to Gas Mark 4/ 180°C/350°F.

2 Place the flour and baking powder in a mixing bowl. Rub in the butter, then stir in the sugar. Make a well in the centre of the dried ingredients and add the egg and vanilla extract.

3 Gradually work in the milk using a wooden spoon. Beat for 1 minute to give a smooth batter, then pour into the prepared tin.

4 Arrange the apple slices on top of the cake mixture, overlapping them to form a circular pattern. Drizzle over the melted butter. Combine the sugar and cinnamon and sprinkle liberally over the top.

5 Bake for 55–60 minutes until risen and set. Remove from the oven and allow to stand for 10 minutes before removing from the tin and transferring to a wire cooling rack.

Apricot Yogurt Cake

Serves: *10*   **Preparation time:** *30 minutes + 45–55 minutes baking + cooling*
Freezing: *recommended*

Amaretti biscuits sprinkled over the top of this cake just prior to baking give a delicious added flavour and unexpected crunch.

115 g (4 oz) dried no-need-to-soak apricots,
   chopped
grated zest and juice of 1 orange
300 g (10 oz) plain flour
2 teaspoons baking powder
½ teaspoon bicarbonate of soda
115 g (4 oz) caster sugar
150 ml (¼ pint) natural yogurt
1 egg, beaten
½ teaspoon vanilla extract
FOR THE TOPPING:
50 g (2 oz) Amaretti biscuits
icing sugar

1 Grease and base line a 23 cm (9 inch) spring form cake tin. Preheat the oven to Gas Mark 4/180°C/350°F.

2 Place the apricots in a small saucepan. Add the orange juice and bring slowly to a simmer. Cover and cook for about 10 minutes until the juice is absorbed. Leave to cool.

3 In a mixing bowl, combine the flour, baking powder, bicarbonate of soda, sugar and orange zest. Make a well in the dry ingredients and add the yogurt, egg, vanilla extract and apricots. Fold together quickly to just combine and spoon into the prepared tin. Level the surface.

4 Place the Amaretti biscuits in a plastic bag and, using the end of a rolling pin, lightly crush to roughly break them up. Scatter over the top of the cake.

5 Bake for 45–55 minutes, until a skewer inserted into the centre comes out clean. Loosely cover with foil or greaseproof paper if the top starts to become too brown.

6 Remove from the oven and leave in the tin for 10 minutes before transferring to a wire rack to cool. Sift a little icing sugar over the top before serving.

Pear and Almond Cake

Serves: *8–10* **Preparation time:** *35 minutes + 1–1¼ hours baking + cooling*
Freezing: *not recommended*

I used a Comice pear, my favourite variety, for this recipe as the texture and taste are both excellent. Whichever variety you use, it is essential that the pear is absolutely ripe.

175 g (6 oz) softened unsalted butter
175 g (6 oz) caster sugar
½ teaspoon vanilla extract
3 eggs, beaten
175 g (6 oz) self-raising flour
½ teaspoon baking powder
50 g (2 oz) ground almonds
1 large ripe pear (approximately 300 g/10 oz)
2 tablespoons milk
FOR THE GLAZE:
1 tablespoon apricot conserve, sieved

1 Grease and line a 20 cm (8 inch) round spring form cake tin. Preheat the oven to Gas Mark 4/180°C/350°F.

2 Cream together the butter, sugar and vanilla extract for a couple of minutes until light and fluffy, then gradually beat in the eggs. Combine the flour, baking powder and almonds and fold into the mixture.

3 Peel and core the pear. Thinly slice one quarter and finely chop the remainder. Fold the chopped pear into the cake batter with enough milk to give a soft dropping consistency.

4 Transfer the mixture into the prepared tin. Do not worry about levelling the surface; instead, arrange the pear slices over the top, pressing down gently so that they are still visible, but lie in the batter.

5 Bake for 1–1¼ hours until risen, golden and set or until an inserted skewer comes out clean.

6 Brush the surface of the cake with apricot conserve and leave to cool in the tin.

Tip: If using apricot jam you may need to warm it before brushing it over the cake.

Photo on page 91

Date and Bramley Loaf

Serves: *8–10*   **Preparation time:** *20 minutes + overnight soaking + 1¼ hours baking + cooling*
Freezing: *recommended*

This is a delicious cake made moist from the apple and soaked dates.

175 g (6 oz) dried ready-to-eat dates
1 teaspoon bicarbonate of soda
250 ml (8 fl oz) recently boiled water
225 g (8 oz) self-raising flour
1 teaspoon cinnamon
115 g (4 oz) margarine
115 g (4 oz) soft light brown sugar
1 medium egg, beaten
1 medium Bramley apple, peeled, cored and
  finely chopped

1 The night before, snip the dates up and place in a small bowl. Stir in the bicarbonate of soda and pour over the water. Cover and leave to soak overnight.

2 The next day, grease and line a 900 g (2 lb) loaf tin. Preheat the oven to Gas Mark 4/ 180°C/350°F.

3 Combine the flour and cinnamon in a bowl. Rub in the margarine and stir in the sugar. Make a well in the centre and add the dates with their liquid, the egg and chopped apple. Beat well with a wooden spoon, just until combined.

4 Pour the mixture into the prepared tin and bake for about 1¼ hours, covering the top with greaseproof paper or foil if it shows signs of becoming too brown. Test that it is ready by inserting a skewer, which should come out cleanly.

5 Remove from the oven and leave in the tin for 10 minutes before turning out onto a wire rack

Orchard Teabread

Serves: *10–12*   **Preparation time:** *15 minutes + overnight soaking + 1–1¼ hours baking + cooling*
Freezing: *recommended*

Old fashioned teabreads are quick to make, do not require creaming or whisking skills and do not have any added fat. Customize your cake with different fruit, such as dried figs, apples or prunes. There is also a vast selection of fruit teas available, many of which would blend beautifully.

80 g (3 oz) dried no-need-to-soak apricots
80 g (3 oz) dried pears
115 g (4 oz) sultanas
300 ml (½ pint) strong hot tea
2 eggs, beaten
115 g (4 oz) Demerara sugar, plus 1 teaspoon for sprinkling
115 g (4 oz) wholemeal flour
115 g (4 oz) plain white flour
2 teaspoons baking powder

1 The night before, chop the dried apricots and pears so that they are roughly the same size as the sultanas. (I find it easier to snip the fruit using a pair of sharp scissors.) Place in a medium sized bowl with the sultanas and pour the hot tea over them. Stir, cover and leave to soak overnight.

2 The next day, grease and line a 900 g (2 lb) loaf tin. Preheat the oven to Gas Mark 4/ 180°C/350°F.

3 Stir the eggs and sugar into the fruit. Mix together the flours and baking powder and beat into the other ingredients.

4 Spoon the mixture into the prepared tin and level the surface. Make a slight indent down the centre and sprinkle all over with the extra Demerara sugar.

5 Bake for 1–1¼ hours until a skewer comes out cleanly when inserted. Cover with foil or greaseproof paper if the cake is browning too much.

6 Remove from the oven and leave in the tin for 10 minutes to cool before transferring to a wire rack.

Tip: Paper loaf tin liners are excellent for baking teabreads. They prevent the outsides from overcooking and help to keep the cake moist for longer.

Apricot and Stem Ginger Loaf

Serves: *10*   Preparation time: *25 minutes +1–1¼ hours baking + cooling*
Freezing: *recommended*

Stem ginger gives this loaf a more subtle flavour than ground ginger. If you prefer a shiny finish, brush the loaf with some of the syrup from the stem ginger while it is still warm.

115 g (4 oz) wholemeal flour

115 g (4 oz) plain flour

1½ teaspoons baking powder

150 g (5 oz) soft light brown sugar

115 g (4 oz) softened butter

pinch of salt

2 eggs, beaten

grated zest of 1 lemon

2 tablespoons milk

175 g (6 oz) no-soak dried apricots, chopped

4 pieces stem ginger

4 tablespoons stem ginger syrup

1 Grease and base line a 900 g (2 lb) loaf tin. Preheat the oven to Gas Mark 4/180°C/350°F.

2 Place the flours, baking powder, sugar, butter, salt, eggs, lemon zest and milk in a mixing bowl. Beat using an electric whisk for 2 minutes, scraping down the mixture halfway through. Fold in the apricots.

3 Finely chop three of the pieces of stem ginger add to the mixture with the syrup. Thinly slice the remaining stem ginger.

4 Spoon the cake mixture into the prepared tin and level the surface. Arrange the sliced ginger down the centre of the top.

5 Bake for 1–1¼ hours or until a skewer comes out clean when inserted. Cover loosely with foil or greaseproof paper if the top becomes too brown.

6 Remove from the oven and leave in the tin for about 15 minutes before transferring to a wire rack to cool.

Tip: If you wish, the loaf may be drizzled with lemon Glacé Icing (page 64) and decorated with additional stem ginger. Alternatively, slice thinly and serve buttered as a tea bread.

Spiced Parsnip and Raisin Cake

Serves: *8–10*   **Preparation time:** *45 minutes + 1 hour baking + cooling*
Freezing: *recommended*

Carrot cake is very popular, so why not parsnip? You cannot taste the parsnip, but it gives an incredible spongy texture. If you are sceptical about how it will be received, serve it without explaining that it contains a whole parsnip and see how everyone reacts!

**1 medium parsnip (approximately 300 g/10 oz),
  peeled, central core removed and chopped**
1 teaspoon bicarbonate of soda
175 g (6 oz) light soft brown sugar
115 g (4 oz) softened butter or soft margarine
1 teaspoon vanilla extract
2 eggs, beaten
300 g (10 oz) self-raising flour
1 teaspoon mixed spice
1 teaspoon ground ginger
¼ teaspoon freshly ground nutmeg
a pinch of salt
80 g (3 oz) raisins
3 tablespoons milk

1 Place the parsnip in a small pan and cover with water. Bring to the boil and simmer for 15 minutes. Drain well, then whizz in a food processor to a smooth purée. Set aside and allow to cool.

2 Grease and line a 20 cm (8 inch) round deep cake tin. Preheat the oven to Gas Mark 4/ 180°C/350°F.

3 Once cooled, stir the bicarbonate of soda into the parsnip purée.

4 Cream together the sugar, butter or margarine and vanilla extract until light and fluffy. Gradually beat in the eggs.

5 Combine the flour, spices and salt. Fold these in, followed by the raisins and parsnip purée. Add enough milk to make a soft dropping consistency.

6 Spoon the mixture into the prepared tin, level the surface and make a slight dip in the centre. Bake in the oven for about 1 hour, or until an inserted skewer comes out cleanly. You may need to cover the cake with greaseproof paper if it shows signs of over browning.

7 Remove from the oven and leave in the tin for 10 minutes before transferring to a wire rack to cool.

Pear, Marzipan and Chocolate Chunk Cake

Makes: *12 portions*   **Preparation time:** *20 minutes + 35–40 minutes baking + cooling*
Freezing: *recommended*

This tray bake can be cut into rectangles or squares. It is moist enough to not need icing, making it practical for picnics and packed lunches.

225 g (8 oz) self-raising flour
½ teaspoon baking powder
150 g (5 oz) caster sugar
115 g (4 oz) softened butter or soft margarine
2 eggs
1 ripe medium pear (approximately 225 g/
    8 oz), peeled, cored and finely chopped
80 g (3 oz) white or yellow marzipan, diced
    fairly small
80 g (3 oz) milk chocolate chunks or chips
3 tablespoons milk
icing sugar, for dusting

1 Grease and base line a shallow 28 x 18 cm (11 x 9 inch) baking tin. Preheat the oven to Gas Mark 4/180°C/350°F.

2 Combine the flour, baking powder, sugar, butter or margarine and eggs in a bowl. Beat with an electric whisk for a couple of minutes, scraping the mixture down halfway through.

3 Fold the pear into the cake mixture with half of the marzipan and half of the chocolate chunks. Add enough milk to give a soft dropping consistency.

4 Spoon the batter into the prepared tin and level the surface, making a small dent in the centre. Scatter the reserved marzipan and chocolate chunks over the top and bake for 35–40 minutes until springy and golden. Remove from the oven and leave in the tin for 10 minutes before turning out onto a wire rack to cool.

5 Dust with sifted icing sugar, cut into 12 squares or rectangles and serve.

Apple Mincemeat Cake

Serves: *8–10*   **Preparation time:** *25 minutes + 45 minutes baking + cooling*
Freezing: *recommended*

This is a beautifully moist cake that needs no icing. There are some lovely luxury mincemeats available, all of which would work well here.

115 g (4 oz) softened butter or soft margarine
115 g (4 oz) soft light brown sugar
grated zest of 1 lemon
2 eggs, beaten
200 g (7 oz) self-raising flour
½ teaspoon baking powder
175 g (6 oz) luxury mincemeat
1 medium Bramley apple, peeled,
  cored and finely chopped

1 Grease and base line a 20 cm (8 inch) round deep cake tin. Preheat the oven to Gas Mark 4/180°C/350°F.

2 Cream the butter or margarine, sugar and lemon zest together until fluffy. Gradually beat in the eggs, adding a spoonful of the flour with each addition if the mixture starts to curdle.

3 Sift together the flour and baking powder and fold in with the mincemeat and apple. Transfer to the prepared tin and level the surface, making a slight hollow in the centre.

4 Bake for about 45 minutes, until an inserted skewer comes out clean. Remove from the oven and leave in the tin for 10 minutes before transferring to a wire rack to cool.

Cider Apple Cake

Serves: *10* **Preparation time:** *30 minutes + 50–55 minutes baking + cooling*
Freezing: *recommended*

The cider does not come across strongly in this cake, but it does provide background flavour. If you have time, bring the cider to the boil the night before, pour it over the sultanas and leave them overnight to soak and plump up.

50 g (2 oz) sultanas
150 ml (¼ pint) cider
175 g (6 oz) soft light brown sugar
115 g (4 oz) butter
2 eggs, beaten
225 g (8 oz) eating apples, peeled,
  cored and grated
115 g (4 oz) self-raising wholemeal flour
80 g (3 oz) self-raising flour
50 g (2 oz) ground almonds
½ teaspoon bicarbonate of soda
½ teaspoon freshly ground nutmeg
15 g (½ oz) flaked almonds
icing sugar, for dusting

1 Line a 20 cm (8 inch) spring form cake tin with baking parchment. Preheat the oven to Gas Mark 4/180°C/350°F.

2 Place the sultanas in a small pan with the cider and simmer for 5 minutes. Set aside to cool.

3 Cream together the sugar and butter. Gradually beat in the eggs, then stir in the grated apples.

4 Combine the flours, almonds, bicarbonate of soda and nutmeg. Fold into the cake mixture with the sultanas and cider.

5 Spoon the mixture into the prepared tin and level the surface, making a slight dent in the centre. Scatter the flaked almonds over the top and bake for 50–55 minutes, or until an inserted skewer comes out cleanly.

6 Remove from the oven and leave in the tin for 10 minutes before transferring to a wire rack to cool. Dust with a little icing sugar before serving.

Sweet Date and Bitter Orange Cake

Serves: *8* **Preparation time:** *1 hour + 1¼ hours baking + cooling*
Freezing: *recommended*

This is a cake of two halves – predominantly sweet from the dates and condensed milk but with an occasional backlash from the candied orange. It has a beautifully moist texture, making it an ideal 'cut and come again' cake.

225 g (8 oz) stoned dried soft dates,
  roughly chopped
50 g (2 oz) candied orange peel, very
  finely chopped
grated zest and juice of 1 orange, juice
  made up to 150 ml (¼ pint) with water
150 g (5 oz) butter
half a 397 g can of condensed milk
1 egg, beaten
150 g (5 oz) plain flour
½ teaspoon bicarbonate of soda

1 Grease and base line a 20 cm (8 inch) round deep cake tin. Preheat the oven to Gas Mark 2/150°C/300°F.

2 Combine the dates, candied peel, orange zest and juice, butter and condensed milk in a pan. Heat slowly to melt the butter, then bring to the boil and simmer for just 3 minutes, stirring constantly. Remove from the heat and allow to cool for 30 minutes.

3 Once cool, beat in the egg. Sift the flour and bicarbonate of soda together and mix in.

4 Pour the mixture into the prepared tin and bake for about 1¼ hours or until an inserted skewer comes out cleanly. Cover with foil or greaseproof paper if the top is browning too much.

5 Remove from the oven and leave in the tin for 30 minutes before turning out onto a wire rack to cool.

Apricot Squash Cake

Serves: *12* **Preparation time:** *50 minutes + 35–40 minutes baking + cooling*
Freezing: *recommended*

This is an everyday recipe with American and New Zealand influences. Butternut squash adds an incredible orange colour to this cake, which is almost torte-like and would make an excellent dessert, served with crème fraîche.

**half a butternut squash (approximately
300 g/10 oz when peeled and de-seeded)**
1 teaspoon bicarbonate of soda
175 g (6 oz) caster sugar
3 tablespoons Acacia honey
150 g (5 oz) butter
½ teaspoon vanilla extract
grated zest and juice of 1 orange
3 eggs, beaten
150 g (5 oz) plain flour
50 g (2 oz) ground almonds
1½ teaspoons baking powder
**115 g (4 oz) ready-to-eat dried apricots,
finely snipped**
15 g (½ oz) flaked almonds
icing sugar, for dusting

1 Cut the squash into chunks and place in a small pan. Cover with water, bring to the boil and simmer for 25–30 minutes until very soft. Drain well and purée in a food processor. Set aside to cool.

2 Base line, grease and flour a 24 cm (9½ inch) round deep sandwich tin. Preheat the oven to Gas Mark 4/180°C/350°F.

3 Mix the bicarbonate of soda into the butternut squash purée and set to one side.

4 Cream together the sugar, honey, butter, vanilla extract and orange zest. Gradually beat in the eggs, adding a tablespoon of the flour if the mixture starts to curdle.

5 Combine the flour, ground almonds and baking powder. Fold this into the egg mixture with the squash purée, apricots and orange juice. The mixture will curdle quite badly at this point. Do not worry, just transfer it to the prepared tin. Level the surface, hollowing it out slightly in the middle and scatter with the almonds.

6 Bake for 35–40 minutes, until the cake shrinks slightly away from the sides of the tin and an inserted skewer comes out cleanly. Remove from the oven and leave in the tin for 10 minutes before turning out onto a wire rack to cool. Dust with icing sugar before serving.

Blackcurrant 'Ribbon' Cake

Serves: *8–10*   **Preparation time:** *30 minutes + 35–40 minutes baking + cooling*
Freezing: *not recommended*

Blackcurrant conserve gives this cake a stunning colour. If fresh blackcurrants are in season, toss some into the cake batter rather than swirling in conserve.

225 g (8 oz) plain flour
1½ teaspoons baking powder
½ teaspoon bicarbonate of soda
284 ml carton of buttermilk
225 g (8 oz) caster sugar
150 g (5 oz) softened butter or soft margarine
3 eggs, beaten
½ teaspoon vanilla extract
115 g (4 oz) blackcurrant conserve
FOR THE FILLING:
50 g (2 oz) softened butter
115 g (4 oz) icing sugar, sifted, plus
    extra for dusting
a few drops of vanilla extract
1 teaspoon milk
2 tablespoons blackcurrant conserve

1 Grease and base line two 20 cm (8 inch) sandwich tins. Preheat the oven to Gas Mark 3/170°C/320°F.

2 Place all the cake ingredients, apart from the blackcurrant conserve, in a large bowl. Beat for a couple of minutes, scraping the bowl down halfway through, until you have a smooth batter.

3 Divide the mixture evenly between the tins. Stir the conserve until smooth and then dot randomly over the surface of the batter. Then, taking a round bladed knife, drag the jam through the cake mixture in a swirling motion.

4 Bake for approximately 35–40 minutes or until the cakes are firm and springy to the touch or a skewer comes out cleanly. Make sure they do not brown too fast. If they look like they are doing so, cover with a sheet of foil or greaseproof paper.

5 Remove from the oven and run a knife around the edge of the tins. Leave them to rest for 10 minutes before turning out onto a wire rack to cool.

6 For the filling, beat the butter until smooth then gradually beat in the icing sugar. Add the vanilla extract and enough milk to give a spreading consistency. Smooth the filling over one of the sponges and top with the conserve. Sandwich the cakes together and lightly dust the top with icing sugar.

Cherry Almond Cake

Serves: *8–10*   **Preparation time:** *25 minutes + 50–60 minutes baking + cooling*
Freezing: *recommended*

This traditional teatime cake is always a favourite. If you prefer a stronger almond flavour, add a few drops of almond essence at the same time as the milk.

175 g (6 oz) softened butter
175 g (6 oz) caster sugar
3 eggs, beaten
200 g (7 oz) plain flour
1½ teaspoons baking powder
175 g (6 oz) natural glacé cherries
80 g (3 oz) ground almonds
2 tablespoons milk

1 Grease and line a 20 cm (8 inch) round cake tin. Preheat the oven to Gas Mark 4/ 180°C/350°F.

2 Place the butter and sugar in a mixing bowl and cream together using an electric whisk for 2–3 minutes until light and fluffy. Gradually add the eggs, whisking well after each addition. Sift the flour and baking powder together and fold in.

3 Rinse and halve the cherries and pat them dry on paper towel. Toss them in the ground almonds and fold them both into the cake mixture. Add enough milk to make a soft dropping consistency.

4 Spoon the mixture into the prepared tin and make a slight indent in the centre. Bake for 50–60 minutes or until an inserted skewer comes out clean. Remove from the oven and leave in the tin for 10 minutes before turning out onto a wire rack to cool.

Tip: Turn the cake out onto an oven glove, remove the lining paper and then tip it back right side up onto the cooling rack, so that the top remains free from markings.

Banana Pecan Cake

Serves: *12–14* **Preparation time:** *30 minutes + 30–40 minutes baking + cooling*
Freezing: *recommended before icing*

This is a cake to be shared with friends – a delicious centrepiece for any occasion. Toasting the pecans first takes very little time and it is well worth it for the additional flavour

300 g (10 oz) caster sugar
115 g (4 oz) softened butter or soft margarine
1 teaspoon vanilla extract
2 eggs, beaten
350 g (12 oz) self-raising flour
½ teaspoon baking powder
½ teaspoon bicarbonate of soda
75 ml (3 fl oz) milk
100 g (3½ oz) toasted pecans, chopped
3 ripe bananas, mashed
FOR THE FROSTING:
250 g tub mascarpone cheese
50 g (2 oz) icing sugar, sifted
¼ teaspoon vanilla extract

1 Grease and base line two 20 cm (8 inch) round sandwich tins. Preheat the oven to Gas Mark 4/180°C/350°F.

2 Cream together the sugar, butter or margarine and vanilla extract for a couple of minutes. Gradually add the eggs, beating well between each addition.

3 Sift together the flour, baking powder and bicarbonate of soda. Fold this in alternately with the milk. Save 15 g (½ oz) of the pecans and fold the remainder in with the bananas.

4 Divide the mixture equally between the prepared tins and make an indent in the centre of each. Bake for 30–40 minutes until risen, golden and spongy to the touch. Remove from the oven and leave in the tins for 5 minutes before transferring to a wire rack to cool.

5 For the icing, beat the mascarpone until smooth. Gradually add the icing sugar and vanilla extract. Use half the icing to sandwich the cakes together. Spread the remainder over the top and sprinkle with the reserved pecans.

Tropical Fruit Cake

Serves: *12* **Preparation time:** *35 minutes + 55 minutes baking + cooling*
Freezing: *recommended prior to icing*

This recipe could easily be named 'Sunshine Cake' – lemon and orange zests give the crumb a warm golden colour, which is flecked with the rich yellows, oranges and reds of papaya, melon, pineapple and mango.

175 g (6 oz) caster sugar
115 g (4 oz) softened butter
grated zest of 1 orange and 1 lemon
2 eggs, beaten
150 g (5 oz) dried sweetened tropical fruit,
finely chopped
225 g (8 oz) self-raising flour
2 tablespoons orange juice
2 tablespoons lemon juice
FOR THE TOPPING:
115 g (4 oz) icing sugar
1 tablespoon orange juice, plus a little extra
25 g (1 oz) dried sweetened tropical fruits,
finely chopped

1 Grease and line a 20 cm (8 inch) spring form cake tin. Preheat the oven to Gas Mark 4/ 180°C/350°F.

2 Place the sugar, butter and citrus zests in a bowl. Cream for a couple of minutes, until light and fluffy, scraping down the bowl halfway through. Gradually beat in the eggs. Fold in the tropical fruit and then the flour and citrus juices.

3 Spoon the mixture into the prepared tin, smooth the surface and make a slight dent in the middle. Bake for about 55 minutes until risen, golden and springy to the touch. Remove from the oven and leave in the tin for 10 minutes before turning out onto a wire rack to cool.

4 For the icing, sift the icing sugar into a small bowl. Add a tablespoon of orange juice and then enough extra to make a fairly thick, yet spreadable, paste. Using a palette knife, spread this over the surface of the cake. Scatter the tropical fruits over the top and leave to set.

Simnel Cake

Serves: *12*   Preparation time: *45 minutes + 2–2½ hours baking + cooling*
Freezing: *not necessary as the cake keeps well for up to a month*

Originally, simnel cake was associated with Mothering Sunday, when girls would take it home to their families.

450 g (1 lb) white or golden marzipan
icing sugar, for dusting
175 g (6 oz) softened butter
175 g (6 oz) caster sugar
grated zest of 1 lemon
3 eggs, beaten
225 g (8 oz) plain flour
½ teaspoon baking powder
1 teaspoon mixed spice
350 g (12 oz) mixed dried fruit (sultanas,
    currants and raisins)
80 g (3 oz) glacé cherries, halved, washed and
    dried
50 g (2 oz) cut mixed peel
1–2 tablespoons milk
1 egg white, beaten

1 Grease and line an 18 cm (7 inch) round deep cake tin. Preheat the oven to Gas Mark 3/170°C/320°F.

2 Divide the marzipan into two pieces, one weighing 275 g (10 oz) and the other 175 g (6 oz). Lightly dust the work surface with icing sugar and roll out the smaller piece of marzipan into a 18 cm (7 inch) circle. Keep the remaining piece wrapped.

3 Cream the butter, sugar and lemon zest together until light and fluffy. Gradually add

the eggs, beating well between each addition. If the mixture shows signs of curdling, add a spoonful of the flour.

4 Combine the flour, baking powder and spice and sift into the mixture. Fold in gently using a metal spoon. Add the dried fruit, cherries and mixed peel. Combine well and stir in a little milk if the mixture looks dry.

5 Spoon half the cake mixture into the prepared tin and level the surface. Lay the rolled out marzipan over the surface and then carefully spread the remaining cake mixture on top.

6 Bake for 2–2½ hours until an inserted skewer comes out cleanly. You may need to cover the top with greaseproof paper or foil if it is browning too much. Remove from the oven and leave in the tin for 30 minutes before turning out onto a wire rack to cool.

7 Roll out half the reserved marzipan into another 18 cm (7 inch) disc. Brush the top of the cake with lightly beaten egg white and lay the marzipan on top. If you wish, lightly score a diamond lattice over the surface.

8 Divide the remaining marzipan into 11 balls. Dip their bases in the egg white and then position them on top of the cake.

Lightly Fruited Christmas Cake

Serves: *16*   **Preparation time:** *35 minutes + 1½ hours baking + cooling*
Freezing: *recommended*

This is a modern take on the traditional Christmas cake recipe – an option for those who like dried fruit in moderation.

115 g (4 oz) unsalted butter
115 g (4 oz) soft light brown sugar
350 g (12 oz) dried fruit (dates, sultanas,
   cranberries, raisins, apricots, prunes)
50 g (2 oz) candied peel, chopped
125 ml (4 fl oz) half rum half orange juice
50 g (2 oz) toasted Brazil nuts, chopped
1½ tablespoons marmalade
2 eggs, beaten
225 g (8 oz) self-raising flour
½ teaspoon mixed spice
½ teaspoon cinnamon
¼ teaspoon freshly grated nutmeg
¼ teaspoon bicarbonate of soda
TO FINISH:
rum or Amaretto
2 tablespoons sieved apricot jam warmed with
   2 teaspoons water
500 g (1 lb 2 oz) marzipan
500 g (1 lb 2 oz) fondant icing

1 Combine the butter, sugar, dried fruit, candied peel, rum and orange juice in a large saucepan. Bring slowly to the boil, stirring constantly, and simmer for exactly 3 minutes. Remove from the heat and stir in the Brazil nuts and marmalade. Leave to cool for 30 minutes.

2 Line an 18 cm (7 inch) round spring form cake tin with a double thickness of baking parchment. Preheat the oven to Gas Mark 2/150°C/300°F.

3 Beat the eggs into the fruit mixture. Sift together the flour, spices and bicarbonate of soda. Add to the fruit mixture and beat for about 30 seconds to make a smooth batter.

4 Pour the mixture into the prepared tin and bake for about 1½ hours or until a skewer comes out cleanly. Remove from the oven and leave to cool in the tin for 30 minutes before transferring to a wire rack.

5 Prick the surface of the cake all over with a skewer. Very slowly drizzle over a couple of tablespoons of rum or Amaretto.

6 Wrap the cake in fresh baking parchment and then foil. Seal in a polythene bag and freeze until 2 weeks before Christmas. Defrost 2 weeks before you require it and 'feed' the cake with rum or Amaretto every other day for about a week.

7 To finish the cake, brush the apricot glaze over the entire surface. Roll out the marzipan to about 3 mm (⅛ inch) thick and cover the top and sides of the cake, sealing so that there are no gaps. Leave for 4–5 days to dry the marzipan out slightly. Finish with fondant icing and decorate as required.

Traditional Christmas Cake

Makes: *one 20 cm (8 inch) round or 18 cm (7 inch) square cake*
Preparation time: *40 minutes + overnight soaking + 3–3¾ hours baking + cooling*
Freezing: *not necessary as this cake keeps well*

Heavily fruited, this cake can be made well before Christmas and marzipaned and iced nearer the day.

700 g (1½ lb) mixed dried fruit (currants, sultanas and raisins)
80 g (3 oz) cut mixed peel
3 tablespoons brandy
225 g (8 oz) plain flour
a pinch of salt
½ teaspoon mixed spice
¼ teaspoon ground mace or nutmeg
225 g (8 oz) softened unsalted butter
225 g (8 oz) soft dark brown sugar
grated zest of 1 lemon
4 eggs, beaten
80 g (3 oz) glacé cherries, halved, washed and dried
50 g (2 oz) toasted flaked almonds
alcohol for feeding the cake

1 The night before, place the dried fruit and mixed peel in a bowl. Pour over the brandy and mix well. Cover and leave to soak overnight.

2 Grease and line a 20 cm (8 inch) round deep cake tin or a 18 cm (7 inch) square cake tin with greaseproof paper. Tie a band of double thickness brown paper around the outside and secure with string. Preheat the oven to Gas Mark 2/150°C/300°F.

3 Sift together the flour, salt and spices. Cream together the butter, sugar and lemon zest until pale and fluffy. Gradually beat in the eggs, adding a little of the flour if the mixture shows signs of curdling.

4 Fold in the flour alternately with the soaked fruit, glacé cherries and flaked almonds.

5 Spoon the mixture into the prepared tin and level the surface. Make a slight dip in the centre. Cover the top of the cake with a double thickness disc of greaseproof paper that has had a small hole cut from the centre. Bake in the oven for 3–3¾ hours, checking with a skewer to test whether the cake is done.

6 Remove from the oven and leave in the tin for 30 minutes before turning out onto a wire rack to cool. Feed the cake with your chosen alcohol (see Tip).

7 Wrap in a double thickness of greaseproof paper, followed by foil, and keep in a sealed polythene bag or an airtight tin.

Tip: 'Feeding' the cake involves pricking all over with a fork or skewer, then very slowly pouring a couple of tablespoonfuls of brandy, rum, whiskey, Cointreau or Amaretto onto the top of the cake, allowing it to soak in. Repeat this every other day for about a week, depending on how alcoholic you like your cake to be!

Royal Icing

Makes: *enough to cover an 18 cm (7 inch) round cake*
Preparation time: *10 minutes*
Freezing: *not recommended*

This is the classic finish for rich fruit cakes. Do remember to apply the icing over a layer of marzipan, which will ensure that it remains snowy white by preventing the cake from discolouring it.

2 egg whites
450 g (1 lb) icing sugar, sifted
2 teaspoons lemon juice
2 teaspoons glycerine

1 Place the egg whites in a large mixing bowl and, using an electric hand whisk, beat to break them up until they are frothy.

2 Add the icing sugar, a quarter at a time, and beat well after each addition. This will take 5–7 minutes.

3 Beat in the lemon juice to flavour and glycerine to soften the icing. Use as required.

Tips: If you wish to flat ice a cake then it is best to make the royal icing the day before. This will then give any air bubbles that have been incorporated time to escape. Stir before using.

You can also now buy royal icing sugar, which only needs water and glycerine adding. Just follow the instructions on the packet.

Fruit and Nut Christmas Cake Finish

For a simple, icing-free finish to your Christmas cake a selection of dried fruit and nuts can be used to give a shiny, jewel-like finish! Brush the top of the cake with a glaze made from sieved apricot jam thinned with brandy, rum, Cointreau or Amaretto. Arrange the fruit and/or nuts attractively in lines or circles. Brush them all well with the glaze.

Choose from dried apricots, pears, cranberries, prunes, dates, etc. Alternatively, you may wish to have a pure nut topping. In this case it is always best to toast the nuts first to bring out their full flavour. Brazils, walnuts, pecans and almonds are all good. A combination of dried fruit and nuts looks and tastes delicious.

Cakes for Puddings

Many of the cakes in this book have dual roles in that they work equally well as an everyday cake but can also be 'dolled up' into a tempting dessert. Most of the cakes in this chapter would benefit from being accompanied by cream, Greek yogurt with a little honey stirred through or a dollop of sweetened crème frâiche.

Lemon Ricotta Cake, page 122

Lemon Ricotta Cake

Serves: *12*   Preparation time: *35 minutes + 70–75 minutes baking + cooling*
Freezing: *recommended*

Close your eyes, take a mouthful and you could almost imagine that you were eating a baked cheesecake. Ricotta gives this cake wonderful body and an underlying creamy taste.

50 g (2 oz) sultanas
225 g (8 oz) caster sugar
175 g (6 oz) softened butter or soft margarine
grated zest and juice of 1 lemon
½ teaspoon vanilla extract
3 eggs, separated
250 g tub of ricotta cheese
225 g (8 oz) self-raising flour
1 teaspoon baking powder
icing sugar, for dusting

1 Grease and line a 20 cm (8 inch) spring form cake tin. Preheat the oven to Gas Mark 4/ 180°C/350°F.

2 Place the sultanas in a small pan and just cover with water. Bring to the boil and simmer for 10 minutes. Drain well and leave to cool.

3 Cream together the sugar, butter or margarine, lemon zest and vanilla extract until light and fluffy. Gradually beat in the egg yolks. Using an electric mixer on slow, blend in the ricotta to make a smooth batter.

4 Sift together the flour and baking powder. Fold into the mixture with the sultanas and lemon juice.

5 Wash and dry the electric beaters and stiffly whisk the egg whites. Fold in, being careful not to knock out any air.

6 Spoon the mixture into the prepared tin and level the surface, creating a slight dip in the centre. Bake for 70–75 minutes or until a skewer comes out cleanly. The crust will have cracked attractively and turned a beautiful golden colour.

7 Remove from the oven and leave in the tin for 15 minutes before turning out onto a wire rack to cool. Dust lightly with icing sugar.

Tip: Treat this cake as a cheesecake and serve with a compôte of red berries

Photo on page 121

Raspberry Almond Cake

Serves: *8–10*   **Preparation time:** *30 minutes + 1–1¼ hours baking + cooling*
Freezing: *not recommended*

This is a very rich, buttery cake. Serve with some sharp crème fraîche to offset its sweetness. Fresh or frozen raspberries both work well.

175 g (6 oz) caster sugar
175 g (6 oz) softened unsalted butter
½ teaspoon vanilla extract
3 eggs, beaten
80 g (3 oz) self-raising flour
½ teaspoon baking powder
115 g (4 oz) ground almonds
175 g (6 oz) raspberries
FOR THE TOPPING:
15 g (½ oz) unsalted butter
50 g (2 oz) flaked almonds
15 g (½ oz) caster sugar
icing sugar, for dusting

1 Line a 20 cm (8 inch) round spring form cake tin with baking parchment. Preheat the oven to Gas Mark 4/180°C/350°F.

2 Cream together the sugar, butter and vanilla extract. Gradually beat in the eggs.

3 Combine the flour, baking powder and almonds. Fold into the cake mixture and then carefully stir in the raspberries. Spoon into the prepared tin.

4 For the topping, melt the butter. Remove from the heat and stir in the almonds and caster sugar. Sprinkle this over the top of the cake mixture, making sure that you reach the edges.

5 Bake for 1–1¼ hours until an inserted skewer comes out cleanly. Remove from the oven and leave to cool in the tin. Turn out onto a serving plate, dust with icing sugar and serve warm or cold.

Rhubarb Cake

Serves: 8   **Preparation time:** 25 minutes + 1–1¼ hours baking + cooling
Freezing: not recommended

Rhubarb upside-down cake is an old favourite. Here the cake is baked with the rhubarb on the top, giving it an interesting appearance.

150 g (5 oz) softened butter or soft margarine
115 g (4 oz) soft light brown sugar
½ teaspoon vanilla extract
2 eggs, beaten
150 g (5 oz) self-raising flour
½ teaspoon baking powder
50 g (2 oz) ground almonds
1 teaspoon powdered ginger
1–2 tablespoons milk
350 g (12 oz) trimmed rhubarb, cut into 2 cm
   (¾ inch) lengths
3 tablespoons Demerara sugar

1 Line a 20 cm (8 inch) spring form cake tin with baking parchment. Preheat the oven to Gas Mark 4/180°C/350°F.

2 Cream together the butter or margarine, sugar and vanilla extract until light and fluffy. Gradually beat in the eggs, adding a tablespoon of the flour with each addition if the mixture shows signs of curdling.

3 Sift together the flour, baking powder, ground almonds and ginger. Fold into the mixture with enough milk to give a soft dropping consistency.

4 Spoon the mixture into the prepared tin and level the surface. Scatter the rhubarb over the top and sprinkle with the Demerara sugar.

5 Bake for 1–1¼ hours until an inserted skewer comes out cleanly. Remove from the oven and leave to cool in the tin. Serve warm or cold.

Tip: For a glossy finish and more gingery taste, once the cake has cooled brush the top with syrup from a jar of stem ginger.

Gooseberry and Walnut Cake

Serves: *8*   **Preparation time:** *25 minutes + 1–1¼ hours baking + cooling*
Freezing: *not recommended*

Vanilla sponge topped with gooseberries and a nutty butterscotch finish. This also makes a lovely winter pudding – use frozen gooseberries and serve with custard.

115 g (4 oz) softened butter or soft margarine
115 g (4 oz) soft light brown sugar
½ teaspoon vanilla extract
2 eggs, beaten
175 g (6 oz) self-raising flour
½ teaspoon baking powder
FOR THE TOPPING:
50 g (2 oz) soft light brown sugar
50 g (2 oz) walnuts, chopped
25 g (1 oz) butter, melted
1 teaspoon cinnamon
350 g (12 oz) gooseberries, topped and tailed

1 Grease and line a 20 cm (8 inch) spring form cake tin. Preheat the oven to Gas Mark 4/ 180°C/350°F.

2 Cream together the butter or margarine, sugar and vanilla extract until light and fluffy. Gradually beat in the eggs. Fold in a tablespoon of the flour with each addition if the mixture shows signs of curdling.

3 Sift together the flour and baking powder and fold in. Spoon the mixture into the prepared tin and level the surface.

4 For the topping, combine the sugar, walnuts, butter and cinnamon. Stir in the gooseberries to coat them. The mixture is quite lumpy but do not worry, the aim is to just take the tartness off the gooseberries. Sprinkle the mixture evenly over the top of the sponge batter.

5 Bake for 1–1¼ hours until a skewer comes out cleanly when inserted. There may well be a little liquid from the gooseberries on the surface; this will be absorbed on cooling.

6 Remove from the oven and leave to cool in the tin. Serve warm or cold.

Plum Cake

Serves: 8–10   **Preparation time:** *1 hour + 1–1¼ hours baking + cooling*
Freezing: *not recommended*

This started out as a cake with a crumble topping. However, on cooking nearly half of the oat mixture sank into the cake. The result was a delicious chewy top with a flavoured cake reminiscent of flapjacks – fabulous!

450 g (1 lb) plums, washed, halved and stoned
2 tablespoons granulated sugar
175 g (6 oz) soft light brown sugar
175 g (6 oz) softened butter or soft margarine
2 eggs, beaten
175 g (6 oz) self-raising flour
½ teaspoon baking powder
½ teaspoon vanilla extract
FOR THE TOPPING:
50 g (2 oz) butter
50 g (2 oz) self-raising flour
¾ teaspoon cinnamon
25 g (1 oz) porridge oats
25 g (1 oz) flaked almonds

1 Line a 20 cm (8 inch) spring form cake tin with baking parchment. Preheat the oven to Gas Mark 4/180°C/350°F.

2 Place the plums, cut side up, in an ovenproof dish. Sprinkle with the granulated sugar and bake in the oven for 20–30 minutes until their juices just begin to run and they have softened. Leave to cool.

3 Place the remaining cake ingredients in a bowl and beat for a couple of minutes, scraping the mixture down halfway through.

4 Spoon the batter into the prepared tin. Lay the plums on top and pour on any juice. (There shouldn't be much.)

5 For the topping, melt the butter in a pan. Remove from the heat and stir in the remaining topping ingredients. Scatter the topping over the top of the plums, making sure you cover the whole cake.

6 Bake for 1–1¼ hours, until the top is golden and an inserted skewer comes out cleanly. Remove from the oven and leave to cool in the tin.

Tip: If the plums you use are very ripe and tender, you may not need to precook them in the oven at all.

Sherry Trifle Sponge

Serves: 8   Preparation time: *35 minutes + 25–30 minutes baking + cooling*
Freezing: *recommended*

Trifle on a plate rather than in a bowl!

3 eggs
80 g (3 oz) caster sugar
½ teaspoon vanilla extract
65 g (2½ oz) plain flour
15 g (½ oz) custard powder
50 g (2 oz) butter, melted and cooled slightly
FOR THE FILLING AND TOPPING:
3–4 tablespoons sherry
2–3 tablespoons red conserve or jam
115 g (4 oz) raspberries, plus extra for
   decorating
1 medium banana, sliced
300 ml (½ pint) double cream
2 tablespoons icing sugar, plus extra for dusting

1 Grease two 18 cm (7 inch) sandwich tins and base line with baking parchment. Preheat the oven to Gas Mark 4/180°C/350°F.

2 In a bowl over a pan of hot water, whisk the eggs, sugar and vanilla extract for about 10 minutes until pale, thick and mousse like. Remove from the heat.

3 Combine the flour and custard powder. Sift half over the surface of the egg mixture and drizzle half the melted butter around the edge. Very carefully, so as not to knock out any of the air, fold in the ingredients. Repeat with the remaining flour and butter.

4 Divide the mixture between the prepared tins, shaking to level the surface. Bake for 25–30 minutes until risen, golden and springy to the touch. Remove from the oven and leave in the tins for 10 minutes before turning out onto a wire rack to cool.

5 Place one of the sponges on a plate and sprinkle with half the sherry. Spread over the conserve. Scatter the raspberries and banana over the top.

6 Whip the cream and icing sugar together. Spread a third of this over the fruit. Place the second sponge cake on top and drizzle with the remaining sherry.

7 Smooth the remaining cream over the top and sides of the cake to cover. Pile a few raspberries onto the top and dust them with some icing sugar. Refrigerate before serving.

Tip: This cake is best eaten on the day it is made.

Chocolate Brazil Nut Cake

Serves: *8–10* **Preparation time:** *35 minutes + 35–45 minutes baking + cooling*
Freezing: *recommended*

This is a flourless cake, so suitable for those on a gluten free diet. It rises beautifully in the oven, the middle sinking slightly on cooling to provide a useful crater for filling. The cake is at its best served slightly warm.

225 g (8 oz) Brazil nuts
200 g (7 oz) unsalted butter
175 g (6 oz) 70% dark chocolate
2 tablespoons instant coffee, dissolved in
  2 tablespoons just-boiled water
175 g (6 oz) caster sugar
6 eggs, separated
½ teaspoon vanilla extract
¾ teaspoon cream of tartar
chocolate curls, to decorate
FOR THE ICING:
175 g (6 oz) mascarpone
2 tablespoons icing sugar, plus extra for dusting
2 teaspoons rum, or to taste

1 Line a 23 cm (9 inch) spring form tin with baking parchment so that the paper comes 5 cm (2 inches) above the rim of the tin. Preheat the oven to Gas Mark 5/190°C/375°F.

2 Spread out the nuts on a lipped baking tray and toast in the oven for 5–10 minutes until just browned – check them frequently. Set aside to cool and then blitz in a food processor until they are very finely chopped – similar in texture to ground almonds.

3 In a bowl, melt the butter, chocolate and coffee over a pan of hot water. Allow to cool.

4 Whisk together the sugar, egg yolks and vanilla extract until thick and mousse like. Fold into the chocolate mixture with the ground nuts.

5 Place the egg whites in a large bowl. Add the cream of tartar and whisk until the mixture forms stiff peaks. Very carefully, so as not to knock out any air, fold one tablespoon of the egg whites into the chocolate mixture to loosen it, followed by the remainder.

6 Pour the mixture into the prepared tin and bake for 35–45 minutes until the cake has risen and the centre just wobbles slightly when you shake the tin. Do not overcook it. The crust will probably crack slightly but do not worry. Remove from the oven and leave to cool in the tin.

7 For the icing, beat together the mascarpone and icing sugar. Stir in rum to taste and cover the top of the cake. Sprinkle with chocolate curls if wished.

Gluten free

Polenta Cake with Lemongrass Syrup

Serves: *12*   **Preparation time:** *35 minutes + 50–55 minutes baking + cooling*
Freezing: *recommended*

Polenta is made from maize, so not only is it an ideal substitute for those unable to tolerate wheat or gluten, it also gives a wonderful warm, orange colour. Accompany with Greek yogurt sweetened with a little clear honey and topped with chopped pistachios.

175 g (6 oz) unsalted butter
175 g (6 oz) golden caster sugar
grated zest of 1 lemon
3 eggs, beaten
150 g (5 oz) ground almonds
115 g (4 oz) polenta
1½ teaspoons gluten free baking powder
a pinch of salt
4 tablespoons milk
15 g (½ oz) flaked almonds
FOR THE SYRUP:
1 lemon
1 lemongrass stalk, trimmed
2.5 cm (1 inch) piece fresh ginger, peeled and
   sliced thinly
50 g (2 oz) golden caster sugar
100 ml (3 fl oz) water

1 Grease and line a 20 cm (8 inch) round spring form tin. Preheat the oven to Gas Mark 3/ 170°C/320°F.

2 Cream together the butter, sugar and lemon zest. Gradually beat in the eggs.

3 Combine the ground almonds, polenta, baking powder and salt. Fold into the mixture with enough milk to make a soft dropping consistency. Spoon into the prepared tin, level the surface and scatter with flaked almonds. Bake for 50–55 minutes until risen and springy to the touch.

4 For the syrup, pare the zest from half a lemon, remove any white pith and cut the zest into thin strips. Squeeze the juice from this lemon and the one used in the cake. Bruise the lemongrass stem with a knife. Place the lemon zest, lemongrass, ginger, sugar and water in a small pan. Heat gently to dissolve the sugar, stirring all the time. Bring to the boil and simmer for 5–6 minutes. Remove from the heat, add the lemon juice and leave to cool.

5 Remove the cake from the oven and prick the top all over with a skewer. Strain the syrup, reserving the lemon zest. Leaving the cake in the tin, slowly drizzle the syrup evenly over the surface. Don't worry that there seems quite a lot, it will all be absorbed. Set the cake to one side to cool.

6 To serve, turn the cake out of the tin and scatter the lemon zest over the surface.

Gluten free

Whole Orange Cake

Serves: *12* **Preparation time:** *2 hours 20 minutes + 45 minutes baking + cooling*
Freezing: *recommended*

This cake uses whole oranges, which are boiled first, to give a beautifully moist crumb. It is equally good served with coffee or as a dessert accompanied by crème frâiche or Greek yogurt.

2 whole oranges
6 eggs, separated
225 g (8 oz) caster sugar
grated zest of 1 orange
200 g (7 oz) ground almonds
50 g (2 oz) polenta
1 teaspoon gluten free baking powder
40 g flaked almonds

1 Scrub the two oranges well. Put them in a pan with enough water to just cover. Bring to the boil and simmer for 2 hours until soft. (Keep an eye on the water level and top it up if necessary.) Remove the oranges from the water and leave to cool.

2 Grease and flour a 23 cm (9 inch) round spring form cake tin. Preheat the oven to Gas Mark 4/180°C/350°F.

3 Cut the oranges in half and remove any pips. Place in a food processor and purée to a smooth pulp.

4 In a bowl, whisk together the egg yolks, sugar and orange zest until pale, thick and mousse like.

5 Combine the ground almonds, polenta and baking powder. Fold into the egg mixture with the orange purée.

6 Wash and dry the beaters thoroughly. Place the egg whites in a large bowl and whisk until they form stiff peaks. Fold in to the rest of the ingredients.

7 Carefully pour the mixture into the prepared tin. Shake to level the surface and scatter the flaked almonds over the top.

8 Bake for about 45 minutes until risen and golden. Remove from the oven and leave in the tin for 10–15 minutes before turning out onto a wire rack to cool. Serve warm or cold.

Gluten free

Honey and Pine Nut Cake

Serves: *8–10*   **Preparation time:** *25 minutes + 45–50 minutes baking + cooling*
Freezing: *recommended*

The drizzle of orange and honey syrup over the top gives added flavour and avoids the need for icing. It makes a lovely pudding accompanied by a dollop of Greek yogurt sweetened with a little honey.

50 g (2 oz) pine nuts, plus 1 tablespoon for topping
115 g (4 oz) softened butter
80 g (3 oz) golden caster sugar
80 g (3 oz) Acacia honey
grated zest of 1 orange
2 eggs, beaten
175 g (6 oz) plain flour
50 g (2 oz) polenta
1 teaspoon baking powder
¼ teaspoon bicarbonate of soda
1 teaspoon cinnamon
75 ml (3 fl oz) milk
FOR THE SYRUP:
2 tablespoons Acacia honey
juice of 1 orange

1 Grease and line a 20 cm (8 inch) round, deep sandwich tin. Preheat the oven to Gas Mark 3/170°C/320°F.

2 Place the 50 g (2 oz) of pine nuts on a baking tray and toast in the oven for 5–6 minutes or until browned. Remove and leave to cool.

3 Cream together the butter, sugar, honey and orange zest for a couple of minutes. Gradually beat in the eggs, then stir in the toasted pine nuts. Combine the flour, polenta, baking powder, bicarbonate of soda and cinnamon. Fold into the mixture alternately with the milk.

4 Spoon the batter into the prepared tin, make a slight hollow in the centre and scatter with the reserved pine nuts.

5 Bake for 45–50 minutes until risen, golden and just firm to the touch or a skewer comes out cleanly. Remove from the oven and leave in the tin for 10 minutes before turning out onto a wire rack.

6 While the sponge is in the oven, blend together the honey and orange juice in a small pan. Bring slowly to the boil and simmer for 5 minutes, without stirring, until syrupy. Leave to cool slightly.

7 While the cake is still warm, prick it all over with a skewer. Pour or spoon the syrup very slowly and evenly over the top.

Tip: Keep pricking the cake with a skewer if the syrup does not soak in. If you do this with the cooling rack positioned over a large dinner plate, you can catch any syrup that runs off and pour it back over the cake.

Buttermilk Cake with Mango and Passion Fruit

Serves: 8–10 **Preparation time:** *40 minutes + 35–40 minutes baking + cooling*
Freezing: *recommended before filling*

Buttermilk gives the sponge a slightly dense texture and a distinctive flavour – not unlike Scotch pancakes. To serve as a cake rather than a pudding, fill with Crème au Beurre (page 39) and a fruit conserve.

225 g (8 oz) caster sugar
150 g (5 oz) soft margarine
grated zest of 1 lime
½ teaspoon vanilla extract
3 eggs, beaten
225 g (8 oz) plain flour
1½ teaspoons baking powder
½ teaspoon bicarbonate of soda
a pinch of salt
284 ml carton of buttermilk
FOR THE FILLING:
150 ml (¼ pint) double cream
2 tablespoons icing sugar, plus extra
    for dusting
2 passion fruit
1 small mango, peeled, sliced and
    roughly chopped

1 Grease and base line two 20 cm (8 inch) sandwich tins. Preheat the oven to Gas Mark 3/170°C/320°F.

2 Cream together the sugar, margarine, lime zest and vanilla extract for a couple of minutes until light and fluffy. Gradually beat in the eggs, adding a tablespoon of the flour with each addition if the mixture shows signs of curdling.

3 Sift together the flour, baking powder, bicarbonate of soda and salt. Fold into the batter alternately with the buttermilk.

4 Pour the mixture into the prepared tins. Bake for 35–40 minutes, covering the cakes towards the end of the time if they are browning too much. The sponges should be firm and just coming away from the edges of the tins.

5 Remove from the oven, loosen the cakes around the edges and leave in the tins for 10 minutes before turning out onto a wire rack to cool.

6 For the filling, lightly whip the cream and icing sugar together until the cream just holds its shape. Halve the passion fruit and scoop out the flesh, seeds and juices into the cream. Carefully fold in.

7 Spread the mango and any juices over one of the sponges. Smooth the passion cream on top and sandwich together with the remaining sponge. Dust the top with icing sugar and serve.

Lemon and Blueberry Drizzle Cake

Serves: *8*   **Preparation time:** *20 minutes + 50–60 minutes baking + cooling*
Freezing: *recommended*

This is a quick to make cake that is drizzled with a simple syrup made by mixing together lemon juice and sugar.

115 g (4 oz) half each of softened butter and
  soft margarine
175 g (6 oz) self-raising flour
1 teaspoon baking powder
175 g (6 oz) caster sugar
2 eggs
grated zest of 1 lemon
4 tablespoons milk
150 g (5 oz) blueberries
FOR THE TOPPING:
80 g (3 oz) caster sugar
juice of 1 lemon

1 Grease and base line a 20 cm (8 inch) spring form cake tin. Preheat the oven to Gas Mark 4/180°C/350°F.

2 Place the butter, margarine, flour, baking powder, sugar, eggs and lemon zest in a bowl and beat for a couple of minutes, scraping down the sides of the bowl halfway through. Fold in the milk. Spoon the batter into the prepared tin and level the surface.

3 Wash the blueberries and pat them dry. Sprinkle evenly over the surface of the cake mixture. Bake for about 50–60 minutes until risen, golden and just springy to the touch. Test with a skewer.

4 While the cake is cooking, mix together the sugar and lemon juice for the topping.

5 Remove the cake from the oven and leave it in its tin. Prick the surface all over with a skewer and slowly drizzle the lemon syrup over the top. Allow the cake to cool in the tin. Serve warm or cold.

Lemon Roulade

Serves: *10* **Preparation time:** *25 minutes + 10–13 minutes baking + cooling*
Freezing: *recommended*

This is a wonderfully tangy dessert for entertaining. It also has the advantage that it can be made the day before and decorated when required.

5 eggs, separated
115 g (4 oz) caster sugar
grated zest and juice of 1 lemon
25 g (1 oz) plain flour
icing sugar, for dusting
FOR THE FILLING:
8 tablespoons good quality lemon curd
250 ml (8 fl oz) double cream, whipped

1 Line a 33 x 23 cm (13 x 9 inch) Swiss roll tin with non-stick baking parchment. Preheat the oven to Gas Mark 5/190°C/375°F.

2 Place the egg yolks, sugar and lemon zest in a bowl. Whisk for 2–3 minutes until pale and thick. Fold in the flour.

3 Boil 2 tablespoons of the lemon juice and fold in at once.

4 Stiffly whisk the egg whites and fold in carefully. Pour into the prepared tin, shake gently to level the surface and bake for 10–13 minutes until the middle is springy to the touch.

5 Remove from the oven and leave to cool in the tin for about 2 hours. The roulade does not require covering.

6 Thickly dust a sheet of baking parchment with icing sugar. Turn the roulade out onto the paper and peel off the lining paper. Spread to the edges with lemon curd and then spread with the whipped cream.

7 Roll up the roulade tightly from the long edge, making sure that the seam ends up underneath. Chill for a couple of hours with the baking parchment still wrapped around the roulade.

8 Remove the paper and dredge the roulade very thickly with icing sugar.

Tip: If you wish, finish with a caramelised lattice pattern. Hold a skewer in heatproof protective gloves and put the other end into a naked flame. Place this directly onto the icing sugar in diagonal parallel lines to make a lattice effect. You will need to use three or four skewers.

Lavender Sugar Swiss Roll with Strawberries

Serves: *8*   **Preparation time:** *40 minutes + 7–10 minutes baking + cooling*
Freezing: *not recommended*

Lavender combines beautifully with strawberries for a summer dessert.

115 g (4 oz) caster sugar, plus extra for dusting
3 heads lavender flowers, plus extra to decorate
3 eggs
115 g (4 oz) plain flour
1 tablespoon recently boiled water
FOR THE FILLING:
225 g (8 oz) strawberries, plus extra to decorate
2 tablespoons icing sugar
150 ml (¼ pint) double cream
a few drops of vanilla extract

1 Line a 33 x 23 cm (13 x 9 inch) Swiss roll tin with baking parchment and grease. Preheat the oven to Gas Mark 7/220°C/425°F.

2 Place the sugar in a food processor. Remove the lavender flowers from the stalks and add. Blitz for just 5 seconds to release the lavender oil. (This is not necessary if the sugar and lavender have been combined already – see Tip.)

3 Place the lavender sugar and eggs in a large bowl set over a pan of hot water. Using a hand-held electric whisk, beat for about 10 minutes until the mixture thickens. Remove from the heat and sift in half the flour. Fold this in very carefully, so as not to knock out any of the air, and then repeat with the remainder of the flour. Fold in the boiled water.

4 Pour the mixture into the prepared tin and gently ease the batter into the sides and corners. Bake for 7–10 minutes until risen,

golden and just firm to the touch. Prepare two large sheets of baking parchment, dusting one heavily with caster sugar.

6 Remove the sponge from the oven and invert it onto the paper sprinkled with sugar. Remove the lining paper, trim just the outside edges, place the other piece of paper on top and roll the sponge up tightly from the short edge, ensuring that the seam is underneath. Leave wrapped in paper to cool on a wire rack.

7 Meanwhile, slice the strawberries into a bowl and sprinkle with 1 tablespoon of icing sugar. Whip the cream together with the remaining icing sugar and vanilla extract until it forms peaks.

8 Carefully unroll the sponge. Scatter the strawberries and their juices evenly over the top and then spread the cream over, making sure you reach the edges. Roll up tightly from the short end, using the paper to help, and refrigerate for at least an hour.

9 Remove the paper, sprinkle the roll with caster sugar and decorate with a few fresh lavender flowers and strawberries. Keep refrigerated until ready to serve.

Tip: If possible pick the lavender flowers a few days in advance and store them in a jar with the sugar to allow the flavours to mingle fully. Fresh or dried flowers work equally well.

Black Forest Chocolate Roulade

Serves: *8–10*   **Preparation time:** *30 minutes + 15–20 minutes baking + cooling*
Freezing: *not recommended*

Black Forest gâteau is a long established favourite. This modern version uses a roulade as the base. Sprinkle a little Kirsch over the chocolate roulade before spreading with jam for a truly authentic flavour.

175 g (6 oz) dark chocolate
2 tablespoons hot water
½ teaspoon vanilla extract
5 eggs, separated
175 g (6 oz) caster sugar
FOR THE FILLING:
284 g jar no-added-sugar
    black cherry jam
150 ml (¼ pint) double cream
115 g (4 oz) mascarpone
1 tablespoon icing sugar, plus extra for dusting

1 Line a 33 x 23 cm (13 x 9 inch) Swiss roll tin with baking parchment. Preheat the oven to Gas Mark 4/180°C/350°F.

2 Melt the chocolate, water and vanilla extract in a bowl over a pan of hot water. Allow to cool slightly.

3 Place the egg yolks and sugar in a bowl and whisk until pale and thick. Stir in the melted chocolate. Stiffly whisk the egg whites and fold into the chocolate mixture.

4 Pour the batter into the prepared tin and ease it into the edges. Bake for 15–20 minutes until risen and just firm.

5 Remove from the oven and cover with a sheet of baking parchment and a damp tea towel. Leave for at least 3 hours or overnight.

6 Dust another sheet of baking parchment with sifted icing sugar and turn out the roulade. Peel off the lining paper and smooth the black cherry jam evenly over the surface. Whisk together the cream, mascarpone and 1 tablespoon of icing sugar until the mixture thickens. Spread this over the jam. Using the baking parchment to help you, roll up the roulade tightly from the short edge. Make sure that you end with the join underneath.

7 Chill the roulade for a couple of hours with the paper still wrapped around to help hold its shape. Remove the paper and dredge with icing sugar before serving.

Mocha Praline Slice with Baileys

Serves: *8*   **Preparation time:** *30 minutes + 10 minutes cooking + chilling*
Freezing: *recommended*

This is an ideal recipe for a novice – praline can be substituted with toasted chopped pecans.

FOR THE PRALINE:
80 g (3 oz) granulated sugar
3 tablespoons water
80 g (3 oz) pecan nuts
FOR THE CAKE:
30 sponge finger biscuits
2 tablespoons instant coffee granules
2 tablespoons boiling water
150 ml (¼ pint) cold water
6 tablespoons Baileys liqueur
50 g (2 oz) icing sugar, sifted
115 g (4 oz) dark chocolate
300 ml (10 fl oz) double cream

1 To make the praline, place the sugar and water in a pan and heat gently to dissolve the sugar, stirring continuously. Add the nuts and bring the syrup to the boil, boiling steadily until it caramelises. Watch it carefully as it will suddenly turn. Carefully pour onto a baking sheet lined with non-stick baking parchment and leave to cool.

2 Line the base of a 900 g (2 lb) loaf tin with baking parchment and arrange one third of the sponge finger biscuits across the tin to cover the base.

3 Dissolve the coffee in the boiling water. Pour in the cold water and Baileys and whisk in the icing sugar.

4 Melt the chocolate in a bowl over a pan of hot water and cool slightly.

5 Whip the cream until it just holds its shape. Halve and set aside one portion in the fridge for decorating.

6 Reserve five whole praline pecans. Put the remainder in a food processor and blitz until finely chopped. Add these to the cream along with the melted chocolate. Fold in carefully.

7 In a steady, thin stream, pour one third of the coffee liquid over the sponge fingers. Spread half the chocolate nut mixture over the top – right to the edges of the tin. Arrange another third of the sponge fingers over the top in a row, filling any gaps. Pour over another third of the coffee mixture and spread the remaining chocolate nut mixture on top. Finish with the remaining sponge fingers and coffee mixture.

8 Cover the cake with clingfilm and lightly weigh the whole thing down. Refrigerate for 3–4 hours to allow the slice to firm up.

9 Carefully loosen around the edge of the cake with a spatula. Turn out onto a serving dish and remove the lining paper. Spread the reserved cream over the top and sides of the cake. Decorate simply with the five reserved nuts in a row down the centre.

Mint Chocolate Roll

Serves: *8*   **Preparation time:** *30 minutes + 10 minutes baking + cooling*
Freezing: *recommended*

Chocolate and mint are a classic combination. You may wish to fold a tablespoon or two of mint liqueur into the cream before spreading it over the chocolate sponge.

25 g (1 oz) butter
3 eggs
115 g (4 oz) caster sugar, plus extra for dusting
65 g (2½ oz) plain flour
2 tablespoons cocoa powder
icing sugar, for dusting
FOR THE FILLING:
250 ml (8 fl oz) double cream
1 tablespoon milk
1 tablespoon icing sugar
115 g (4 oz) After Eight chocolates, each broken into six pieces

1 Line a 33 x 23 cm (13 x 9 inch) Swiss roll tin with non-stick baking parchment. Preheat the oven to Gas Mark 6/200°C/400°F.

2 Melt the butter and set aside to cool slightly.

3 Place the eggs and sugar in a large bowl over a pan of hot water. Using an electric hand whisk, whisk the mixture until thick and foamy. You should be able to leave a trail of mixture on the surface if you lift up the beaters. This will take about 10 minutes. Combine the flour and cocoa powder.

4 Drizzle half of the butter around the edge of the egg mixture and sift in half the flour. Very carefully, so as not to knock out any of the air, gently fold in. Repeat with the remaining butter and flour.

5 Scrape the batter into the prepared tin and shake or tease it into the corners and edges. Bake for 10 minutes.

6 Prepare two sheets of baking parchment, each just a little wider than the Swiss roll tin. Sprinkle one of these with caster sugar.

7 As soon as the sponge comes out of the oven, turn it out onto the sugared paper. Remove the lining paper and trim the edges using a sharp knife. Place the other sheet of paper on top and roll the sponge up tightly from the short end, making sure that the join is underneath. Place on a wire rack to cool.

8 For the filling, whip together the cream, milk and icing sugar until thick. Fold the After Eight chocolates into the cream.

9 Unroll the cooled sponge, remove the central paper and spread evenly with the mint cream mixture. Reroll tightly, making sure that the seam is again tucked underneath. Leave the outer paper around the sponge and chill for a couple of hours to set. When ready to serve, remove the paper and dust with icing sugar.

Chocolate Cream Cheese Icing

Makes: *enough to top a 20 cm (8 inch) round cake*
Preparation time: *5 minutes*
Freezing: *not recommended*

The beauty of this icing is that it is so quick to make. As it contains cream cheese it is best to keep the cake in the fridge once iced. However, this will take the gloss off the icing, so ice just prior to serving if possible.

115 g (4 oz) full fat cream cheese
50 g (2 oz) icing sugar, sifted
50 g (2 oz) plain chocolate, melted

1 Beat together the cream cheese and icing sugar until smooth.

2 Stir in the chocolate and spread over the cake before it has time to set.

Citrus Julienne Strips

Makes: *enough to top a 20 cm (8 inch) round cake*
Preparation time: *10 minutes + cooling*
Freezing: *not recommended*

These are very useful for finishing off orange or lemon flavoured cakes – whether for teatime or to be served as a dessert. You can vary the length of the strips to suit the type of cake –smaller pieces work better on individual cakes.

1 lemon or 1 orange
2 tablespoons granulated sugar
90 ml (3 fl oz) water

1 Take a sharp knife or vegetable peeler and pare the rind from the fruit. Carefully cut away any white bits of pith as these will make the peel taste bitter.

2 Cut the peel into very thin strips.

3 Dissolve the sugar in the water. Add the citrus strips and bring to the boil. Simmer gently for 5 minutes. Drain and leave to cool.

Tip: If you prefer your strips to be sticky and candied, then simmer the zests for a further 5 minutes.